Everything is Permitted, Restrictions Still Apply

This book applies historicised psychoanalytic thinking in a non-reductive way to better understand the dominant emotional trends in contemporary cultural and socio-political life, with a specific focus on the relationship between social dislocation, narcissism, and "post truth".

Rapid social dislocation and change are ubiquitous in late capitalist societies, though these processes may be felt unequally. Following the work of the late Christopher Lasch, *Everything is Permitted, Restrictions Still Apply* suggests there are powerful narcissistic trends in contemporary life mitigating against the capacity to acknowledge and face these changes; in other words, against the capacity to face reality and to mourn. There is a tendency to assert the primacy of a compelling emotional narrative over the claims of evidence and expertise, and to relate to others, past and present, as alternately idealised and/or denigrated aspects of the self. These trends permeate across socio-cultural divides and the political spectrum – underpinning phenomena as apparently divergent as free-market fundamentalism, certain forms of anti-capitalism, and contemporary identity and victim politics of both nominal right and left: movements that have more emotional and intellectual underpinnings in common than their proponents may care to admit. The contrast between liberal progressiveness and post-truth populism ignores the inter-relationship of these phenomena and begs the question of those powerful subjectivist and relativistic trends amongst sections of radical and "progressive" opinion that have long sought to problematise the very notion of truth. This book links these phenomena to contemporary social defences against facing limitation, loss, and internal conflict. More specifically it argues that in a pseudo-therapeutic culture preoccupied with narratives of victimhood, the losses associated with "traditional" manufacturing and its attendant associational cultures have neither been acknowledged nor mourned.

Everything is Permitted, Restrictions Still Apply will appeal to all readers interested in history, politics, and socio-cultural analysis, and in new ways of thinking about contemporary issues. It will be of particular interest to researchers applying a psycho-social perspective on contemporary conflict and to a psychoanalytically informed readership.

Ian Thurston is a registered psychoanalytic psychotherapist, currently working as a Principal Adult Psychotherapist at the Department of Psychotherapy, Newcastle-upon-Tyne, UK. He has worked extensively in public sector mental health care, initially as a psychiatric nurse, and later as clinical manager of an Acute Day Hospital in East London.

Everything is Permitted, Restrictions Still Apply

A Psychoanalytic Perspective on Social Dislocation, Narcissism, and Post Truth

Ian Thurston

Routledge
Taylor & Francis Group

LONDON AND NEW YORK

First published 2018
by Routledge
2 Park Square, Milton Park, Abingdon, Oxon OX14 4RN

and by Routledge
711 Third Avenue, New York, NY 10017

Routledge is an imprint of the Taylor & Francis Group, an informa business

British Library Cataloguing-in-Publication Data
A catalogue record for this book is available from the British Library

Library of Congress Cataloging-in-Publication Data
A catalog record has been requested for this book

ISBN: 978-1-78220-612-5 (pbk)

Typeset in Times New Roman
by Apex CoVantage, LLC

To my wife, Hedge, for all her help and unflagging support, and without whom the completion of this book would not have been possible.

In memory of my father, Tommy Thurston, and of Ian Cooke, an inspirational psychiatric nurse, thinker, and good friend.

Contents

Acknowledgements

With gratitude and appreciation to my mother and father, family, and to colleagues and friends, past and present, with whom I have discussed, over the years, politics, psychoanalysis, football, literature, music, and many other things besides. With thanks to Mr Ken Robinson, Mr Michael Rustin, and Ms Fiona Henderson for comments offered on earlier writings. I would like to thank Rod Tweedy at Karnac Books for his support of the idea, and comments. With many thanks, also, to patients seen in many settings. Please note that though there are a very limited number of brief clinical vignettes these do not refer to any actual individuals, but are rather composites of a number of different situations.

About the author

Ian Thurston was brought up in the north east of England and studied English Literature at Newcastle University, obtaining a first class honours degree. He trained and worked as a psychiatric nurse within the National Health Service (NHS), in acute adult mental health, in Newcastle upon Tyne. Following further training in counselling and then psychodynamic psychotherapy, he worked as a therapist and clinical manager within the NHS and voluntary sector in London. His interest focused on the practical application of psychoanalytic principles to generic mental health work, and wider socio-cultural analysis. He was the clinical manager of a psycho-socially orientated acute day hospital in East London during the period of an extensive European wide randomised control trial during the 1990s. His paper based on this experience, "Developing the therapeutic alliance in acute mental health care", published in the September 2003 volume of the Association for Psychoanalytic Psychotherapy in the NHS (APP) quarterly journal *Psychoanalytic Psychotherapy*, won the inaugural prize in 2003 for the best essay on applying psychoanalytic ideas to the public sector. Since 2002 he has worked within the regional department of psychotherapy at the Centre for Specialist Psychological Therapies at Newcastle upon Tyne. His current role is that of principal adult psychotherapist, as part of the Northumberland, Tyne and Wear NHS Foundation Trust. He is a registered psychoanalytic psychotherapist with the Psychoanalysis and Jungian College of the United Kingdom Council for Psychotherapy (UKCP), and a member of the Forum for Independent Psychotherapists in London.

Introduction

This book is written as a psychoanalytically informed response to the increased polarisation of politics in contemporary life between apparently very different positions, between "Brexiteers" and "Remainers", between metropolitan liberals and "post-truth" populists, written from the belief that, in the wake of the protracted demise of neo-liberalism, self-designated categorisations of "right" and "left", "reactionary" and "progressive", are frequently beset by contradiction and cannot be taken at face value. In my analysis I write from the belief that a genuinely progressive political project must have its foundation in the rationalism and universalism of the bourgeois Enlightenment, but that this requires foundations in a robust and dynamic understanding of the vicissitudes of human subjectivity, and the way in which, as Tom Main (1967) noted, ideas, even good ideas, can become emotional objects, apt to be used for emotional purposes.

My analysis has its foundations in my experience of working in mental health care in the National Health Service (NHS) as a psychiatric nurse, clinical manager, and psychoanalytic psychotherapist. In an era in which there is often a reductive understanding of human subjectivity, a psychoanalytic perspective on the complex and dynamic relationship between the individual and the social, between the inner and the outer world, of the way in which intra-psychic dynamics are externalised in intra-personal relational patterns, is, I believe, deeply necessary. From this perspective, the patient's difficulties, arising out of the infinitely complex interplay of temperamental endowment and lived interpersonal environment, are evident as a characteristic pattern of relating to self and others. A precondition for improvement is the presence of staff open to the often disturbing projection of feelings from the patient, and a setting where these dynamics can be reflected on, better understood, and embodied in effective treatment interventions and structures. Such work, difficult at it can be, is helped if there is a culture in which there is acceptance that not all the disturbance resides in the patient: that there is in human beings ultimately more in common than in difference.

In a psychotherapy setting containment of disturbance, though a prerequisite for change, is not, however, enough. There is also a requirement that the patient has some motivation and capacity to consider his own contribution to his difficulties, rather than as seeing these simply as the product of illness, or the failings, past and present, of others. Accordingly, the psychoanalytic perspective emphasises the centrality of facing reality, internal and external, as far as is possible, as a pre-condition for learning and development. This involves the painful recognition that reality does not care to answer to human wishes – that though in the unconscious mind everything is permitted, in reality restrictions still apply. It involves the capacity to see other people in a nuanced way as separate from, rather than exten-sions of, the self. It involves, too, tolerance of the inevitable presence of conflict-ing, and sometimes disturbing emotions, thoughts, and wishes without too much self-reproach; and without the excessive projection and externalisation of these conflicts into others. Most centrally of all, from this perspective, development is inseparable from the capacity to mourn, to gradually and painfully relinquish that which has been lost as an external object, as a precondition for internalisation within the self, as part of personality, memory, and identification.

These are lifelong struggles; we all oscillate between relating to others in a balanced and realistic way, and relating to others as an extension of the self. We all have to find ways of tolerating and living with parts of the personality we may not like, and with conflicting wishes and feelings, in particular those related to normal ambivalence: the inevitable co-existence of both loving and hating feel-ings towards others.

Psychoanalytic and systemic approaches to groups and organisations have highlighted the ubiquity of psychotic processes – the confusion between internal and external reality, the suffusion of perception with emotion, the breakdown of reflective and symbolic thinking – at times of transition, or when the ordinary work-related task of the group is compromised. They have highlighted the way in which just as in psychotic patients there is also a healthier part of the personality, if it can be located, so in seemingly healthy individuals there are psychological fault lines, and more disturbed parts of the personality.

However whilst there are now long and rich traditions of applying psychoanalytic understandings to groups, organisations, workplaces, and of applying some of these principles to national and international conflict resolution these contributions tend to be comparatively neglected in public discourse. Rather, in such discourses – in response to the phenomena, for example, of homegrown nihilistic terrorism – there appears to be an impoverished conception of human subjectivity. In place of an attempt to apprehend the dialectical and dynamic relationship between the individ-ual and his social world, there is a tendency towards biological and/or social deter-minism; that is, the individual as, on the one hand, a victim of genetic destiny, on the other, a blank slate (Pinker, 2002), or holy innocent, subject to the oppressions and distortions of an unjust social order. There is, too, a tendency to overvalue con-scious motivation and ideology at the expense of attention to unconscious emotional motivations. There is a requirement, in this context, for a more robust and dynamic understanding of human subjectivity, the relationship between certain types of social dislocation, and the emergence of individual and group psychopathology.

I want at this point to make clear that this book is not intended as a work of psychoanalytic theory – the integrative account that I provide in the first part of the book of the psychoanalytic understanding of human mind and development will be familiar to many psychoanalytically informed readers. Rather, the book aims at a more general applicability, and represents an attempt to apply psychoanalytic thinking in a non-reductive way to the better understanding of emerging and dominant emotional trends in contemporary cultural and socio-political life. A psychoanalytic perspective, however, though necessary is not sufficient. There is also a requirement for meaningful and conceptually coherent integration with other modes of enquiry. Without such integration there is a danger of overextending concepts derived from clinical settings, of category error, and of reductionist and repetitive accounts. Above all else, however, it is essential, in my view, to maintain a historical perspective, and to recognise the dynamic and changing nature of the phenomena under investigation. It is just such an integrated and historicised psychosocial perspective that I seek to provide in this book, not as a totalising explanation, as some of these phenomena may continue to elude full understanding, but as a means of a least throwing some light on the situation. And while a psychoanalytic perspective might at best provide a signpost to what remains largely unchartered and unpredictable terrain, a reliable signpost in a hostile landscape can be a lifesaver, particularly at a time when the weather is about to turn.

This book is also inescapably and necessarily political, not in a party political sense, but in the sense of representing an attempt to apply a robust understanding of human subjectivity to increasingly dominant, though not exclusive, trends in socio-political and cultural life. Indeed, it is one of my central contentions that in the current climate such an understanding is required not least because assigned and self-designated political labels of right and left, reactionary and progressive, cannot be taken at face value, and can function, consciously or otherwise, to disguise the sometimes surprising new class configurations, interests, and alliances that are emerging under the current form of globalisation. In this sense the book represents an attempt to think about what a genuinely rather than pseudo progressive political project might begin to look like in such a context. The perspective that I bring to bear on these matters, influenced as it is by psychoanalytic, historical, and political vantages, is, of course, ultimately my own.

My specific focus is that of the relationship between social dislocation, narcissism, and the contemporary preoccupation with what has been called "post truth". Rapid socio-economic and cultural change is of course highly characteristic of late capitalist societies and globalisation, though the impact of these shifts may be felt unequally. I suggest, following the work of the late American historian Christopher Lasch (1977, 1979, 1984), that there are powerful narcissistic trends in contemporary life mitigating against the capacity to acknowledge and face these changes, in other words against the capacity to face reality and to mourn. I suggest that, although there are also strong countervailing forces, these trends permeate across socio-cultural divides and the political spectrum – underpinning phenomena as apparently divergent as free-market fundamentalism, certain forms of anti-capitalism, and contemporary identity and victim politics of both nominal right and left; movements that have more common emotional and intellectual underpinnings than their proponents may care to admit. These powerful trends distort perception, limit engagement with reality, and influence the way in which social problems are experienced and conceptualised. They have a tendency, through mutual projective processes to self-perpetuate, creating at best a situation of impasse, at worst of malignant social regression.

Narcissism, in the psychoanalytic literature, is a notoriously complex subject; the term refers to a universal developmental stage; and to an equally universal tendency to withdraw into the body, or the self, particularly at times of stress, illness, and loss – including loss of love. Narcissism also refers to self-regard – we all require a degree of narcissistic self-investment in order to function, and in this respect a deficit of narcissism is as much a problem as an excess. However, the term is also used to denote what has been called a pathological organisation (Steiner, 1993) of the personality. This is typically characterised by the manifest or hidden presence of a grandiose self, alternating with feelings of inferiority and shame; of a sense of "special" entitlement and righteous grievance; and, interpersonally, a tendency to relate to others not as separate and different, but as alternately idealised and denigrated extensions of the self.

In what has been termed the "thin-skinned" hypersensitive state (Britton, 1998; Rosenfeld, 1987) there is an expectation of total agreement, of unconditional empathic validation of the subjective self, and a tendency to withdraw and/or explode when the other asserts a different perspective. This can oscillate with a "thick-skinned" state, infused by a sense of superiority and emotional untouchability whilst vulnerability and neediness are projected into others, who are then treated with contempt and disdain. At worst, in this picture, that of severe malignant narcissism, there is an idealisation of destructive parts of the self, held to be superior to normal life.

The concept of malignant, or destructive, narcissism (Kernberg, 1984, 2004; Rosenfeld, 1971), has been thoughtfully applied (Manne, 2015) to the better understanding of the psychology of contemporary terrorism. More widely, it is becoming something of a received wisdom that narcissistic traits are writ large in the trend towards a "post-truth" society, in the omnipotent contempt for the claims of reality and truth, the mutual contradictions held without apparent conflict, in much of the rhetoric of a newly resurgent populist right. However, these latter accounts, though containing important insights, can also lend themselves to a familiar picture; that of liberal, secular, tolerant democracies besieged by the forces of unreason, to the notion of a Manichaean struggle of cultures. Such a picture neglects the clear evidence of underlying connections between apparently very different phenomena. What if states of narcissistic irrationality are not accidental to late capitalism but integral to it? What if the emotional wellspring of nihilistic terrorism comes not just from "Islamic fundamentalism", but from the intensely subjectivist fixations with righteous victimhood characteristic of some forms of "progressive" Western identity politics? Most fundamentally, it could be argued that the tendency towards "post truth", the assertion of the compelling power of an emotional narrative over the claims of expertise or objective evidence, has long been the default position of sections of progressive and radical opinion.

I suggest that there is, in contemporary life, a tendency towards a hypersensitivity characteristic of thin-skinned narcissism, a fixation on trauma, offence, and insult – the evolution of what the late Robert Hughes (1993) called a "culture of complaint". The latest manifestations of these trends are in preoccupations with "cultural appropriation", "micro-aggressions", and "micro-invalidations". The concomitant of these tendencies is an antipathy towards claims of evidence and objective knowledge, a tendency to defensively retreat to the politics of identity and victimhood, and to relate to others not in realistic way but as alternately idealised and denigrated aspects of the self. Such a mindset is characterised both by fundamentalism – states of emotional certainty and concretised thought – and extreme relativism. These "post-truth" tendencies, latent to varying degrees in all human beings, limit the capacity to engage with reality, and indeed heighten the danger of further social regression – well evident in recent political events across the developed world – unless their emotional basis is better understood.

I begin my analysis, therefore, with a focus on the embodied psychological processes of the individual, and then move into psychoanalytically orientated group and systemic perspectives before widening into historical and socio-cultural analysis.

In Chapter One I introduce an integrated psychoanalytic perspective on human subjectivity, emphasising that development is simultaneously interpsychic and intrapersonal, and involves the dynamic interaction of internal and external worlds. In Chapter Two I illustrate the complexity of the psychoanalytic understanding of human subjectivity, of the inextricable mix of biology and culture in specific historical contexts, through a brief discussion of the life and works of two great modernist writers, Franz Kafka and Samuel Beckett. This leads to a consideration of the relationship between narcissistic retreats and the pain of attachment and loss. In Chapter Three I consider contemporary objections to psychoanalysis. I suggest that, though there remain important conceptual differences, findings emerging from neuroscientific research on embodied emotional experience support the contemporary psychoanalytic conceptualisation of an internal relationship between a self and object representation linked by a dominant emotion, or affect, becoming enacted as a characteristic pattern of interpersonal relationship. I introduce the concept of social defences against anxiety (Jacques, 1955; Menzies-Lyth, 1959) as a conceptual bridge between individual and social analysis. In Chapter Four I discuss the co-existence of progressive and malignantly regressive trends amidst the social changes and dislocations of recent history, and the importance, in seeking to better understand these phenomena, of a multidisciplinary approach. I describe psychoanalytic accounts of psychotic anxieties and processes in large groups. I suggest that these analyses, hugely important yet neglected in much contemporary debate, in turn require integration with historical and socio-political study.

In Chapter Five I turn to a prime example of such an integration – the rise of millennial groups in late medieval Europe as described by the late historian Norman Cohn (1957) – and link this analysis to psychoanalytic accounts of psychotic processes in large unstructured groups. Cohn's analysis suggests a link between certain historical forms of social and psychic dislocation and the emergence of pathologically destructive social movements. Such movements, arising out of the collapse of "traditional" social bonds and securities, a collapse associated with the onset of early "primitive" capitalism, have common aetiologies, despite differing outward forms, common structures, unconscious (and sometimes conscious) fantasies, and emotional motivations. I argue that the distinction made by Cohn (1957) between those reformist and revolutionary groups that faced reality and had potentially realisable aims, and those that looked forward to a blissful state of satiation, outside of human history, following the purging of the unrighteous, have a contemporary resonance and implication.

Cohn (1957, 1967) made a link between the millennial fantasies and the ideology, such as it was, of Nazism. In Chapter Six I consider the way in which in recent years Nazism has been much talked about, whilst at the same time being removed from historical context. I explore the historical backdrop to the emergence of Fascism; the rise of virulent and emotionally based exclusivist ethnic nationalism, contrasting this with more benign and inclusive models of nationhood. In Chapter Seven I discuss the film *Downfall* (Hirschbiegel, 2004), an account of the last days of the Third Reich. The film reveals, in its structure, content, and critical reception, contradictory and complex attitudes towards guilt, victimhood, and the problem of destructiveness. I refer to the work of the historians Richard Evans (2005, 2008) and Ian Kershaw (1985, 1987) but also suggest that one way of viewing *Downfall* is as a devastating portrayal of the nihilistic implosion of a destructive narcissistic organisation (Rosenfeld, 1964). In Chapter Eight I suggest that such a reading, also influenced by the work of the psychoanalyst Janine Chasseguet-Smirgel (1990), does not replace the need for careful historical and political analysis, but rather suggests that such analysis might be complemented by a better understanding of the emotionally motivated irrationality that underpins such movements, and of their relationship with social dislocation and loss.

In Chapter Nine I explore the way in which theories of totalitarianism, themselves emerging out of post-war liberalism, contrasted two "cold war" worlds; on the one hand, a single party state, ruthlessly suppressing and controlling voluntary associations, with a command economy; on the other, open institutions, interest group politics, free markets, confessional pluralism, cultivation of creativity, and so on. I suggest that the distinction between liberal pluralism and totalitarian one-party states, though still crucial, was increasingly undercut by the ascendancy of a fundamentalist free-market capitalism that was itself a totalising system, which, albeit in a different way, increasingly intruded into everyday life, into human subjectivity and relationships.

As a way of exploring these changes I turn in Chapter Ten to the lives and works of the Italian writer and filmmaker Piers Paulo Pasolini, and the historian

Richard Cobb. Pasolini projected his own psychodrama on to the outskirt estates of post-war Rome, in his identification with what now might be called the semi-criminal underclass, and his opposition to the new "respectable" consumer society. Cobb (1988) also perhaps idealised the anarchic underclass; but in so doing recorded the loss of the small-scale Paris of hidden lanes and courtyards, small artisan establishments, and mixed class and ethnic configurations, where a certain degree of social connectedness was possible – even for alienated intellectuals. I suggest that the lives and work of these restless figures both expressed a real social loss that was otherwise unarticulated, and may also have formed part of an individual "psychic retreat" (Steiner, 1993) from loss, and from more intense human contact. I make clear in this discussion that the social world, past and present, real and imagined, also forms part of the inner world of the individual, and is a source of complex and often contradictory personal identification.

I then turn in Chapter Eleven from the experience of the solitary intellectual and to wider socio-cultural responses to social change, as manifest in popular culture through the medium of professional football. I return to my native Tyneside and the decline of the famous Swan Hunter shipyard. As the shipyards fell into inactivity, the local football team, Newcastle United, a largely sleeping giant of unfulfilled expectations, began to rise again, playing football of unparalleled excitement and creativity. The team's attacking football, and the fans identification with it, expressed a creativity, a joie de vivre, and an inclusive collective spirit that was denied expression elsewhere. As such it functioned as a cultural riposte to commodification and part of a creative defence against the experience of loss. I suggest, however, that the real achievements of Newcastle United took on a quality of manic grandiosity, on the part of both the club and a large section of their fans; as the club was burdened with a level of emotional investment that, in the destruction of other sources of identification, it could not meet. This was manifest, in football terms, as a particular Achilles heel – problems with the defence.

If the market was idealised by the fundamentalist neo-liberal right, the old centres of manufacturing, their industries, attendant communities, and social institutions, were denigrated, not least by sections of what termed itself the progressive left, as bastions of patriarchy, ignorance, prejudice, and xenophobia – in what was a radical retreat from the notion of a shared public history, into the politics of identity. I suggest in Chapter Twelve that this was indicative of a major shift on sections of the left, contributing to a growing disconnect with sections of the population, often those most negatively affected by globalisation.

I go on in Chapter Thirteen to analyse these phenomena with reference to the late Christopher Lasch's writings on the "narcissistic" culture of late capitalism – and its critics. Lasch (1977, 1979, 1984) famously argued that narcissistic personality traits, latent to varying degrees in everyone, were adaptive to the requirements of late capitalist culture in which consumption was the dominant mode, and where the business of making things was being increasingly outsourced to other parts of the world. They were the psychological correlate, too, of a "therapeutic state"; shorn of the tragic realism of Freud, emphasising the values of self-actualisation and personal authenticity ; at a time when "traditional" institutions formed in the crucible of an earlier era were being hollowed out by the totalising forces of market and commodity.

I suggest that Lasch's analysis, though subject to critique and inevitably dated in some respects, nevertheless remains central to any understanding of dominant psychological, emotional, and intellectual trends in contemporary life. These, I suggest, are particularly manifest in a collective estrangement from a public past, in the assertion of subjectivity and emotion over intellect, in the pervasiveness of narratives of victimhood, in the denigration of paternal authority, and in the prevalence of extreme relativism. These trends, I suggest, are related to the fundamentalist free market ideology of which postmodernism, as Frederick Jameson (1991) has argued, is the cultural logic, and they form the emotional and intellectual backdrop to today's "post-truth" society.

In Chapter Fourteen I explore my own area of professional experience, in the light of these trends. I consider the treatment of severe mental illness and personality disorder, where a "consumer" model of human relating is grossly inadequate and risks collusion with pathology. In Chapter Fifteen I discuss the way in which postmodernism has permeated into some forms of psychotherapeutic theory and practice. I suggest, influenced by the writings of Ronald Britton on narcissism (1998), that postmodern psychotherapy and postmodernism itself, occupy the dyadic world of epistemological narcissism, in which risk is seen as "false compliance with a powerful object" (p. 166) and the traumatising impingements of the external world upon the authentic vulnerable self. In such a situation the paternal object and paternal functioning are avoided and/or denigrated and become unavailable for internalisation. I argue that these essentially narcissistic trends tend to substitute wish-fulfilment for the apprehension of reality, and to relate to others as extensions of the self, thus limiting the capacity to deal realistically with social conflicts.

In Chapter Sixteen I consider the different arguments for and against the Iraq war, and subsequent responses to it, to illustrate the role of subjectivism and relativism in contemporary life. I argue that neither the proponents nor the opponents of the war engaged with reality. Tony Blair appeared to be arguing from genuine conviction, but he also gave the impression of answering to God rather than to any more ordinary human authority, or to the claims of objective reality. Many opponents of the war, however, retreated into self-righteousness and the kind of moral relativism that equated George Bush with Saddam Hussein. The position of old-fashioned positivist science and rationality was represented by the weapons inspector Hans Blix – either there were weapons of mass destruction or there weren't – and his sceptical, empirical voice was increasingly drowned out by louder clamouring and assertions of will.

This illustrates a central concern of the book: in a world where the power of a compelling narrative takes precedent over the claims of objective evidence or truth, the danger is of a situation where subjective reality can be willed to power without a basis in external reality, and where some voices may be louder, and more powerful, than others. As an example of this, I discuss, in Chapter Seventeen, the way in which the economic crisis of 2007, starting in the deregulated housing and derivatives markets of the United States of America (USA) was reconceptualised as a crisis of social democracy, and has given rise to the politics of austerity. This might be seen as the fundamental contemporary post truth from which all other post truths follow.

I then turn, in Chapter Eighteen, to the events of 2016, and in particular the progressive reaction to the European Referendum in the United Kingdom and the election of Donald Trump in the United States. I suggest a view that contrasts liberal progressiveness with post-truth populism is based on a false dichotomy, as it ignores the interrelationship of these phenomena; in particular, the way in which a tendency towards post-truth, and the privileging of emotional narratives over the claims of expertise and evidence, permeates across the political and socio-cultural divides. Such a view dismisses the possibility of a progressive populism and treats Brexit and Donald Trump, which are, in this picture, crudely conflated, as causes rather than as symptoms of an underlying process of socio-cultural dislocation. Most fundamentally, however, the accusation of the "post-truth" politics of the populist right begs the question of those powerful subjectivist and relativistic trends, not least amongst sections of radical and "progressive" opinion that have long sought to problematise the very notion of truth.

A question that arises from the current polarisation over "Brexit" is whether, in the face of the fractures and social dislocation that are the downside of globalisation, the best available form of protection against narcissistic and paranoid group regression is an empowered, democratic, and inclusive nation state, or a supranational body. That this substantive issue has largely gone undebated, and indeed has been drowned out by what has become another form of identity politics, speaks to the failure, I suggest, on both sides of the debate, to engage with reality. Meanwhile, the continuing denigration of the "traditional" working class and its associational culture, not least by sections of "progressive opinion", leaves the field open for the authoritarian right to articulate the unexpressed language of social dislocation and loss.

In my concluding chapter I put forward the notion that there are some positions held on the contemporary "progressive liberal left" that are in practice neither classically liberal nor of the left. Here I make a differentiation between cosmopolitanism as a way of life and cosmopolitanism as a self-conscious identity; between liberal pluralism, where there is an attempt to live with and accommodate different views, and an authoritarian or fundamentalist mindset in which there is a thin-skinned intolerance of a different perspective. Indeed, to offer a different perspective is experienced as the violation or invalidation of the self. I consider that here we are in the presence of a particular form of projective identification, which buttresses itself behind an apparently unimpeachably correct moral position, and which perpetuates a pathological splitting between the righteous and the profane, between victims and victimisers. These projections serve a psychological purpose and the aim is not integration and progress but to perpetuate the split.

I consider whether there may be a connection between certain forms of extreme political correctness and religious fundamentalism as a violent variant of Western "identity politics". Contemporary nihilistic terrorism may be motivated by resentment, grievance, and a sense of personal trauma and shame, identified with national and religious humiliation, redeemed by an act of purifying violence and self-immolation. The acts of terror that result do not appear to have achievable political or strategic aims. Rather, they appear to be ends in themselves, given meaning by the impact they have on the object of attack. In response there is a danger of overvaluing the conscious ideologies of the perpetrators, of colluding with grandiosity, and of giving such "beliefs" unmerited credibility. There is a need therefore to better understand the unconscious emotional motivations that might be at play, and the socio-cultural conditions from which they arise.

I conclude that a genuinely progressive response to such phenomena needs to maintain an empathic capacity, in the psychoanalytic sense, but also requires the replacement of culture wars with political analysis, and the robust reassertion of the universalist values of socio-economic justice, civil rights, everyday civility, respect, pluralism, and the rights of people to have their own opinions even if we disagree with them. It requires understanding but also moving beyond the toxicity of contemporary politics of identity. I suggest that universalism is more likely to thrive where there is a secure basis, an attachment to the local, and a sense of shared, though not exclusive, history and values.

Chapter 1

Psychoanalytic perspectives on subjectivity

The mode of the European Enlightenment was, as the literary critic Ian Watt (1957) has pointed out, "critical, anti-traditional, and innovating, its method has been the study of the particulars of the experience of the individual investigator, who, ideally at least, is free from the body of past assumptions and traditional beliefs" (p. 13). In setting itself against the old hierarchies of birth, rank, and class, against the primacy of tradition, and the vested interests of property and church, the bourgeois Enlightenment had as its centrepiece the empirical investigation of external reality, of nature. No longer would truth be conditional upon abstract reasoning, arguments from authority and from ancient texts. As the motto of the newly established Royal Society in London put it, "*Nullius in verba*", loosely translated as "Take nobody's word for it".

The industrial revolution was strongly linked to these rationalistic progressive and democratic developments, to the belief in a world where the productive capacities of men could be set free, setting in train a world of potentially endless growth and development. This combined both academic and practical methods, scientific investigation and theory, artisan skills and experience, natural philosophy and technical innovation. Many of the protagonists of the early world of capitalist development were radical, self-educated men of modest or low background, progressive in social attitudes, tolerant, democratic, and able to bring their energies and talents to fruition in the new conditions. This was the case on my native Tyneside, for example. The Stephenson Brothers, William Armstrong, Charles Parsons were amongst the heroes of this age of capitalism, an era built on scientific innovation and the skills of the workforce in producing things. Indeed it could be argued that globalisation started with Robert Stephenson, and the revolution in transport, and the development of the railways. These men created a historic transformation, as artistically represented in the apocalyptic biblical paintings of the Tyneside artist John Martin, in what Marshall Berman (1982) and, later, Christopher Lasch have termed the Promethean transformation of nature and reality through technological development.

As Ernst Gellner (1983) has noted, the changes involved in industrialisation embodied rationality, efficiency, and, at a deeper structural level, "a universal conceptual currency" (p. 21) in which "all facts are located within a single continuous logical space" (p. 21), so "that in principle one single language describes the world and is internally unitary" (p. 21). This was very different from a premodern agrarian world in which multiple "hierarchically related sub worlds" co-exist, often with specialised language and rituals, but were not integrated or subject to the expectations of a putative "ordinary reality" (p. 21). Indeed, such integration and subjection to "reality" would have been regarded as blasphemous or outrageous.

These profound socio-cultural changes in the West found expression in new cultural and literary forms (Watt, 1957). In contrast to the classical and renaissance workings and reworkings of myth and past history as means of fidelity to more general and universal truths, separate from the mere contingencies of historical time and place, the new form of the novel placed unique and irreducible individual experience, and consciousness, at the centre, in terms of both form and content. The novel as a genre brought with it originality of plot, the importance of time, attention to individual characterisation, and the delineation of the specific social environment. The "bourgeois novel" thus aimed at verisimilitude to individual experience, to life as it really was. Correspondingly Daniel Defoe's heroes, for example, were also ordinary unheroic Everymen, and Everywomen.

If the rise of the novel was part of a movement towards philosophical and literary realism, and active engagement with the world, at the same time, however, it was also part of a move towards subjectivism and solipsism. It is this contradiction that is at the heart of the work of Defoe (1719). As Watt pointed out, whilst the prototypical Robinson Crusoe might be self-reliant:

> His inordinate egocentricity condemns him to isolation wherever he is. The egocentricity, one might say, is forced on him because he is cast away on an island. But it is also true that his character is throughout courting his fate and it merely happens that the island offers the fullest opportunity for him to realize three associated tendencies of modern civilization – absolute economic, social, and intellectual freedom of the individual.
>
> (p. 96)

This is the line stretching right through the form and content of the novel, from *Robinson Crusoe* (1719) to Michel Houellebecq's *The Possibility of an Island* (2005), a dystopian science fiction in which the cloned narrator, Daniel24, lives alone in a compound with his cloned dog.

The spirit of rational enquiry and individualism of the bourgeois Enlightenment, and the industrial revolution, thus pointed in two directions: one towards public engagement and improvement, to "good works", and the other towards solipsism. Richard Sennett (2003, p. 105) points out that "individualism" was in fact a term first used by De Tocqueville in the 1830s to invoke the social isolation he observed in America, a situation where people might love their family and friends but be indifferent to wider social relations. Back in England the young Frederick Engels (1845) wrote of the atomised and egoistic crowds of people in London, their indifference to, and isolation from, others in the face of their common humanity.

Joseph Conrad, in *The Secret Agent* (1907), has his anarchistic and nihilistic terrorists with their idealisation of destruction and death as a purifying force, moving in unhappy isolation around a phantasmagorical London – a place that is presented as overwhelming, alienating at the same time as being crushingly banal. Conrad's darkly impressionistic portrayal of London is that of a city as an impersonal force, forever changing and of reach, as implacable in its indifference to human wishes as a force of nature. Conrad's view of the revolutionaries is that of atomised individuals, who, though they speak in the name of the people, are of no more substance than the world they inhabit.

Or as T. S Eliot (1922) later put it:

Unreal City,
Under the brown fog of a winter dawn,
A crowd flowed over London Bridge, so many,
I had not thought death had undone so many.

Gellner (1983) argues that industrial society is, in historical terms, the only society ever to be based on the notion of perpetual growth, of "expected and continued improvement" (p. 22), and in this way "its favoured mode of social control is universal … buying off social aggression with material enhancement". Such a homogenised world appears open to endless possibilities and combinations. The danger of this situation, as Gellner points out, is of loss of legitimacy, "if the cornucopia becomes temporarily jammed and the flow falters" (p. 22). In such a world there is a need for mobility, adaptability, and the capacity to move away from "traditional" roles and occupations. There is no place for unchanging stratification based on rank and hierarchy. However, if this world is, in formal terms, more egalitarian than pre-capitalist societies, the price to be paid is in terms of the omnipresence of social dislocation, of material and psychic insecurity.

From these perspectives capitalism was, and is, a constantly revolutionising process, utilising pre-capitalist and "traditionalist" structures (for example, of family, the Protestant work ethic) and then discarding or undercutting these as they become less adaptive to workings of the system. In the post-war years this inherent turbulence was balanced by a broadly social democratic settlement, itself a reaction to the conditions that helped foster the rise of Fascism. To be clear, capitalism, or certain versions of it, can be supremely creative. Left to their own devices, however, that is, without adequate checks and balances, and effective opposition, the forces of the market and commodity value tend to hollow out, undermine, and commodify "traditional" social bonds and patterns of attachment – bonds that have themselves arisen as bulwarks against the vicissitudes of the market, and of life.

I write this book from the perspective that any genuinely progressive political response to the contemporary manifestations of these dislocations must have its foundation in the rationalism and universalism of the bourgeois Enlightenment. It was the practical application of these values that created, for the first time, the chance for the mass of the population to have a life that was something other than nasty, brutish, and short. It was these principles that underpinned the heroic but savage era of early productive capitalism, and it was the same traditions that created the basis for critiques centred on the application of reason and principles of human equality, of the inequities of unregulated capitalism and imperialism. And, in the context of the rise of emotionally motivated identity politics, it is more important than ever to maintain the rationalist distinction between historical claims, subject to evidence, from those that are not.

It is essential, however, that such a project has foundations in a realistic and robust understanding of human subjectivity. A psychoanalytic perspective on the ubiquity of emotionally motivated irrationality in organisational and group life, particularly during periods of change and dislocation, is an essential component of such an understanding.

A common contemporary cultural response to Freud and psychoanalysis, a response influenced by subjectivism and the postmodern relativisation of all truth claims, is that psychoanalysis universalised the particular socio-cultural milieu of late bourgeois Vienna; and a historically specific character structure was used to generalise about "the human condition". However, it is a basic contention of this book that truths about the world are not dependent on perspective (Bell, 2009), and that there are existential "facts of life" (Money-Kyrle, 1968) that exist in all cultures, albeit that they may be represented and expressed in different ways.

Such a "traditional" psychoanalytic view, emphasising the universals of human experience rooted in biology and human vulnerability, rather than what is culturally specific, has become unfashionable. The obvious truism that there are biological as well as social limits to human aspiration – that we have to acknowledge generational and sexual difference, the reality of ageing and loss – sets itself against the many forces in contemporary intellectual, cultural, and social life that seek to present human beings as Protean, self-inventing, shape-shifting, changing identities at will, or as disembodied minds or selves. These ideologies of the independent autonomous self are reinforced by medical and technological innovation that promise to liberate human beings from the presumed burdens of the human body and the biological.

Meanwhile the idea of a dynamic "unconscious", with repression as it main agency, can still attract opprobrium in the wider cultural sphere, as if the notion of the unconscious was "socially constructed" by psychoanalysis. However, that beliefs, emotions, and wishes can motivate human behaviour whilst they are partially or fully out of conscious awareness is the stuff of literature and folk culture the world over – "the heart has its reasons that the mind knows not".

In this chapter I introduce a condensed and necessarily simplified description of some of the central themes of the psychoanalytic perspective on human mind and development, as they relate to the themes of this book, with the immediate caveat that there are many different psychoanalytic schools of thought; though a degree of pluralism is desirable, not all approaches are amenable to meaningful integration – in other words there are some schools that are mutually exclusive. An attempt, for example, to integrate contemporary American self-psychology with Freudian drive theory would lack the internal conceptual coherence necessary to offer a credible explanatory account (Hanly, 2009). I have endeavoured in my summary to bring together ego psychology – born out of Freud's work, and continued by Anna Freud, focusing on the functioning of the ego in managing, modifying, and expressing drives and impulses – and object relations theory, emphasising relational development.

There are four areas of the psychoanalytic theory of the mind that I want to highlight. The first is that all mental events and phenomena are potentially meaningful and intelligible, within the context of the life history of the individual. This applies even to the most apparently bizarre and meaningless psychotic symptoms. The second is that of unconscious mental functioning, of a part of the mind that is omnipresent and dynamic, outside of awareness. The third is of inherent psychic conflict between different parts of the self: although there is, usually, a supraordinate "I" of subjective self-consciousness, the self is not a unitary subject. The fourth concerns a compulsion to repeat the relational patterns derived from early relationships throughout life, to transfer feelings initially aroused in relation to early attachment figures on to people in the present. Sometimes this is in the service of communication and development, a process that can become, particularly in a treatment setting, subject to reflection and modification. Sometimes, however, in what Freud termed the "compulsion to repeat" (Freud, 1920g), this is in the service of a destructive and/or self-sabotaging impulse.

If what makes us characteristically human is the capacity to reflect on experience, and to employ the flexible and symbolic properties of language, we also have to acknowledge the omnipresence of a part of the psyche that remains outside of conscious awareness and which is not available, unlike that which is preconscious, for normal introspection. **There is a difference between the descriptively unconscious – feelings and thoughts that are not yet conscious – and the dynamically repressed unconscious**. Freud believed that this part of mind is characterised by primary process thinking, in which "everything is permitted" and the pleasure principle dominates – there is no time, there is no death, there is mutual contradiction, wish fulfilment holds sway over the frustrations and delayed gratifications of reality. In the realm of the unconscious there are no constraints – anything is possible.

The ego by contrast is that part of mental functioning that is concerned with "secondary process" thinking. This is governed by the "reality principle", and involves the testing out of internal perceptions and thoughts with external reality, the recognition of time, limitations, and the separateness of other people. It is orientated towards external reality, reason, and "common sense", and the need to inhibit and control impulses, exercise restraint, delay gratification, appraise evidence, and test out perception. The ego, however, is not synonymous with conscious mental functioning. In all of us there are, for example, what Freud, later followed by his daughter Anna Freud (Freud, A, 1936) called "ego defences" – repression, denial, sublimation, displacement, and so on; protecting against anxiety and the consciousness of what might be inadmissible psychic conflict.

The dynamic repressed unconscious, an implacable force that can never be known directly, nevertheless gains expression through dreams, everyday slips of the tongue, and so on, and through psychological symptoms. Such phenomena have a symbolic meaning, and represent compromise formations between the forces seeking expression and fulfillment, and the forces of repression. They are multi-determined, and their true meaning is disguised through mechanisms such as condensation, the bringing together of different images and thoughts into a single motif, and displacement, where emotions are directed to an alternative object. The meaning of symptoms requires decoding; emotions can be divorced from their conceptual and ideational content, impulses, and wishes may be turned into their opposite, or turned against the self.

At the beginning of life there is only a rudimentary "ego" and the infant tends to relate to the other not as a "whole object", or complete person, but as a "part object" or a function. At this point thinking is archaic (dominated by bodily processes and expressed in bodily terms), concrete, and dominated by anxiety and wish fulfilment. The first anxieties are those connected with helplessness and painful frustrations, somatic and instinctual tensions, and these are usually assuaged intuitively by the actions of the mother, or primary caretaker, to manageable proportions. A well-known example of this is the smiling response between mother and child. The child looks for the mother's smiling response and when rewarded the smile broadens. When the mother does not respond in this way, the infants smile fades and is replaced with perplexity and unpleasure. Another anxiety associated with the growing bond with mother, is "stranger anxiety", in which the infant clings to mother in the presence of new faces. A further anxiety is aroused by mother's absence. As Freud put it, the child "cannot as yet distinguish between temporary absence and permanent loss" (1926d, p. 169). He famously described the game of peek-a-boo, played between child and mother, as a way of repeating and mastering this unpleasurable feeling state (1920g).

The origins of the ego, then, are in the mental representation of bodily experience and physical sensations. As development occurs, the growth of the ego is through a process of identification, and this becomes, in the orthodox psychoanalytic account, a way of representing the link between the individual and the social, between biology and culture (Frosch, 1987). Classically, it is the Oedipus complex that is the crucible of this process. In the male version of this constellation the child's wish for an exclusive relationship with mother involves also his rivalry with a simultaneously loved and hated father. The wish to kill off father also provokes guilt and fear of retaliation. Normally, reality prevails and the wish is renounced and becomes subject to repression, and there is identification with father and paternal authority. These processes are complex; a part of the psyche may relinquish oedipal wishes and accept reality, whilst another part may remain in willful ignorance or outright opposition. At the same time there is also in human beings a "negative" version of the Oedipus complex, in which the desired object is of the same sex, and the rival becomes the parent of the opposite sex. This can lead, in boys, to a feminine identification, against which there may then be a masculine protest. The universal existence of such complex identifications, as Freud believed, attested to the innate psychic bisexuality of all human beings. From a psychoanalytic perspective these unconscious and often conflicting identifications permeate mental life and personality development.

The dissolution of the Oedipus complex involves the identification of son with father, and the sublimation of feelings towards mother, a process that involves the internalization of parental, and in particular, paternal authority. The heir to the Oedipus complex is the superego, that part of the psyche concerned with adhering to moral values, ideals, and prohibition. The father, representing the social order, past and present, has to be internalised in a relatively benign way. A key developmental factor is normally the strength of the superego; too weak leads to failures of conscience, and the internalisation of moral values, but too harsh and there will be savage internal judgements on self and others. Freud believed that this harshness was a sign of a primitive superego, infused with inner directed aggression, as is the case, as we shall see later, with melancholic states.

The contemporary object relations psychoanalytic understanding of human mind and development has its foundation in biology – the individual is decidedly not a *tabula rasa* or blank slate, the passive subject of social conditioning, but is also intersubjective and inescapably intrapersonal. The developing child requires the presence of at least another interested mind in order to internalise and identify with reflective thinking and mental functioning, in order to develop the capacity to think about rather than act on their emotions, and to imagine the mind and different perspective of another. In this way, what some psychoanalysts (Fonagy et al., 2002) have called the capacity to "mentalize", to represent the mental state of self and others through thinking and words, is rudimentarily developed. From this perspective, relationally based emotional regulation is, optimally, gradually internalised as part of development.

In an averagely expectable environment there is instinctual reciprocity between child and mother that enables age specific maturational developments to take place. Although the child is initially unable to distinguish between self and other, it is intrinsically "object-relating" from the onset, and such relating and the maturational steps that follow are biologically primed. The structuring of experience is developed through the "psychic reciprocity" of mother and child interaction, in a dynamic intersubjective context. The child is predisposed to respond to mother's voice, to the cadence of nursery rhymes, and perhaps to the taste of mother's usual food, and to seek out information generally. The mothers face is clearly recognised at two days old.

For Melanie Klein (1975), and clinicians working in her tradition, the child has a need to separate loving and hating parts of the self, to protect good parts of the self from bad. There is therefore a psychologically necessary splitting of self and object, and the utilisation of the "primitive" defence mechanisms of denial, splitting, and projective identification. A positively invested emotional relationship with an idealised all-providing mother is separated from a negatively invested relationship with a depriving one. The infant projects unmanageable and inchoate emotions into the primary carer, usually but not always the mother, where they can be contained and metabolised, before being returned in a more digestible form; that is, the mother is able to receive, manage, and process the infant's projections of feeling without premature distance or discharge, without returning the feelings in unmodified form straight back. This process is seen as being crucial for a securely established primary relationship, and as the foundation for further personality development. Optimally the infant is able to take in good experience, as part of the building blocks of the developing personality, and to allow separateness. The divergence between the objective reality of the external world, and of other people, and the internal representation of this world becomes smaller as the child's mind and personality becomes more integrated.

It is the oedipal configuration, as we have seen, that faces the child with a three-person triangular situation in which exclusion, smallness, and reality have to be negotiated. The capacity to accept the depredations of the Oedipus complex, to be the excluded third, requires the capacity to mourn what has been lost, as a prelude to further maturation. This capacity to mourn itself involves the capacity to bring together loving and hating feelings towards the same person, to face up to the destructive attacks made on the otherwise loved object. The capacity to work through the oedipal position and relinquish infantile omnipotence is thus indivisible from the capacity to reach what Klein called the "depressive position", in which integration of ambivalent feelings (love and hate) towards others, and of ordinary reality; awareness of destructive aspects of the self without feeling overwhelmed by them; the capacity for realistic guilt, and for creative reparation, are possible. Throughout these processes mourning involves the relinquishment of the lost person or thing as an external object, as a precondition for internalisation and identification.

There is an innate resilience to human beings that is at odds with many of the assumptions of contemporary victim and identity politics. However, it is also true that, in part because of the lengthy period of development and maturation in human beings compared with other mammals, things can go wrong; whether as a result of intrinsic constitutional factors, or environmental deficits, or, more usually, a complex combination of both. In psychotic states of mind, for example, the more reality-orientated parts of the personality, associated with "ego functioning", are overwhelmed with anxiety and powerful emotions or affect, or "unimaginable storms" (Jackson & Williams, 1994). In the "prodomal" phase of increasing psychotic anxiety, "bad" or inadmissible aspects of the self are projected into the external world, creating a persecutory environment in which attack is feared, activating more internal aggression, leading to more projection, in what can be, if left unchecked, a vicious spiral of decline. Such can be the basis of psychotic breakdown. This can bring in its wake an attempt to repair what Freud described as a rent in the ego with, for example, a paranoid delusional system in which "bad" aspects of the self are concretely identified with people and objects in the external world; whilst the "good" parts of the self are idealised in grandiose or megalomaniacal fantasy. Alternately there may be a shutting down, a withdrawal from life and relationships that can become, if there is not effective intervention, a chronic situation – the "defect" states evident in some forms of psychotic illness.

In what Otto Kernberg (1984) has termed borderline personality organisation (which can manifest as borderline, narcissistic, schizoid, and other personality disorders) there is contact with external reality but a distorted view of self and others leading to a repeating pattern of dysfunctional interpersonal and work relationships. In contrast to people with neurotic difficulties, for whom the primary defence is repression, such people make excessive use of the developmentally earlier defences of projective identification, splitting, and denial. Whether due to temperamental or environmental factors, or more usually the complex interaction of both, there is a "failure of containment" in the primary relationship leading to pathological splitting of experience of self and others. There is a need to split and dissociate positive loving feelings and experiences on the one hand, and negative and hating feelings and experiences on the other, for fear that the latter will prove more powerful than the former. These defences may protect from the feared catastrophe but lead to a state of what Kernberg (1984) has termed identity diffusion, in which there is a flat, impoverished, and contradictory sense of self and others, with a concomitant instability in interpersonal relations, and a tendency towards the repetitive re-enactment of dysfunctional and ultimately distressing (to self and others) relational patterns.

In these situations an internal relationship between a representation of self and other, linked by an affect, is re-enacted, via projective processes, in the intrapersonal environment. These relationships tend to be dichotomised; experienced in extreme terms as either positive or negative. Perhaps most typically, a relationship between a victimised self and a victimising or malignantly misunderstanding other is re-enacted as a characteristic relational pattern. Although there may well have been real disturbance – and often the experience of abuse and neglect – in the patient's actual background, the repletion of this pattern in a new situation, where the reality may be different, can create a repetitive and self-sabotaging situation. The projective processes involved are powerful; the recipient of the projection may find himself "inhabited" by a powerful set of feelings, and feel pushed into those very "angry" and "misunderstanding" responses that actualise the internal fantasy. Alternately, there may be "role reversal", with the recipient of the projection in the role of the besieged victim.

The driving force in these situations is the need to avoid bringing together loving and hating, positive and negative, experiences of self and of others: to maintain a split. It is important to realise that these defences have a function and are, from the person's perspective, necessary for survival. People may find it very hard to face their internal realities if they believe their hate will prove much more powerful than their love. Kernberg links these difficulties to a high level of constitutional aggression and a difficulty in integrating loving and hating feelings towards the other, originating in the primary relationship with the primary caretaker, usually mother, and to later problems in the interpersonal environment, often, though not always, greatly exacerbated by early trauma and/or neglect. Whatever the causation, and this is a subject to which I will return, if there has been a failure to adequately secure the primary relationship and identify with good experience then the oedipal situation cannot be negotiated; nor can, in a parallel process, the depressive position be securely established (even if it has also to be noted that all human beings oscillate between these positions throughout their lifetimes).

Recent psychoanalytic literature on severe personality disturbance has balanced the psychoanalytic preoccupation with, and possible idealisation of, the role of the mother with an increased awareness of the importance of paternal functioning, and the centrality to development of internalisation of the father (Campbell, 1999). The presence of "good authority" and effective paternal functioning provides a model for identification and an alternative source of help in the face of the regressive pull towards a hostile dependent relationship with the maternal object, by the setting of limits and the ensuring that, although endless permission is sought, restrictions in the end do apply. However, internalisation of paternal functioning and identification with father is rendered more difficult in a contemporary world in which good paternal authority is often absent, and frequently subject to social marginalisation and cultural denigration when it is present. These are themes that I will return to later.

Optimally, in normal development the appearance of neurotic defences such as repression, suppression, and reaction formation (cleanliness as a defence against messiness, for example), together with unconscious identification with both parents, begin to structure "personality" and the acquisition of character. Later, social identifications during the latency period and adolescence occur with peers and the wider social milieu. For everyone, though, in these developmental challenges there will be moves back and forwards between more and less integrated states, with necessary periods of chaos and regression leading to further periods of integration. Anna Freud and later clinicians writing in her tradition (Yorke et al., 1989) concentrated on the notion of "developmental lines" of cognitive, emotional, and psychomotor advance and regression; leading to further consolidation, subject to disruption linked to the balance of instinctual forces (including level of innate affect), strength and flexibility of the ego defences, and the availability or otherwise of helpful figures in the environment.

In psychoanalytic terms the hallmark of maturity includes the capacity to realistically appraise reality; to reflect on emotional experience and to be able to take a different perspective; to have a coherent and nuanced view of self and others; to inhibit and delay reactions, responses, and wishes. However, although such maturity may be achieved, there is an inherent, never fully resolvable, tension between the individual and the social world, and between different aspects of the personality. The move between the paranoid-schizoid position – characterised by denial, splitting, and projective identification, and in which others are related to as idealised and/or denigrated aspects of the self – and the depressive position – where separateness and ambivalence are tolerated – is subject to disruption, and constitutes a lifelong struggle. The deep unconscious can never be fully known and the human being remains to some extent a stranger in his own house. Such is the "tragic realist" psychoanalytic understanding of the human personality, the treatment aim of which is not "happiness" or "empowerment", but to convert "neurotic misery into ordinary unhappiness" (Freud, 1895d, p. 305) or, more positively put, to better enable the individual to work, love, and play.

Psychoanalysis has been accused of reductionism but as the liberal critic Lionel Trilling wrote, "man, as Freud conceives him, is not to be understood by any simple formula … but is rather an inextricable tangle of culture and biology. Such is not a view that narrows the world ... but on the contrary opens and complicates it" (Trilling, 1947, cited in Shengold, 1988, p. 5). Freud's case histories are perhaps still the best illustration of the labyrinthine complexity of developments, of mental life, and of the dynamic interaction of individual and environment; here we have impulses and wishes turning into their opposites, polymorphous sexual currents and their fusion with aggressive instincts, the co-existence of immature and mature defences, conflicting identifications with parental objects altered by projective processes; all of this in interaction with a specific interpersonal and cultural environment.

Such a view of the dynamic and dialectical relationship between individual and environment, and of the importance of unconscious emotional motivations, is precisely what is lacking, however, in much current discourse on human subjectivity. Thinking of the better understanding of some forms of contemporary terrorism, for example, a psychoanalytic perspective would suggest that there is in human beings an innate drive towards attachment, development, and the acquisition of knowledge. There is, too, an innate resilience that is at odds with the contemporary fixation on victimhood – the pathogenic impact of trauma cannot be assumed. There is also in human nature, however, a capacity for what philosopher and psychoanalyst Jonathan Lear has called "motivated irrationality" (2005, p. 4), particularly during periods of social transition and dislocation, for which intellectual reflection and political ideology may provide convenient rationalisations:

> The terrorist thinks it is *because* his people have been humiliated that he is justified in his acts. But might the situation be just the reverse? That is, because he takes a certain pleasure in destructive hatred, he has become attached to his sense of humiliation.
>
> (Lear, 2005, p. 4)

As I will discuss in more detail later the psychoanalytic perspective, if culturally besieged, is congruent with much of the research and evidence emerging from the recent advances in neuroscience. As the cognitive neuroscientist Steven Pinker (2002), no particular friend of psychoanalysis, writes:

> More generally, the interplay of mental systems can explain how people can entertain revenge fantasies that they never act on, or can commit adultery only in their hearts. In this way the theory of human nature coming out of the cognitive revolution has more in common with the Judeo-Christian theory of human nature, and with the psychoanalytic theory proposed by Sigmund Freud, than with behaviourism, social constructivism, and other versions of the Blank Slate. Behavior is not just emitted or elicited, nor does it come

directly out of culture or society. It comes from an internal struggle among mental modules with differing agendas and goals.

(2002, p. 40)

In historical terms, though, psychoanalysis emerged out of late bourgeois culture and what has been termed "high modernism", and it is perhaps in modernist literature that the psychoanalytic perspective on human subjectivity is most fully expressed. It is to two prime exemplars of this tradition, and the link between narcissism and loss, one of the central themes of this book, therefore, that I next turn.

Chapter 2

Narcissism and loss

Conventional contemporary readings of Franz Kafka's *The Trial* (1925), represent the novel as an allegory or premonition of twentieth-century totalitarianism or at the very least a representation of the arbitrary bureaucratic iniquities and absurdities of the old Austro-Hungarian Empire. There is important truth to such readings but the originality and power of Kafka's work is that he is also describing internal persecutors, or persecutory objects, aspects of the psyche that the protagonist can neither integrate nor escape from. In the final chapter Joseph K is taken by "two old second rate actors" (1925, p. 205) to a desolate stone quarry at the edge of town. Just before the final denouement he glimpses a figure at a casement window. "Was it a friend, a good man, someone who wanted to help? Where was the judge he had never seen? Where was the court he had never reached?" (1925, p. 210). At one level this final scene might be seen as a brilliant premonitory account of the wickedness and evils of the twentieth century, and of today – a world of arbitrary summary executions by nameless forces on the edges of unnamed towns. At another level, though, both the court, and the possibly helpful figures glimpsed in the distance, are aspects of Joseph K's psyche; they are objects from his internal world. The oppressors are more powerful than the pull, however risky, towards libidinal and human contact.

The historian Saul Friedlander (2013) suggests that Kafka was most of all a "poet of his own disorder" (2013, p. 4), dramatising his own conflicts between, in psychoanalytic terms, masochistic submission before, and rebellion against, the world of father, between feminine and masculine identification, and between heterosexual strivings and ego dystonic homoerotic wishes. Such a reading recognises the indivisibility of content and form. For Kafka's deconstructing of the expectation of narrative explanation and continuity is itself an attack of the bourgeois world of the father. The cruel and arbitrary treatment – yet still, the book suggests, somehow justified – meted out to Joseph K is a representation of the punishment this rebellion draws, a punishment with masochistic and perhaps sexualised attractions. Such a reading is only reductive if it fails to place such personal conflicts within a specific historical, socio-cultural, and ideological context – broadly that of a German-speaking Jewish minority in the era of the growth of Czech nationalism. However, the limits of such crude sociological brushstrokes are illustrated by

Kafka's own famous comment, in his 1914 diary entry, on his relationship with his Judaism: "What have I in common with Jews? I have hardly anything in common with myself" (cited in Gilman, 2005, p. 30).

As the late Anthony Storr (1979) has movingly written, Kafka may have belonged to a group of people for whom the demands of human intimacy are too much – "a desperate need for love combined with an equally desperate fear of close involvement" (1979, p. 101). Such "schizoid" people may give an impression of a certain aloofness and coldness, but this is usually not the case. Rather, intimacy is feared and experienced as overwhelming and engulfing, and therefore threatening to the autonomous self. Beneath the apparent detachment is an intense neediness, which is denied and instead projectively identified with the other, then experienced as insatiably demanding. This then provokes a distancing, which in turn leads to loneliness and isolation, and a return of a tentative wish for contact. Such "claustro-agoraphobic dilemmas", or "core complex anxieties" as they have been termed (Glasser, 1998; Rey, 1994), are universal but are particularly marked in some individuals. The tragedy of these situations is that, contrary to appearances, such people frequently feel not too little, but too much. Withdrawal may express both a wish to avoid the pain connected to attachment and an unconscious addiction to self-punishment and failure.

If Kafka evokes in deadpan, indeed at times comic, concrete detail a bizarre social world, and invokes socio-political interpretation, then Samuel Beckett seems to strip away any social specifics. His work, early critics ventured, concerned the absence of God, the futility of man – universal themes transcending any social context. Voices – or perhaps multiple voices – speak in the darkness, and in an apparent absence of time, identity, and place, evoke memories, or memories distorted by wishes, Beckett suggests that there is simultaneously a desire for expression and a sense of its futility. Speech, drama itself, is a way of killing time. These monologues, however, are lyrical, and have their own rhythmic cadences, moving in form and content between engaging and not engaging.

Anthony Cronin's (1996) superb biography offers a compelling study of a more specific set of anxieties and conflicts. Kind, generous, and loyal to his friends, Beckett was also, Cronin suggests, aloof, emotionally and sexually inhibited, and prone to nihilistic despair, psychosomatic maladies, and debilitating ennui. His was in some senses a refusal of the world. Cronin makes it clear, however, that this position was also a defence against the pain of living and of loss, particularly that of his parents – a subject Beckett reportedly returned to on his deathbed. Beckett had great love for his sporting sociable father and an intense ambivalent attachment to his mother, an attachment he clearly found both engulfing and impossible to relinquish; throughout his life he moved back and forth between Paris and the family house in a suburban Protestant ascendancy enclave of Dublin.

Beckett was well capable of sociability and liveliness and, of course, intense creativity. He, however tentatively, sustained relationships and marriage. He is one of the few great modernists to also appear as a player in Wisden's cricket almanac. He took part in the French resistance. He enjoyed capacious nocturnal pub crawls through Paris, particularly when in the company of the formidable

Irish acting and drinking duo Patrick Magee and Jack MacGowran. Beckett's work and life might be read as in part a dramatisation of the psychological conflict between the pain and joy of living and the reality of attachment and dependence on others, and an addiction to death-like states or at least states of what the psychoanalyst Betty Joseph termed "near death" (1982).

In *Krapp's Last Tape* (1958) the sixty-nine-year-old protagonist is in a darkened room illuminated only by a single light above a wooden table. "Past midnight. Never knew such silence. The earth might be uninhabited" (p. 221). As in all Beckett's work the dramatic form itself, its staging, setting, the non-verbal activities of the actor, are forms of poetic expression and communication. Thus the room, the table with the light above it, become images of the self, and of the withdrawn and solipsistic nature of Krapp himself, and by implication, of all human experience. Activity, even the activity of speaking, may be communication, may be communicative, but is also a way of filling empty space and time. The dramatis personae of the play are all figures from Krapp's mind, and from his history, represented not simply as they are, or were, but refracted through consciousness, memory, and time. He listens to, and offers thoughts and commentary on, a tape (box three, spool five), made by his thirty-nine-year-old self, recorded the year his mother died. The play is resonant with autobiographical hints and allusions; the father who died young, the blinds shutting, an allusion to the death of his mother in a nursing home on Dublin's Grand Canal, an epiphany – or not – on the pier at Dun Laoghaire. There is a dog on the canal towpath who makes off with a black rubber ball – a lost memento mori. There is "a girl in a shabby green coat, on a railway station platform" (p. 222), possibly a version of his cousin Peggy Sinclair. "Could have been happy with her, up there on the Baltic, and the pines and the dunes. [Pause.] Could I? [Pause.] And she?" (p. 222).

The play superbly dramatised the lifelong conflict between engagement and withdrawal, and the costs of both positions. Krapp's regular protestations that he is best done with all that, that the misery is best left behind, is belied by his revisiting and reliving of the past. The central recurrent memory of the play is of a woman in a punt: "I lay down across her with my face in her breasts and my hand on her. We lay there without moving. But under us all moved, and moved us, gently, up and down, from side to side" (p. 221). This could be understood as a multi-determined image, the woman representing both the maternal object, a version of the lost mother, and a sexual partner with a mysterious scratch on her thigh. Here we have the oedipal dimension; evidence of the unsettling presence of a third party. Soon after, her image becomes distorted, her eyes become slits in the glare. This glare is perhaps also the too-bright glare of human contact. However, her eyes open and she lets him in. Is this a real memory or a memory altered by wishes? Perhaps, though, best not to think too much, to embrace the solace of isolation and hopelessness "all over and done with, at last" (p. 220).

The emergence from narcissism is one of the major tasks of psychological development, and it is difficult because, amongst other things, the awareness that one's life depends on others over whom one has ultimately little or no control is a source of terrible anxiety. Emerging from narcissism means confronting this reality and the terror that accompanies contact with it.

(Caper, 2008, p. 44)

As a patient, from an extremely deprived and impoverished background who very much identified with Beckett's protagonists, said, if isolation and loneliness could be painful they were as of nothing compared to the mental agony and conflict afforded by the possibility of emotional contact. The difficulty of this struggle should not be underestimated. It may feel safer to remain detached, or even to idealise deathly solutions (Joseph, 1982). Such a retreat can provide its addictive pleasures. Cronin describes the characteristic "Beckett man" – melancholic, pared down, isolated from, and indifferent to, any sources of consolation. Reality and human nature are reduced to their basics: bodily functions, cruelty, hunger, suffering, and death:

> He does not smart under indignity; it is axiomatic with him that one is insulted and humiliated at every turn. He is used to physical suffering and the degradations of the body; indeed he is something of a connoisseur of these and they might also be said to give him pleasure.

(Cronin, 1996, p. 381)

Melancholia, in the psychoanalytic literature, refers to a form of depression and pathological mourning, in which inadmissible hostility towards the object of loss is instead turned against the self. Freud (1917e) made the point that the sufferings of the melancholic, the endless tormenting reproaches (to others as well as to the self), are also undoubtedly pleasurable, at least in a masochistic sense. And a pleasure, Freud also notes, is not easily relinquished. It is to the relationship of narcissism and loss that I turn next.

In the psychoanalytic literature pathological narcissism is sometimes seen as an expression of an innate hostility to that which is other, separate, and different from the self, sometimes as a defence against vulnerability and a terrifying dependency on others. It has been conceptualised, as we have seen, as one manifestation of what Otto Kernberg (1984) has termed a "borderline personality organization", in which radically different views of self and others co-exist but are not integrated into a realistic appraisal. What distinguishes narcissism from borderline personality disorder, in this account, is a relatively stable, or entrenched, personality structure in which there is the overt or covert presence of a pathological grandiose self.

It was Freud (1914c) who first developed a clinical theory of narcissism as a way of understanding some universal tendencies in human development and mental functioning and in extreme character pathology. He formulated the notion of a universal "primary narcissism" (Freud, 1914c), associated with the earliest infantile states, in which there is no ego, no difference between self and environment, there is no pain, but rather a state of infantile megalomania, the prototype of which is the state of intra-uterine bliss. He invoked narcissism, therefore, to capture an "infantile state of mind that pre-existed object relations" (Britton, 1998, p. 171). There was only the self. These ideas, though, were problematic and not widely accepted, as they seemed to suggest that there was an "object-less" state, before relationships, and this seemed to go against research into infant development, which, rather, established that the infant was primed for attachment.

The French psychoanalyst Bela Grunberger (1989) bridged the gap between Freud's ideas of primary narcissism and later "object relations" theory (in which the infant is inherently object-seeking) by suggesting that primary narcissism is related to the need for a dyadic untroubled relationship with mother, or the primary carer; a wish for a symbiotic link, which has as its prototype the meeting of all needs in the existence in the womb. Such a wish might be seen individually in those patients who seek to create such a womb-like place, or symbiotic link, in their therapy, or within the psychiatric system; or even in the (hitherto) infinite bosom of the NHS, "from cradle to grave". These tendencies might be seen culturally, it could be argued, as the idea, projected into the past, of a lost Eden, and into the future, of a utopian paradise. From this perspective narcissism involves the search for pure bliss, man being at one with nature, the harmonies of the universe, a fantasy based on primal intra-uterine bliss, together with a disavowal of biological origins and drives. Indeed, Christopher Lasch (1977, 1979, 1984), to whom I shall return in more detail later, argued that such regressive wishes were characteristic of some counter-cultural movements in the West, with the idealisation of the natural world, and the denigration of paternal authority and scientific objectivity.

Freud (1914c) also described a process of "secondary narcissism", when "libido" is withdrawn from the external world and redirected towards the ego. Narcissism, then, is related, as in the popular usage, to self-absorption or withdrawal into the body. In its more benign versions a narcissistic struggle may mean the person – all of us – oscillating between being able to engage with people and the world, and withdrawing from relations and external reality. As Jean Michel Quinidoz (2004) points out in his discussion of the subject, temporary libidinal withdrawal from the world can also be characteristic of times of illness, organic pain, and sleep: "the condition of sleep ... [implies] a narcissistic withdrawal of the positions of the libido on the subject's own self, or more precisely, on to the single wish to sleep" (Freud, 1914c, cited in Quinidoz, 2004, p. 130). This can be a defensive reaction, and a response to a frustrating or traumatic situation, when, for example, love is not reciprocated. In this understanding, the patient's self-love replaces the love of the mother, and the motive for the narcissistic regression is protective, rather than representing an innate hostility to relating to others.

Freud's controversial account (1910c) of one of his beloved "greats", Leonardo da Vinci, illustrates his thinking about a complex type of narcissistic defence against loss and separateness; Leonardo, Freud conjectured, loved his apprentices as he hoped his mother would love him, and in so doing, one part of him was identified with the youths with whom he was enamoured, and another was in identification with his mother. In this way, Freud thought, Leonardo could undo the loss he might otherwise have experienced of his primary love object, mother:

> The child's love for his mother cannot continue to develop consciously any further; it succumbs to repression. The boy represses his love for his mother, he puts himself in her place, identifies himself with her, and takes his own person as a model in whose likeness he chooses the new objects of his love.
>
> (Freud, 1910c, p. 100)

This is a complex intra-psychic and intrapersonal dynamic – a certain type of narcissistic configuration, one that also involves the themes that Freud was to further explore in "Mourning and melancholia" (1917e). The other person, people generally, are not related to as separate objects but as projected aspects of the self; something of their separate reality, their separateness and difference, is denied. Such an apprehension of separateness and difference might mean the experience of loss, vulnerability, and the collapse of omnipotence. I will consider later in this book whether these sorts of dynamics might be paradigmatic of powerful emotional and cultural trends in contemporary life, and, in particular, the ways in which those groups seen as "victims" can become depersonalised, the object of the projection of needy parts of the self, the concomitant of which is the vitupera- tive denigration of those held to be the victimisers.

As we have seen, in the psychoanalytic understanding it is the oedipal configu- ration that is crucial for development:

> The early efflorescence of infantile sexual life is doomed to extinction because its wishes are incompatible with reality and with the inadequate stage of development the child has reached. The efflorescence comes to an end in the most distressing circumstances and to the accompaniment of the most painful feelings. Loss of love and failure leave behind them a permanent injury to self-regard in the form of a narcissistic scar.
>
> (Freud, 1920g, cited in Chasseguet-Smirgel, 1986, p. 21)

The infant has to experience disillusionment and psychic pain. The immature infant cannot please or satisfy mother in the way that father can. This brings in its wake a sense of exclusion and smallness, in short a narcissistic injury. The child has to accept the hopelessness of his task, and therefore the verdict of reality over wish fulfilment. The task of the parents, as in each developmental stage of the child (and development requires the relinquishment and mourning of previ- ous satisfactions) is to wean off and allow disillusionment to occur, whilst also encouraging the child with the belief that in the future he will be able to mas- ter new challenges and attain satisfaction; to become like the parents, in time. A degree of healthy narcissistic self-regard is essential for normal functioning, and for these developments to be able to take place. The infant and the child has to tolerate "getting it wrong" in the secure conviction that he will eventually learn to "get it right", and that his failures will be tolerated and tolerable rather than sources of narcissistic mortification, shame, and humiliation. In both individual and social terms there are no developmental short cuts to this gradual period of trial and error, learning, and mature identification.

In the intermediate stage of development the father and other idealised figures in the familial world, peer group, and socio-cultural environment becomes the source of what Freud described as the "ego ideal": how the individual himself would like to be seen, how he would aspire to be. In this more mature personality structure there is an inevitable tension between the observing and judging part of the self, and the ego, related to the failure of the ego to meet the aspirations of the ego-ideal.

For some people, however ("the narcissistic type", as Freud put it) the tension between the ego (how they are) and the ego ideal (how they would like to be) is weak or missing entirely, because they become their own ego ideals. Here we begin to enter the realm of pathological narcissism. These are the people who are, in Freud's terms, "special cases" for whom special conditions should apply. They have identified themselves with their ego ideals. They worship at their own altars. In the therapeutic situation it is the therapist that really needs them, not them the therapist. However, running alongside this apparent invulnerability and grandiosity is usually also the opposite: a devastated self-esteem, and a neediness for others, albeit one that is usually projected out, and attributed to others, where it is treated with contempt. This instability and underlying sense of inferiority may be related to the psychic reality of a pseudo-maturity and pseudo or shallow identification with parental figures, and in particular with the father. In contemporary life there may be a socio-cultural leaning towards such pseudo-identifications (Chasseguet-Smirgel, 1985) and the exclusion and the denigration of paternal functioning, a subject to which I will return later in this book.

Britton (1998) describes a certain kind of narcissistic presentation, in which the patient appears to be "thin skinned", easily hurt, and hypersensitive. Absolute agreement is expected, and when the analyst, or anyone else, moves from a position of empathic validation of the patient's experience to express his own independent view this can produce violence or withdrawal. The scene is set for an impasse; if the analyst asserts his reality the patient will act as if traumatised, may explode or masochistically submit. If the analyst submits to what might be a tyrannous omnipotent expectation of complete agreement on behalf of the patient he loses his own integrity, and a collusive pseudo-analysis may ensue:

> It appears to be the case in such clinical contexts that the patients fear the analyst's psychic reality, if emergent, will destroy their own. The complementary counter transference of the analyst is that if he or she adopts the psychic reality of the patient the analysts own reality will be annihilated.
>
> (Britton, 1998, p. 43)

For Britton, a coming together of maternal and paternal functioning, of the empathic validation of the patient's point of view with a more objective view in which the analyst communes with his own thoughts, or supervision, or theory (the symbolic counterpart of parental intercourse) is feared by such patients as a catastrophe. This brings in its wake what Bion (1962, p. 116) called "nameless dread", an inchoate annihilatory anxiety. By communing with his own thoughts, for example, the analyst introduces separateness and exclusion into the idealised dyadic relationship. Symbolically, the "good" empathic mother is now having a dialogue (or intercourse) with the "bad" objectifying father.

Britton (1998) points out that many patients move between a thin-skinned position (the narcissistically vulnerable, exquisitely sensitive self) to a more "thick-skinned position", in which paternal objectivity is identified with, but the subjective feeling self is now split off, rather than integrated into the personality structure. The patient presents as intellectually able to talk about himself from an objective position, but is emotionally untouchable. In this position "an inter-subjective relationship with the primary object of an empathic kind is avoided and the third object, personifying objective knowledge, is sought as the source of understanding" (Britton, 1998, p. 50).This thick-skinned position may under-pin the kind of arrogant and grandiose narcissistic presentation delineated in the symptomatic classification of "narcissistic personality disorder" in the American Psychiatric Association's *Diagnostic and Statistical Manual of Mental Disorders (DSM-5)* (American Psychiatric Association, 2013), in which the patient remains emotionally untouchable and cut off from empathic feelings for self and others. The patient no longer needs anyone, except, in an idealised and snobbish way, for narcissistic supplies of admiration, and in a contemptuous way as a vehicle for the projection of inadmissible, vulnerable, and denigrated aspects of the self.

Turning to the subject of destructiveness, Herbert Rosenfeld (1971) distin-guished between a "libidinal narcissism", in which "good" parts of the self (and others) are idealised and seen as the repository of all that is good; and a more "destructive narcissism", in which "bad" parts of the self, associated with destruc-tion, death, and various forms of triumphing over life, are idealised, and identified with. In the former, the grandiose self of the libidinal narcissist is the result of an appropriation of the admirable qualities of others, through a process of omnipo-tent identification, a process in which undesirable aspects are disowned and pro-jected. The world is therefore full of idealised and denigrated people and things. In the latter situation, that is, in the more destructive narcissistic state, there is an idealisation of destructive as well as good parts of the self, creating a state in which potentially good experiences, and good internal "object relationships", can be enslaved by a mad omnipotent, grandiose, and cruel self.

Rosenfeld's (1971) powerful description of an internal mafia gang is a vivid personification of a destructive organisation within the personality. The metaphor is that of a powerful organisation, under the control of a leader, intent on securing its continuation, and neutralising any threat. Such an organisation is idealised, as a source of superior strength and invulnerability; the internal gang is tightly held together, not least by the threat of reprisals; if a more healthy part of the personality seeks independence, and tries to make contact with others, this may be followed by a deterioration or negative therapeutic reaction. The presence of such an organisation, appearing to offer protection from emotional pain and conflict, has been characterised in the psychoanalytic literature in a number of closely related ways, as a "narcissistic organization" (Rosenfeld, 1971; Sohns, 1985), a "pathological organization" or "psychic retreat" (Steiner, 1993), or as an "ego-destructive superego" (Britton, 2003). They all involve pathological spitting and projective identification, omnipotent control, and powerful defences against the experiences of need, vulnerability, and envy that come with an apprehension of the separateness of the object and the nature of human dependency.

Such organisations comprise particular anxieties, and sets of internal and external object relations, these tending to be re-enacted in the interpersonal sphere via projective mechanisms. The central point, however, is that the saner, needy, vulnerable, and relationship-seeking part of the personality is held captive by a more destructive part, and that there may be a degree of addictive pleasure in this situation; indeed such a process may have become sexualised. Aggression or sadism towards others may be overt and direct, and may, less directly, include triumphant attempts at suicide and self-harm.

There is usually a conflict within the individual between such pathological organisations and more healthy parts of the self – as we have seen, the human psyche is not unitary. However, a more dangerous situation occurs when there is an ego-syntonic identification with a destructive part of the self. Here, severe malignant narcissism links to anti-social personality disorder (Clekley, 1941). This is the psychological profile, Kernberg also argues, of some charismatic terrorists. "An idealized self-image and an egosyntonic sadistic, self-serving ideology rationalize the anti-social behavior and may coexist with the capacity for loyalty to their own comrades" (Kernberg, 2004, p. 57). I will return to this subject in a later chapter.

In the meantime, a defining characteristic of pathological narcissism is the excessive use of projective identification, and the tendency to relate to others not as separate and different but as alternately idealised and denigrated aspects of the self. The projection of aspects of the self, good and bad, leads to depletion of personality, and to a distorted sense of self and others. This picture of narcissism, then, is inseparable from the idea of loss, from the exclusions and pain of the oedipal situation, and from the requirements of mourning.

The central task of mourning as identified by John Steiner (1993), is that to progress, the "object" (thing, person, wish, ideal) has to be given up in the external world, in order to be installed in the internal world, the corollary of which is that functioning through narcissistic projection ultimately leads to distortion of reality and depletion of the self:

> The process of regaining parts of the self lost through projective identification involves facing the reality of what belongs to the object and what belongs to

the self, and this is established most clearly through the experience of loss. It is in the process of mourning that parts of the self are regained, and this achievement may require much working through. Thus a true internalization of the object can only be achieved if it is relinquished as an external object. It can then be internalized as separate from the self and in this state can be identified with in a flexible and reversible way. The development of symbolic function assists this process and allows the individual to identify with aspects of the object rather than its concrete totality.

(Steiner, 1993, p. 9)

Here we come once more to the distinction between normal and abnormal mourning and Freud's absolutely crucial distinction beween mourning and melancholia. Freud (1917e) noted that in normal mourning there is a temporary withdrawal of what he termed "libido" from the world, a period of grief, which differs in time and nature in different people and in different cultures, in which the lost person is gradually and painfully relinquished in the external world. Though grief may always remain, energy and libido are slowly reattached to life, and to new relationships and projects. Such a process may never be complete, in that sharp grief comes and goes in waves. But life goes on.

In melancholia, by contrast, the remorseless and endless imprecations against the self – "You are the worst person in the world", "You should be run off the face of the earth" – speak of a very different internal reality. Here, Freud suggested, the lost person or "object" has been loved narcissistically with a high degree of ambivalence and becomes unconsciously identified with the self, or the body, which is then subject to lacerating remorseless attack. In this way, an unconscious conflict between loving and hating feelings is transformed into a conflict between different parts of the self, in the process of which the object of loss is kept alive, albeit in a tormented state. As Freud famously and evocatively put it:

the shadow of the object fell upon the ego, and the latter could henceforth be judged by a special agency, as though it were the object, the forsaken object. In this way an object-loss was transformed into an ego-loss and the conflict between the ego and the loved person into a cleavage between the critical activity of the ego and the ego as altered by identification.

(1917e, p. 249)

An elderly patient on an acute in-patient ward was convinced that she had cancer of the stomach and that her insides were literally rotting away. Her thinking was quite concrete and certain about this, and these nihilistic delusions were entirely unaffected by the verdict of reality: that medical tests had repeatedly shown that no such cancer was present. Taking the personal history, it turned out that her husband had died some six years previously, of cancer of the stomach. She was able to say that she had always loved her husband, he had been a perfect life partner, and there was nothing bad she could possibly mention about him. What could he have possibly done to deserve a wife like her?

States of depression, like any other form of mental illness, are multi-determined, and biological factors play a part. However, from a psychological perspective it might be understood that this lady was unconsciously identified, in her symptomatology, with the lost husband, whilst at the same time was able to give vent to her inadmissible (ego dystonic) feelings of disappointment and rage with him through very public self-recriminations. In this way she defended herself from becoming aware of her anger and hatred towards this otherwise loved figure and kept the two emotions separate. Such an awareness would have been unacceptable to her and given rise to what must have felt like irreconcilable conflict. Her symptoms had both a defensive and an expressive purpose, though in disguised form. They expressed her hatred of her husband, if only for leaving her alone, whilst at the same time protected her from full awareness of these feelings and from emotional conflict, that is, of her own psychic reality. Her symptoms also kept her relationship with her husband going, and delayed the verdict of reality: the need that she relinquish husband and engage with new things.

Melancholic states can be self-perpetuating; despair begets hate, which begets more despair, and so on. Ignês Sodré (2005) points out the underlying situation behind such an impasse; "the melancholic suffers from an unconscious feeling of being incapable of loving, and feeling unlovable is a consequence of this" (Sodré, 2005, p. 127). The picture, as Sodré paints it, is of black and red coal seams in the dark underground state of melancholia, the interpenetration of despair and hate. This reaches its apogee in frankly suicidal states in which the person feels unloved, abandoned, and only able to pine away and die.

A patient suffered a split-up from a girlfriend who was now studying abroad. Still obsessed by her, he sent her an email late at night, under the influence of alcohol, which he then re-read the next morning as full of unconsciously expressed hostile feelings. Having sent the email he was unable to retract the communication, which he thought would both fatally damage and wound his ex-partner, and also show himself, in her eyes, to be irredeemably bad. He had destroyed any possibility of re-establishing a relationship with her. The situation was compounded by his not hearing back from her. He felt internally and externally condemned, without mercy. In other words, he was now at the mercy of a harsh and unforgiving superego. He felt that suicide might be his only option. Fortunately, this patient was able to discuss these feelings in his psychotherapy sessions, where they became progressively diminished.

Frequently, the clinical picture is that melancholic states alternate with states of mania. Manic defences operate in all human beings; increased activity in the external world serves as a defence against depression or other troubling affects, and substitutes a mastery of external events for an internal state of depletion. In a more chronic and pathological situation, though, there is a cruel triumphalism, with the lost person or thing denigrated and treated with contempt. The "manic feast" cannot be sustained, and lacking a foundation in the secure internalisation of what has been lost, burns itself out, leading to an underlying depletion, a collapse into depression, and another manic defence, in what can be, if there is not an effective intervention, an increasing cycle of mood instability.

If, on the other hand, loss can be faced then this provides for the possibility of development, in that what has been lost externally is taken into the self as experience, memory, and a form of positive identification. Another way of putting this is that the "lost object" has to be painfully relinquished as an external object in order to be internalised. For this to occur – a process that may be subject to life-long oscillation – the separateness of what has been lost has to be recognised, and an inevitable degree of ambivalence – the presence of both loving and hating feelings – has to be tolerated without too much self-reproach.

Freud's conceptualisations of narcissism and melancholia, in introducing the central psychoanalytic notion of an internal world consisting of relationships between different parts of the self, provide a further conceptual bridge between the individual and the social. These "objects" are, in part, internalisations of emotionally invested relationships with others: internalised not as they are in an objective sense, but under the influence of powerful affect states. Such internal relations tend in turn to be re-externalised, through unconscious projective processes, in the interpersonal sphere; for example, the harsh superego of the melancholic may be projected into others who are then experienced as critical and severe in judgement, while the self is identified with a degraded object. In manic states it might be the vulnerable and needy part of the self that is projected into others, where it can then be treated with contempt. In borderline states internal conflict is denied and externalised via projective mechanisms, as a dyadic relationship between, for example, victim and victimiser. Such an internal object relationship can be actualised through behavioural provocation, the recipient of the projection stirred to the anger and criticism that "makes real" the projection.

The compulsion to repeat these patterns, often occurring with rapid role reversal, is sometimes in the service of communication, that is, of a state of mind being recognised and better understood, "contained" in psychoanalytic terms; but it also sometimes involves more destructive processes. It may involve splitting off of "bad" or inadmissible parts of the self into others who are then subject to devaluation and omnipotent control.

Integrating psychoanalysis and systems theory Elliot Jacques (1955) and Isabel Menzies-Lyth (1959) outlined the way in which such processes could occur at a systemic level within organisations. Influenced by the work of group analysts such as W. R. Bion (1961), to whom I will come later, they emphasised the importance to the psychological stability and functioning of members of a realistic, achievable, and reality-orientated work task. The overall culture of a work environment involves the nature of the primary task and the structures and routines of work organisation, including, crucially, the explicit and implicit roles individuals are expected to take up:

> In developing a structure, culture and mode of functioning, a social organization is influenced by a number of interacting factors, crucial amongst which are

its primary task, including such environmental relationships and pressures as that involve; the technologies available for performing the task; and the needs of the members of the organization for social and psychological satisfaction and above all, for support in the task of dealing with anxiety.

(Isabel Menzies-Lyth, 1959, p. 50)

In all organisations there are also emotional systems defending workers against the unconscious anxieties inherent in the particular work task, and this involves the development of socially structured defence mechanisms:

An important aspect of such socially structured defence mechanisms is an attempt by the individuals to externalize and give substance in external real-ity to their characteristic defence mechanisms. A social defence mechanism develops over time through collusive interaction and agreement, often uncon-scious, between members of the organization over what form it should take. The socially structured defence mechanisms then tend to become an aspect of external reality with which old and new members of the institution must come to terms.

(Menzies-Lyth, 1959, p. 51)

In her most famous study Menzies-Lyth (1959) analysed the social defences of a university teaching hospital. She noted that splitting of tasks and roles, detach-ment and denial of feelings, the resource to ritual task performance, depersonali-sation, the denial of the patient-nurse relationship protected the nurse from the difficult emotions attendant upon relating to the ill patient as a human being – attachment, disgust, the evocation of anger at those who do not respond to treat-ment, and so on. These were organisational defences, institutionalised into role functions, clinical practice, and professional relationships, with which new staff had to come to terms, or not. They involved the projection of authority upwards into management and the infantilising of junior nursing staff, who had to be sub-ject to constant scrutiny and checks for any manifestations of irresponsibility. Such a defence system protected against some of the core anxieties attendant upon the task, but also served to pre-empt opportunities for development and emotional learning, in both patient and nurse; a process that inexorably led to both ineffi-ciencies in care and the loss to the organisation of some of the most talented staff.

The work of Jacques (1955) and Menzies-Lyth (1959) opens up an important con-ceptual bridge for a non-reductive psychosocial application of psychoanalytic ideas to organisations and to the wider cultural and ideological domain within which they operate. Such a perspective requires a historical context; Menzies-Lyth's analysis, recognised as classic in the field but strangely neglected in wider cultural analysis, was written in the late 1950s and identifies emotionally repressive trends associated with modes of British professional life that were even then in decline. It is a conten-tion of this book that new defences have emerged in the years since, often disguising themselves as liberations from the old "paternalist" systems.

It is not hard to see echoes of Menzies-Lyth's findings in contemporary life. In the field of health care there may be therapeutic, or it could be argued, pseudo-therapeutic mantras of self-expression and personal empowerment, but there has also been an obsessive monitoring of performance and practice, as if when a blind eye is turned the old irresponsibilities, or worse, will emerge. This culture of monitoring has at times undercut professional autonomy and traditions. I will look in a later chapter at the inadequacy of those apparently progressive consumerist models of the therapeutic relationship, which tend to ignore the nature of human attachment and dependency.

Meanwhile, in recent times, Freud and the psychoanalytic tradition – which is not, as we have seen, in any case, a unitary one, nor without constant revision and development – have often been subject to opprobrium and attack. In part these attacks are culturally driven; the "tragic realist" nature of classical Freudian thought, the embodied nature of human experience, the ubiquity of disappointment, the limitations of reality, the inherently divided nature of the self, and the innate nature of human destructiveness, are not views of the human condition easily commensurate with the disembodied Protean shape-shifting selves of postmodern discourse, nor with thin-skinned hypersensitivity of contemporary victim politics.

Before moving further forwards it is necessary, therefore, to consider further, and respond to, some of the objections that there have been, and continue to be, to psychoanalysis and in particular to its classical "tragic realist" traditions.

Chapter 3

Embodied experience

We have seen that in the psychoanalytic account character and personality are multi-determined, arising out of the infinitely complex interplay of internal and external world. However, in contrast with this dynamic and dialectical understanding of the relationship between the individual and his environment, between biology and culture, much contemporary political and socio-cultural discourse appears to have foundations in impoverished, reductionist, and often determinist views of human subjectivity. On the one hand, there is loose general reporting of scientific research in the media, in which a crude genetic reductionism is rampant, to an extent that is often at odds with what scientists are actually saying: newspapers report simple gene transmission for complex behavioural or characterological traits such as manic-depression, schizophrenia, and alcoholism. Correlative changes in brain functioning are treated as though they are causative. On the other hand, the traditional liberal-left view has tended to see people as *tabulae rasae*, as innocents oppressed by, or impinged upon by, a malign society, the victims of social neglect and/or repression, of inequality, poverty, discrimination, and the internalisation of prejudice and stigma. These factors may be of central importance, but they are not sufficient for an explanatory account of, for example, the nihilistic violence that is a feature of much that goes under the name of contemporary terrorism. An effective understanding of, and response to, these phenomena is made more difficult still by a presumption of rationality and the motivating power of conscious ideology, when the true motivations may be unconscious.

However, even amongst those not ideologically or emotionally hostile to the notion of a dynamically repressed unconscious, and to the possibility of unconscious motivations, there is a tendency to present psychoanalysis as a monolithic and unchanging set of beliefs or pseudo-scientific dogmas most of which remain, in Karl Popper's terms, unfalsifiable. The irony of the attacks on Freud and psychoanalysis, however, is that they have been coming at a time when the findings emerging out of neuroscience are tending to lend support to many psychoanalytic principles; the embodied nature of consciousness, the ubiquity of unconscious mental functioning, the importance of emotion in decision-making, and the complex and conflicted nature of the human psyche.

Mark Solms and Oliver Turnbull (2002) have argued that a materialist neuroscientific view of the human mind, which links it to brain functioning from an objective perspective and allows scientific investigation and validation, can complement an approach that seeks to understand the human mind subjectively, from the perspective of introspection and, amongst other forms of enquiry, psychoanalytic exploration. This is not to collapse one mode of understanding into another. The relationship between subjective mental states and neurological brain processes is correlative not causative, and therefore cannot explain questions of aetiology of these mental states – although growing understanding of the dynamic localisation of brain functioning could explain how damage to certain parts of the brain through trauma, lesions, and so on, could compromise certain mental functions and personality structures. Nor is the unconscious mental functioning of neuroscientific research the same as the dynamic repressed unconscious of Freud.

Nevertheless both the neuroscientific and the psychoanalytic understanding of mind/brain emphasise that human consciousness has a foundation in bodily experience, involving relationships with "objects" in the external world, under the sway of emotions and drives. Such a view runs quite against socio-cultural behaviourist models of the human being as a blank slate conditioned by society, or the popularised view of the human brain as being analogous to a computer with complex cognitive circuits, feedback loops, and so on. Indeed Solms and Turnbull (2002) point out that this latter model is wholly implausible, because the computer, although capable of intelligent behaviour, does not have a visceral body capable of feeling and thus of generating reflective consciousness.

Jan Panksepp (1998) has outlined four basic emotion command system in mammals and humans; fear, panic, rage, and seeking. The seeking system involves exploring the environment for "objects" that might meet need, and is associated with "libidinal" energy, arousal, and appetite. It is this emotion command system, Solms and Turnbull suggest, that links most closely with Freud's notion of the drives. Freud described "the drives" or the "*triebe*" as "a concept on the frontier between the mental and the somatic, as the psychical representative of the stimuli originating from within the organism and reaching the mind, as a measure of the demand made upon the mind of work in its connection with the body" (1915c, p. 121). These systems interact with other systems, and in particular with conscious and unconscious memory of earlier "affectively tinged" experiences of objects in the world. The vast majority of mental activity associated with them goes on outside of the threshold of conscious awareness, either unconsciously or preconsciously; in the latter state they can become known, when subject to introspection.

Solms and Turnbull (2002) mordantly note that, for reasons that appear to be socio-cultural rather than scientific, the drive theory has recently become unpopular in some schools of psychoanalytic practice, as it has in the wider culture. The idea of biologically based drives may be unpopular, I would suggest, in part because it goes against the postmodernist notion of a world of free-floating selves constituted only by their disembodied and virtual relationships with each other. However the drives, like them or not, cannot be willed out of existence – they are part of the basic emotion command systems of all mammals, and human beings are the product of evolution.

The neuroscientist Antonio Damasio (1999) has argued that it is only because we are embodied creatures that we are able to have what he calls "core consciousness", a sense of self, including a background sense of feeling "good" or "bad", based on a "virtual" map of the current state of the internal milieu and viscera of the body. He suggests that this generation of core consciousness is physiologically associated with the evolutionarily older parts of the brain, the brainstem, and the extended reticular and thalamic activating system, and is probably present in all mammals. Hypothalamic registering of the current state of the body's homeostatic regulating systems indicates the state of the internal milieu of the body, temperature, hunger, sexual need, and so on, in part through the generation of subjective feeling. In this way the visceral state of the body and its representation, Damasio argues, can be said to form the basis of core consciousness, the essential state of self – through the generation of subjective feeling states. This system is essential to adaption to the environment and survival, as it is only within certain homeostatic physiological ranges that the human or animal organism can survive.

From an evolutionary perspective, that of survival and reproduction of the species, the evaluation, through subjective feeling, of the internal milieu of the body also needs to be related to the external environment. Damasio (1999) suggests that what he calls core consciousness, based on visceral experience, also involves an evaluative emotional link between self and "objects" in the external world, so that these objects are imparted with positive, negative, or neutral emotional value; as Solms and Turnbull put it, "Consciousness is not only what you feel, it is what you feel *about* something" (Solms &Turnbull, 2002, p. 92). They conclude, following Damasio, that "it consists of fluctuating *couplings* of the current state of the self with the current state of the object world" (2002, p. 92).

In this sense, without minimising the conceptual and methodological differences that also exist, findings in contemporary neuroscience in relation to the embodied nature of human experience tends to lend support to contemporary psychoanalytic theory; the foundations of the emerging personality reside in bodily needs, experiences, and sensations, in which an inner world based on the bodily self is innate and gradually evolves to include the internalised representations of self in relation to others, dominated by a particular affect:

> In childhood an individual internalizes a self-representation in interaction with an object representation dominated by an affect. These self-object-affect units ultimately form a kind of mosaic that comprises the individual's sense of self in a series of relational patterns with others. These internalized object relations are unconsciously repeated in interactions throughout adult life.
>
> (Gabbard, 2000, p. 159)

Damasio makes the point that what distinguishes human beings from animals is not the capacity to experience emotions, as other mammals certainly share some of these feeling states, but the capacity to have awareness of these emotions. The capacity of human beings "to be conscious of their consciousness" and to "transform concrete perceptions into abstract concepts" is heavily dependent upon the use of language to retrieve, classify, evaluate, relate, and abstract specific experiences. This, Damasio terms extended or reflective consciousness; linked to the evolution of the cortex, the association cortex especially, the language zones of the left cerebral hemisphere, and the superstructure of the prefrontal lobes. With the growth of this part of the brain, development is then possible in the realm of thinking and cognitive elaboration of past, present, and likely future experience; so that past experience is not simply relived and repeated. This allows the essential human capacity to modify, delay, and mentally "test out" instinctual responses rather than immediately enact them. It is this capacity that means that biology is not simply destiny.

In some people, however, these capacities may never fully develop, and in all of us they are subject to regressive processes, particularly at times of stress and transition. In line with Freud's idea of the somatic basis of disturbance, inchoate anxiety may not be verbally represented at all but instead connects itself to parts of the body, or to aspects of the environment. Thus the experience of anxiety may never develop into an emotion that can be thought about and potentially modified. The mind may attack its own capacity to think, and thinking itself becomes diseased. An example of this is in severe obsessional states where the agonised and tormented intellectual introspection of the patient is itself a symptom and fails to afford insight or to ameliorate suffering from guilt. A depressed patient may find ever more reasons for being depressed.

There are also physiological events that can compromise reflective, symbolic functioning. For example, Solms and Turnbull (2002, pp. 101–104) suggest that the neurological correlates of reality-orientated inhibitory ego functioning are the diencephalic and ventromesial frontal structures of the brain, which systematise the retrieval of memories in a way that accords with reality and reason, rather than with the more loosely associated unconscious organisation of memories evident, for example, in dreams. These reality-orientated features are involved in the retrieval process, and accord with secondary process thinking and the reality principle in Freud's terms. It is only with relative developmental maturity that these "goal directed, rational, realistic, selective and chronologically sequenced" aspects of memory retrieval are consolidated. Damage to the ventromesial frontal lobes (through lesion, strokes, brain trauma, and so on), they argue, leads to the patient regressing to primary process thinking, in which mutual contradiction, timelessness, and the replacement of external reality by psychic reality (and by wish fulfilment) can all be readily seen.

Peter Fonagy and colleagues (Fonagy et al., 2002), working on the theory of mind, have postulated that people with severe emotional and personality difficulties may have an early pattern of insecure attachment, due to a combination of temperamental and environmental factors. The former may include hypersensitivity of the amygdale and limbic system to even neutral stimuli, so that when the attachment system is activated the person is flooded with affect. At the same time there is a toning down, or lack of development, of the reflective mental functioning associated with the suborbital areas of the prefrontal cortex. Such a scenario, if unchecked, leads to chronic emotional dysregulation. More specifically, Fonagy and colleagues (2002) argue, these people may not be able to "mentalize", to represent the actions and behaviours of self and others in psychological and/ or emotional terms. Such a situation may arise out of a disturbed interpersonal context; neglect, abuse, deprivation, and persistent emotional misattunement on the part of primary carers.

Whatever the causative factors – and they are likely to be multi-determined - some people lack the capacity, as Ronald Britton (1998) has suggested, to reflect on their experience from a different perspective, to adopt the "third position" related to recognition of the oedipal couple and exclusion. Thus, they may find it difficult to really empathise with another, and put themselves in that person's shoes, and this may be linked to an insecurely established relationship with the primary caretaker, usually, though not always, mother. This insecurely established relationship gives rise to pathological splitting, denial, and excessive use of projective identification.

We all of course project feelings into others but optimally this process can also be reflected upon, we obtain feedback from others, and this becomes part of communication and reality testing. However, if the force of projective identification is too great, this cannot take place. The outcome is that, though there may still be contact with external reality, the picture of self and others is depleted and distorted. "Good" as well as "bad" aspects of the self can be projected into others and, being located externally, become unavailable for the self.

Thus, from a psychoanalytic perspective the hallmark of psychological maturity is a capacity for reflective functioning and to understand and employ the symbolic properties of language. In psychoanalytic terms this entails the capacity to distinguish reality from wish fulfilment, to see other people in realistic terms, to be able to see things from another point of view, to distinguish between belief and certainty, and to be able to inhibit gratification and tolerate limitation and disappointment. We also have, as best as is possible, to tolerate internal conflict without externalising it into others through projection. As we have seen, such maturity is not a once-and-for-all achievement but is subject to regressive processes and lifelong oscillation.

I now want to draw out some socio-cultural implications of the psychoanalytic understanding of human subjectivity in an era of "post truth". The first is that, from a psychoanalytic perspective, as we have seen, a human being is not just individual or just social but both. The links between the individual and the social are mediated through the human body and its vicissitudes, unique temperamental endowment, internalised "object relations" (which are not simply a taking in of what is "out there" but are under the sway of projection, introjection, and affect), and complex largely unconscious processes of psychic identification with significant individuals and with social structures and ideals; all of this taking

place within the changing contexts created by objective dynamic forces of economics, class, formation, and human history. Such identifications, as we have
seen, are related to temperamental substrates; early interpersonal relationships;
and a changing socio-cultural milieu, and thus are inevitably contradictory and
multifaceted. This complexity begs many questions of the apparently essentialist assumptions of contemporary exclusivist identity politics. At a deep level all
claims to identity, normative or transgressive, may rest on shaky ground – in other
words, we all contain multitudes. This also informs our potential to identify with
and empathise with others who may be outwardly very different.

The second is that it is the capacity to face reality that is the key determinant
of mental health in individuals, and the same is true, with appropriate conceptual
translation, of groups, organisations, and societies. The capacity to face reality
inevitably involves mourning what has been lost and what has not been, or may
never be, achieved. It involves acknowledging that though in the banner headlines
of the unconscious mind "everything is permitted", in the small print of reality
"restrictions still apply". Such an assertion does not imply a return to problematic
nineteenth-century ideas of positivistic truth, of separation between subject and
object, but rather that reality does not care to answer to human wishes and that
there are universal existential "facts of life" (Money-Kyrle, 1968), with which we
all have to come to terms, or not:

> The struggle between patient and analyst is not, from this perspective, to find
> useful narratives but as far as possible to be truthful. This struggle has to be
> distinguished from fundamentalist assertions of absolute truth with a capital
> "T", which derive from omniscience and are an attack on the capacity for
> truthfulness. The truth is complex and the struggle never ending. But recog-
> nising the complexity of reality is not the same thing as believing that what
> constitutes truthful descriptions of reality are a matter of choice.
>
> (Bell, 1999, pp. 6–7)

We all require defences against overwhelming experiences, and inadmissible
conflict. However, in extremis, the denial of painful internal and external reality
leads to psychotic states, where the capacity to distinguish between what is inside
and what is outside the self is lost. More often, however, and to greater or lesser
extents in all us, part of the personality is curious for knowledge and truth, whilst
another part remains in opposition, or willful ignorance. Here the difference is not
in kind but in degree, between temporary regressions in response to personal and/
or environmental stressors, and more embedded, though not necessarily unchanging, distortions associated with disorders of the personality.

The third is that it is in the experience of loss, above all else, that there is an
inescapable collision between the world as it is and the world as it is wished to be.
The object of loss cannot be hallucinated back into existence, at least not without
significant consequences for our mental health. Grief involves inevitable and necessary ebbs and flows. Optimally, however, the process of mourning allows the

object of loss to be painfully relinquished, in the course of which it is in internalised within the self, as a source of memory and identification. Thus, the apparent paradox that facing loss can also become a source of enrichment and that there is no development that does not also entail a degree of loss. The capacity of an individual – and a society – to mourn, in turn rests on the capacity to acknowledge the separateness and difference of the object of loss, to tolerate ambivalence – the presence of loving and hating feelings – and to see what has been lost in realistic terms, rather than as the subject of idealisation and denigration.

The "object of loss" in grief is most often thought of as another person. However, an individual may mourn a lost ideal, a part of the self, a place, a community, a landscape, or any object to which he has become, consciously or unconsciously, attached, or "cathected" as Freud would have put it. At a conscious level the streets where we have lived may be written with personal memory (including that of aspects of ourselves that we have lost) and be signifiers of temporal change. At a still deeper level we unconsciously project aspects of ourselves into the social environment, into buildings and landscapes. This is both an individual and collective process, and mourning is made more difficult if what has been lost has been rendered invisible, or subject to denigration, as has undoubtedly been the case, as I shall discuss later, with the old heartlands of traditional manufacturing and industry in the UK and the USA.

This brings us to the fourth implication: the requirement that mourning at a social level – and the opportunities for learning from and internalising past experience – should not be confused with the pathological immersion in past historical traumas, real and imagined, that can form the basis of some forms of contemporary victim and identity politics. Nor should it be confused with the sanitised commodification of the past as heritage industry; or with the specious fashion for the retrospective apologising for the actions of distant forefathers for which the apologiser can have no meaningful responsibility. Indeed, as Tony Judt points out (2009), these pseudo connections with the past serve to obscure what would otherwise appear to be a process of active forgetting; in which the public past can only be seen, if at all, through the prism of present concerns, particularly those of victimhood, or alternately, guilt. In these circumstances the personal and public past, or certain versions of it, can become a refuge, a source of defensive identification on the one hand, and an object of denigration and contempt on the other. That is, in the timeless present of late capitalism the past is related to narcissistically.

Finally, it is also one of the truisms of psychoanalysis that, without collapsing the difference between mental health and illness, staff and patients usually have more in common than they have in difference; that is, even in severe illness and disturbance there is often a part of the personality that is more healthy and adaptive if it can be located. Equally, even though relative maturity may have been reached, this is subject to regression under stress, and there remains, to a greater and lesser extent in everyone, a part of the personality where thinking is suffused with emotion; where there is hatred of reality and truth, where perception is distorted by wishes, where separation of self and object is confused by projective processes, where everything is permitted and where the restrictions imposed by reality do not apply. Moreover, there may be certain sorts of group, organisational, and social situations where these propensities, latent to varying degrees in all of us, become emergent or even dominant.

It is to this subject that I turn next.

Chapter 4

Psychoanalytic perspectives on social dislocation and group regression

Cultural pessimism is rife these days, the more so since the European referendum in the United Kingdom (UK) and the election of Donald Trump in the USA. In some ways this is clearly overdone. On most indices things are substantially better for more people than they have ever been, in part due to globalisation and techno-logical advance. Steven Pinker (2011) has recently argued the case that contrary to much perception we live in an increasingly peaceful age, with, in most parts of the world, declining rates of violence and murder in everyday life.

It is, however, a feature of contemporary life that radically different realities co-exist. The historian, Eric Hobsbawm (1994), has argued that the twentieth century – despite the massive and revolutionary gains in health and quality of life, associated with technological development – was, nonetheless, "without doubt the most murderous century of which we have record" (1994, p. 13). This was not sim-ply a matter of civil discord, world war, and so on, but of a regression from those agreed civilised codes of conduct, whose origins lay in the liberal values of the bourgeois Enlightenment. In the late eighteenth century national statutes abolished torture. In the nineteenth century there had increasingly been a mutually agreed non-targeting of civilian populations during outbreaks of war. Hobsbawm recalls the antipathy expressed by Marx and Engels, both on moral and political grounds, against individual and group terrorism, against the targeting of ordinary people. In the twentieth century, by contrast, "wars have been increasingly waged against the economy and infrastructure of states, and against their civilian populations" (Hobsbawm, 1994, p. 13). The same was also increasingly true of the campaigns waged by terrorist groups. Episodes of seemingly irrational and, at times, nihilistic destructiveness permeate recent history, whether at the level of national and civic conflicts, or in the more random activities of disaffected groups and individuals.

Misha Glenny in his account of *The Fall of Yugoslavia* (2002) writes of the poor rural flatlands in the interior of the Dalmatian coast. A long-disputed territory and military frontier,

> the Vojna Krajina can claim to be one of the most active and disruptive histor-ical fault lines in Europe. Apart from forming the border between the empires of Islam and Christendom for three centuries, it is also the line of fissure

between Rome and Constantinople, the Roman Catholic and Orthodox Christian faiths.

(Glenny, 1992, p. 6)

It was here that there was the most fearsome fighting between Tito's partisans and the Croat Fascist movement, the Ustasha, whose capacity for genocidal activity had managed to shock even the German authorities. And it was here that some of the bloodiest fighting and atrocities took place in the 1991 conflict. On one side of this line were twentieth-century ideas of democracy and economic growth, on the other were more ancient atavistic struggles based on pre-feudal enmities and battles for land.

I have a photograph at home of a largely abandoned stone village in the remote Mani district of the Peloponnese peninsula in Greece. The stark, austere, and minimalist architecture of old warlord communities can be seen in the deserted stone villages, highly fortified houses, and tall towers; an urban world built around defence and attack, reprisals and counter reprisals, anticipatory defensive strikes, and the revenging of lost honour over the generations. Such communities can embody fraternal care and hospitality, alongside utter murderous ruthlessness and the capacity to redress vendettas and grievances in a way that ensures their endurance. As Steven Pinker notes, it then becomes a matter of having to respond to a threat before you are annihilated, a culture of the mutually reinforcing pre-emptive strike: kill or be killed.

The powerfully held Western cultural paradigms of the human being as a *tabula rasa*, "socialised" into pathological behaviour by malign social forces, has resulted in difficulties in thinking about, and formulating a response to, the eruptions of violence in society. As Pinker (2002) has also said, this view of violence tended to be based on a "blank slate" view of human nature which we now know to be false. As Pinker argues, "if anything, it is the belief that violence is an aberration that is dangerous, because it lulls us into forgetting how easily violence may erupt in quiescent places" (2002, p. 314). And, as he says, "condemning violence is all to the good but not if it is disguised as an empirical claim about our psychological makeup" (2002, p. 316). The capacity for violence can be in people's inherent psychological make-up as a genetic endowment, rather than as a simple response to disadvantage; violence, too, can be in people's interests, and conflicts of interest are inherent in human society.

However, even allowing for Pinker's account of violence as an inherent and non-pathological aspect of human nature, a distinction has to be drawn between aggression for a "rational" purpose and aim (even if we, as observers perhaps, do not agree morally with the aim); such as defence against an actual or perceived attack, or a battle for land, or a pre-emptive strike; and something more intrinsically destructive and nihilistic. As Ronald Britton, writing from a psychoanalytic perspective, notes, there is a difference between a fight for survival and a xenophobic intolerance of that which is experienced as different and alien to the self:

Aggression may result from predominantly defensive or predominately destructive narcissism. But there is a difference between fighting to retain love and the wanton violence of object hostility. In the social realm, war can be defensive and patriotic aggression can be misguided love, but genocide is neither; it is prompted by the wish to annihilate otherness, from a xenocidal impulse.

(Britton, 2003, p. 157)

Misha Glenny's account (2002) of the breakup of Yugoslavia shows a conflict that goes beyond the more "normal" conflicts of interest between human social groups that might underpin wars and civil and political struggles. After the fall of a Communist regime that had tried to balance and suppress conflicts between different ethnic groups, Yugoslavia very quickly regressed into ancient fissures; the upshot was a decline into mutually reinforcing patterns of barbaric behaviour, underpinned by ethnic narratives of victimhood that often appeared to have extremely tangential relationship with objective truth. As Glenny wrote, "even for those like myself who have observed not merely the war itself but the dense web of political intrigue which led to it, the nature of the violence is beyond any framework of moral comprehension" (1992, pp. 172–173).

It has been difficult, though, to find a public language in which these seemingly irrational and nihilistic phenomena can be realistically conceptualised. Pinker recounts the continuing social power of a view of human nature based on the idea of the individual as a Rousseauesque holy innocent, corrupted by the social world and civilisation. In the era of romanticism, pathology was located in the social system, in need of reform and change, and denied in the individual, frequently seen as a victim of malign social process. In the twentieth century the awful historical realities of the eugenics movement and the "social Darwinism" of the National Socialist German Workers (Nazi) Party made any discussion of innate and universal factors in human personality difficult, and lent themselves to environmentalist approaches to understanding human difference. There was a fear of anything that might smack of genetic determinism, and, on the left, an antipathy to anything that appeared to suggest that there might be a limitation on the capacity of social reform and progress to impact on human nature.

However, forewarned is fore prepared, and it might therefore be best to begin with some salutary realities. In writing from a psychoanalytic perspective on the issue of emotionally motivated irrationality in cultural and socio-political life I want to stress, however, that though such a perspective is necessary, it is not sufficient. It cannot substitute for historically contextualised political analysis – though it can, if judiciously applied, form an integral part of such an analysis.

In psychoanalytic theory aggression is not normally considered to be inherently pathological. Indeed, a degree of aggression is necessary for normal functioning. Aggression in the service of development has therefore to be differentiated from aggression in the service of destructiveness. Two sorts of aggression have been noted, although these often co-exist in the same individual. Self-preservative aggression is a developmentally innate and hardwired response based on flight-fight mechanisms (flee or attack) to perceived threats in the environment. The threat to the integrity of the self may be a physical and/or a psychological one (for example, a shaming or exposing situation where the fragile self feels in danger of annihilation). Such threats may, however, be perceived in error, and this form of aggression may be particularly dangerous, as the fate of the threatening "object" is a matter of indifference; it simply needs to be annihilated.

Sadomasochistic aggression is linked to "core complex" anxieties regarding closeness and distance, and involves a developmental step up from this position; there is a relationship with an "object" (usually, but not always, a person; it could be an organisation or group) that needs to be controlled, tormented, and, usually, kept alive. In the self-preservative state of aggression a man may lash out at his partner if that person gets "too close" to his vulnerability. In the sadomasochistic state of mind, he may treat his partner (and at times himself) in a cruel and torment-ing way, in a manner that seeks to maintain both the relationship and the distance.

There is a third form of aggression, but this has very different neural and affec-tive substrates to the other two. This is that of cold blooded "reptilian" predation, the calm and methodical hunting of a prey or victim, characteristic of what used to be called psychopathy, (and is now associated with extreme antisocial personality disorder) (Reid Meloy, 1998).

Turning back to the subject of severe malignant narcissism and antisocial per-sonality, Shakespeare's study (1603) of the "motiveless malignancy" of Iago in destroying the lives of Othello and Desdemona just because he could, has been regarded as paradigmatic of the emptiness and negation that are often at the heart of destructiveness. If there is any emotional content, it is the slight and personal injury of being passed over and excluded, and the envious impulse to destroy in others the happiness that cannot be experienced by the self.

The personification of evil in Western culture is of course the Devil, and the most notable and rounded portrayal in literature is that contained in John Mil-ton's *Paradise Lost* (1667). It is through the discussion of this figure that psycho-analysts like Ronald Britton (1998) and Hannah Segal (2002) have been able to approach the subject of radical evil. In the romantic era Milton's Satan was seen as a Promethean figure, rebelling against the father and paternal authority, against tradition – provoking the famous admiring comment by Blake that Milton "was of the devil's party without knowing it". Blake's prophetic poem *Milton* (1804) is a romantic rewriting of *Paradise Lost* in which Milton returns as "the bard" to liberate the human imagination from the fallen intellect, and helps create, through visionary fight, a New Jerusalem. Britton (1998), however, views Milton's por-trayal of Satan in *Paradise Lost* not as an unconscious expression of the urge to rebellion (though it may in part be such), but as a sympathetic and devastating portrayal of "destructive narcissism". Lucifer, the most beautiful of the angels, out of envy rebelled against God, furious that he has been displaced and usurped by the son. Full of pride and malice, he cannot bring himself to submit to the father, and a war follows, ending with Lucifer – now Satan – consigned for eternity to a hell that is both a place and an internal state.

As Ignês Sodré (2005) has suggested, when describing suicidal and destructive states of mind, the ego hates, and hates itself for hating. The situation becomes chronic and cannot change without outside help. Tragically, in the case of Milton's Satan, outside help (in this case, God) cannot be allowed to help because he is both denigrated and made more fearful by what is projected into him, and also because to accept dependence upon him would produce terrible humiliation and guilt. This beautifully describes a clinical situation familiar to many clinicians working with severely narcissistic patients, and arguably also describes a pervasive dynamic of contemporary life, in which paternal authority, in particular, is denigrated and thus becomes unavailable for positive identification.

The work of clinicians at the Portman Clinic in London (Campbell & Hale, 1991; Campbell, 1999; Glasser, 1998), with forensic patients, has helped the develop the psychoanalytic understanding that melancholic states contain murderous as well as despairing states of mind; and it is this murderousness that helps explain how the suicidal person is able to overcome the instinct for self-preservation and to treat his own body as an object, thus allowing himself to kill himself; or in a different but related configuration, to kill the body of another. In the suicidal state of mind the body that is attacked is frequently identified at an unconscious level with a hated other – as we see in the case of the psychotically depressed woman mentioned previously, whose cancerous body, as she saw it, was identified with her dead husband. Pathological splitting into all good and all bad states allows the bad feelings to be equated with the hated body.

Campbell and Hale (1991) suggest that a common fantasy in suicide is that the hated body is killed off, and that a surviving self is united in a state of oceanic bliss or oneness with the primary all-providing good mother. The fantasy of a surviving self that will exist after the body's death is not normally conscious, and is in Campbell and Hale's terms clearly a psychotic belief. Yet this account fits the clinical facts: the often unusually calm and untroubled suicidal – or murderous – patient has stilled his anxiety and self-doubt, his state of internal conflict. He is resolved upon an action, and is now steadfast and beyond the reach of others and of normal human compassion and empathy. A member of a psychotherapy group remarked that she had been thinking about suicide but had also thought that if she succeeded we would not accept her back into the group. This patient clearly had in mind a surviving self. Her remark also expressed, at the same time, her more healthy connection and attachment to the group, and to life.

Aspects of this fantasy are conscious, or at least preconscious, when revenge dominates the picture. Here there is a frequently ego-syntonic wish to triumph over life, over the parents that have failed to provide or attune, or the lover who has betrayed, or over the services that have not done enough, and the sometimes conscious fantasy is of watching the response of others to the suicide.

These hard-won and vital understandings rarely, however, appear in cultural discourse, in attempts to better understand, and effectively respond to, suicide and murderousness as social phenomena. Such a perspective is particularly important as a potential means of understanding the motivations and actions of lone wolf and other nihilistic terrorists. Indeed, I suggest later in the book that the attribution of these actions with political motivations and significance may be part of the problem, as this only serves to exacerbate the process; as a form of unconscious collusion with the deluded grandiosity of the perpetrators of what might be also understood as emotionally motivated acts of criminality.

The psychoanalytic model of the mind would suggest, however, that there is not an absolute difference between the well and unwell; in otherwise well-functioning people there are areas of difficulties and disturbance, and in mentally unwell people there are parts of the mind that remain in touch with reality. Another way of putting this is that there are psychotic parts of healthy people, and non-psychotic parts of mentally unwell people. This is not to fall into the romanticisation of mental illness evident in counter-cultural anti-psychiatry; or to assert there is no difference between states of mental health and ill-health. Mental illness is a destructive process in which the person, far from attaining higher truths, becomes progressively more estranged from internal and external reality. They become less able to engage with the world and to address, personally and collectively, socio-political issues.

In *Group Psychology and the Analysis of the Ego* (Freud, 1921c) Freud suggested that the mutual, libidinally invested, identification of all the members of a group with each other in their joined identification with the leader, on to whom they collectively project their superego, allows a regression to more primitive and atavistic behaviour than those individuals would usually display in their personal and family lives. The projection of the superego (including what might be more normally termed "the conscience") on to the leader allows groups to destroy and kill at the leader's behest; bestows a sense of belonging, security, and strength; and creates an exhilaration at being freed from normal moral constraints.

Later psychoanalytically informed authors (Barnett, 2007; Dicks, 1972) have highlighted the corruption of the superego, which allows otherwise "ordinary" individuals (as opposed to sadistic psychopaths and criminals) to carry out, or be part of, atrocious acts of cruelty without apparent conscience or conflict; and to rationalise that in so doing they were only carrying out orders. In their descriptive accounts, these writers note the kinds of splitting and dissociation of differing self-states that enable individuals to carry out acts of cruelty, and then show civility and kindness in their ordinary family lives. The capacity for such splitting, self-deception, and disavowal of unacceptable aspects of the self is of course regularly seen in everyday clinical situations, and in everyday life. These authors suggest, following Freud, and influenced by the experience of the two great wars, that there is a frailty to normal human functioning, and to the operation of rational thought, conscience, and delayed gratification essential to social life; and that developmental achievements, and identifications with the familial and social world, can become quickly undone at times of social unrest and large group regression.

Contemporary psychoanalytically informed approaches to group regression, and intergroup and social conflict, have stressed the way in which the natural human propensity for the splitting of loving and destructive aspects of the self can run along the channels of the idealisation of the social group the individual identifies with, and the projection of "bad" parts of the self with out-groups and other societies. The universal personal propensity for splitting takes shape during latency in particular, buttressed by stories and myths, in which others become objects of denigration or hatred. Such a splitting process is seen as defending against the guilt that might accrue if these "bad" parts of the self are taken back and aggressive conflicts and rivalries with others in the same social or familial group are acknowledged, rather than projected.

Extremes of splitting are, however, in an averagely expectable environment, modified by experience and the developing capacity to empathise with the experience of others, and particularly by an awareness of the universal aspects of human existence, based on similarities rather than differences. In optimum circumstances the ordinary socialisation structures of everyday life offer a protection from this kind of regressive pull, allowing for elaboration, sublimation, repression, and reaction formations dealing with primitive aggression, the toleration of ambivalence, demonstrating the dominance of love over hatred.

Kernberg (2003) suggests, though, that in individuals and social groups there remains a persistent unmetabolised core of aggression, primitive object relations, and primitive defensive operations – a latent psychotic core, a channel or a fault line that can be exposed in certain historical conditions, both in individuals and in social groups and structures. The processes of socialisation and empathy with others who are "different" can be disrupted by traumatic social experience, during the course of which an individual can identify his own inherent developmental "narcissistic wounds" with a communal or social trauma or historical injustice (Volkan, 1988). At times of social unrest and crisis, and large group regression, more mature identifications can collapse – sometimes with shocking suddenness – into these more ancient fissures, and a regression takes place. This is more likely, as we shall see later, if the communal or national traumatic experience has involved the reality or perception of gross and "unnatural" injustice and/or unfairness, rather than a "natural" calamity. These can then form the basis of a deep sense of personal and national grievance, and become part of a "psychotic core" of revenge, retaliation, and violent gratification, going on, if unchecked, for centuries. As for the individual, this destructive and self-destructive cycle can become, over time, a source of identity and a means of secret pleasure.

W. R. Bion (1961) noted that in small groups there is a propensity for regression when the basic reality-orientated task of the group is frustrated or fails. A clear, realistic, and achievable work task; congruent organisational and technical resources; and institutional authority allow mutual affiliation and the emergence of effective and empowered leadership. However, if there is an unrealistic task, overwhelming demands, or challenges to basic security, then more "primitive" emotionally driven responses can rapidly occur. These are what Bion termed the "dependent basic assumption group" and the "fight-flight basic assumption group" (1961). Kernberg (2003) sees these as narcissistic and paranoid regression respectively; the former involving a passive, entitled, mutually rivalrous, and infantilised dependency on a narcissistic and glib leader; the latter involving a hypervigilant response to perceived internal and external threat and a tendency to factionalise or alternately unite against an external enemy. Such a group tends to have as its leader a dominant, aggressive, paranoid person. A third constellation, "the pairing basic assumption group", represents a hope for the future, by way of a fantasised relationship between a couple, on whom the group's interest becomes focused.

Investigations of large groups (Rice, 1969; Turquet, 1975, cited in Kernberg, 2003) have demonstrated how the collapse of a realistic work task can, with great suddenness, and amongst members seen as psychologically healthy and mature, lead to states of intense anxiety, and excessive reliance on projective identification, omnipotent control, and other more primitive defences. In such a situation there is little tolerance of rationality, and the presence of resentment against individuals who try to bring rationality and reflection to bear. There is thus a parallel between the defensive processes of people with severe personality disorder and the behaviour of unstructured small and large groups at times of stress and regression (Bion, 1961).

According to Kernberg (2003) these regressive processes in failing unstructured large groups tend to produce, as a "solution", either a narcissistic or a paranoid group, with accordingly narcissistic or paranoid leaders. He describes the narcissistic group as dependent on the banalities of the messianic and self-loving leader, as infantile, passive, and assuming a right to be fed and taken care of. The paranoid group, on the other hand, is mobilised by primitive flight-fight mechanisms, hostile, alert, ready to find threats within the group and in the external world, creating a paranoid atmosphere, tending to factionalise, and choosing an appropriately aggressive, and paranoid leader. Kernberg (2003) suggests that a regressed unstructured large group, in selecting a paranoid leader and adopting a paranoid ideology, can become an embryonic political mass movement. The worst-case scenario, according to Kernberg, is that of a combination of a malignantly narcissistic leadership and a paranoid political ideology; a situation that differentiates "ordinary" dictatorships and authoritarian rule from terroristic totalitarian regimes.

Kernberg (2003) makes clear that the extent to which a large group shifts in a paranoid or narcissistic direction is dependent upon a number of interrelating factors: socio-cultural, economic (what pressure and constrains are group members under?), the stability or otherwise of the physical and social environment, the composition of the group, and the nature and quality of the leadership available. It is a basic contention of this book that at times of particular social and psychic dislocation, group regressive phenomena may become dominant; at times where there is also, paradoxically, great potential for a positive developmental step. It is also a contention of this book, further elaborated in the following chapter, that some psychoanalytic views of group functioning have inherited a liberal individualist tendency to see the crowd as an actual or potential irrational mob. Regressive outcomes are not inevitable and there have been, and continue to be, many situations where the crowd is a progressive force for change, and where societies have found ways of living with and accommodating difference, with inevitable tension and conflicts at times, but, overall, well enough. The question of whether the process is regressive or progressive is therefore simultaneously political and psychological, both historically contingent and universal, and also raises questions of ideology, class formation, socio-economics, and political leadership. It is to a paradigmatic example of such an integrated analysis that I turn in the next chapter, a historical study in which the distinction between realistic and regressive social movements arising as a response to social dislocations and deprivations becomes clearer.

Chapter 5

Destructive narcissism in history

Norman Cohn's study of millennialism

Norman Cohn's *The Pursuit of the Millennium: Revolutionary Millenarians and Mystical Anarchists of the Middle Ages* (1957) has long been regarded as the starting point for the study of millenarian sects and movements in medieval Europe, those movements which developed amongst the rootless poor in Western Europe between the eleventh and sixteenth centuries. Although Cohn's views have come under revision from later historians I think that they provide a prototype for the study of the conditions that allow for the eruption of a more malignant form of narcissism in human society, and of the social structure and dynamics of such a movement.

Cohn begins with the militant eschatological traditions that had roots in the oppression and/or perceived oppression of early Jewish and Christian religious groups. These were the fused religious and political ideologies of oppressed peoples, for whom religious and social transformation was indivisible. After the failure of the uprisings for national independence in AD 31 Jewish apocalyptic millennial tendencies declined in force and appeal. Instead, these millennial traditions became an essential part of early Christianity. Early Christians saw history as divided into two periods; before and after the triumphant coming of the Messiah. The apogee of this is in the Book of Revelation where, as Cohn puts it, "Jewish and Christian elements are blended in an eschatological prophecy of great poetic power" (Cohn, 1957, p. 24). A ten-horned beast symbolises the last world power, the persecuting Roman state; a second beast, the provincial Roman priesthood, vanquished by Faithful and True, a figure on a white horse, leading to the general resurrection of the dead, the last judgement, the new millennium, and "the holy city, new Jerusalem, coming down from God out of heaven, prepared as a bride adorned for her husband" (p. 25). In the second century, the early Bishop of Lyon, Irenaeus, consolidated these traditions by pulling together messianic prophecies from the Old and New Testaments and stressing the view that these would actually take place on the earth, and that the oppressed and righteous would receive their due reward. The key element of such beliefs was the view that transformation was not simply in the spiritual realm but would take place in history on earth, and would involve the actual overthrow and/or destruction of sources of "corrupt" and oppressive earthly power.

In the Montanist movement, for example, a self-proclaimed prophet gathered round him visionaries and ecstatics, and proclaimed the imminent arrival of the New Jerusalem. In common with later movements, this was a "fiercely ascetic movement, which thirsted for suffering and even for martyrdom" (Cohn, 1957, p. 25), the latter being seen as a pathway to the new millennial age. This movement was strengthened by its provocation of actual persecution and oppression, and spread through Asia Minor, Africa, Rome, and Gaul. In these movements religious and socio-political discontents merged into a revolutionary movement, threatening the position of the newly established Church.

Theological attacks on these millennial tendencies first began in the third century, by stressing the spiritual and allegorical nature of Christian eschatological writings. By the fourth century the church was established and prosperous, ascendant in the Mediterranean world, and the official church of the empire, "and the men responsible for governing it had no wish to see Christians clinging to outdated and inappropriate dreams of a new earthly paradise" (Cohn, 1957, p. 29). Orthodox doctrine was established by St Augustine in his treatise *The City of God*; in this work the Book of Revelation was regarded as spiritual allegory, not political blueprint. The millennium had already been established by the Church.

The Catholic Church could never, however, wholly suppress these movements, which continued to exist "in the obscure underworld of popular religion" (Cohn, 1957, p. 30). The Sibylline Books or oracles (originally books of Hellenic Judaism, which then attracted Christian apocalyptics) continued where the Book of Revelation had left off. These books were tremendously influential during the Middle Ages, "indeed save for the Bible and the works of the Fathers they were probably the most influential writings known to medieval Europe" (1957, p. 33), which, despite being transcribed in Latin in the West, penetrated down to "the lowest strata of the laity" (1957, p. 33).

These millennial movements had many different outward forms and characters but, Cohn argued, similar aetiologies, structures, and fantasies. In what Cohn calls the "central phantasy" (1957, p. 21) of religious millenarianism there is a world that "is dominated by an evil, tyrannous power of boundless destructiveness" (p. 21): a force that is perceived as more than human, as "demonic". The sufferings of the victims become ever more outrageous and extreme until the "saints" – "the holy people", "the righteous" – rise up and overthrow the tyranny, establishing a new kingdom, a dominion over the whole earth, a harmonious and peaceful world, a world of endless bounty and satiation, where there will be provision for everyone in a new Eden. Such a fantasy increasingly involved the presence of a "Messiah", a saviour, a warrior-king, a "son of man", and a "lion of Judah". It also involved the annihilation of those deemed to be unworthy. Enemies would be put to the sword. The establishment of the New Jerusalem required the violent purging of the unrighteous.

There appear to be several recurring features of such movements, at whatever time and in whichever geographical locality these movements emerged. There was usually a leader or prophet who tended not to be (unlike the leaders of popular political uprisings) a peasant, artisan, or manual worker, but rather was often a priest or a former priest, or preacher, or petty noble, or simply an impostor. Many of these leaders claimed that they were divinely inspired, or identified themselves with mythologised historical figures, such as Frederick II, or Charlemagne, or Count Baldwin IX, or the mythical "emperor of the last days". They tended to have been obsessed with millennial eschatological fantasies, and identified themselves, at times to a delusional extent, with figures of messianic divine retribution. At times of great social upheaval they sometimes succeeded in recruiting the rootless poor as followers. Needless to say, such leaders often possessed charisma and personal magnetism, to the extent, Cohn, argues, that followers, often from atomised and abject social conditions, became "enthralled". Out of these conditions might then emerge a

> new group – a restlessly dynamic and utterly ruthless group which, obsessed by the apocalyptic fantasy and filled with the conviction of its own infallibility, set itself infinitely above the rest of humanity and recognised no claims save that of its own supposed mission. And finally this group might – though it did not always – succeed in imposing its leadership on the great mass of the disorientated, the perplexed and the frightened.
>
> (Cohn, 1957, p. 285)

Cohn gives a number of detailed accounts of the historical trajectories of these groups and the success they did have in winning support and threatening the established power of the church and established vested interests. Although these groups tended to start from a righteous position, with an ascetic and puritanical character, they tended to degenerate into violence and, in particular, to violent murderous attacks on those they characterised as corrupt and damned, members of the Catholic laity, and the small but significant Jewish community in medieval urban centres.

The conditions favouring the growth of millennial groups, Cohn suggests, was remarkably consistent over the centuries; population increase, the beginnings of industrialisation, the weakening or shattering of traditional social bonds, and where there was an increasingly huge gap between rich and poor:

> Then in each of these areas in turn a collective sense of impotence and anxiety and envy suddenly discharged itself in a frantic urge to smite the ungodly – and by doing so to bring into being, out of suffering inflicted and suffering endured, that final Kingdom where the Saints, clustered around the great sheltering figure of their Messiah, were to enjoy ease and riches, security and power for all eternity.
>
> (Cohn, 1957, p. 60)

Cohn points out that many peasants lived at near subsistence level, and a bad harvest might mean a mass famine. There were regular invasions, and wars between private barons. Many peasants were serfs trapped into dependence on ecclesiastical or lay lords. Land had to be rented and protection earned through hard labour. There was great inequality within and between different villages. Although life could be difficult, and might be at times be full of poverty and oppression, there had also been some stability and social cohesion in the feudal world. There was material and emotional support provided through kinship groups, village communities, and guilds, and traditional institutional methods for voicing grievances and pressing claims. Life was dominated by age-old communal routine and custom:

> Social relationships within the village were regulated by norms which, though they varied from village to village, had always the sanction of tradition and were always regarded as inviolable. And this was true not only of relationships between the villagers themselves but of the relationship between each villager and his lord.
>
> (Cohn, 1957, p. 55)

Cohn makes it clear that at times when the population was sparse and labour much in demand, peasants has a certain leverage in this. There were, in short, some conditions of material and emotional security. The extended family may have worked the same plot of land for generations, and this provided continuity, cohesiveness, and a sense of belonging. Hardships were accepted as part of the nature of things, and horizons were narrow, and "in an economy which was uniformly primitive, where nobody was very rich, there was nothing to arouse new wants; certainly nothing which could stimulate men to grandiose fantasies of wealth and power" (p. 56).

As Ernest Gellner (1983) has pointed out, in relatively stable agro-literate pre-industrial societies there are horizontal cleavages of the population into estates, castes, and millets. Although massive inequalities exist, these are endowed with an aura of "inevitability, permanence, and naturalness", and "that which is inscribed into the nature of things is consequently not personally, individually, offensive, nor psychically intolerable" (Gellner, 1983, p. 12). This situation began to change in Western Europe with the rise of commerce and early industrialisation from the eleventh century onwards in parts of north west France, in what is now Belgium, and in the Rhine valley. Trading stimulated the growth of urban centres, and increased population saw the beginning of a rural and urban proletariat. For many these developments, particularly those associated with the cloth industry, offered the opportunity of escape from the restrictive conditions and low horizons of the past, and the opportunity, too, for rapid social ascent. If new wants and aspirations were stimulated, however, then these could not always be met. Conditions in the new urban centres were insecure, and the new industry could not absorb the surplus population, creating a situation of marginalization and chronic insecurity. There were beggars and roaming bands of mercenaries, but even artisans felt unprotected. As Cohn argues, if this was an era of small workshops under the usually benevolent patriarchal authority of a "master", it was also an era of a form of "uncontrolled primitive capitalism" in which a newly dominant merchant class provided the raw material and sold the finished product in an international market, and in which the position of even skilled workers was insecure.

At any moment war or slump might send these workers into the ranks of the destitute, even though they had their guild organisations. For the mass of unskilled workers, journeymen, and casual workers there were no traditions to fall back on, no social network, and therefore they lived naked before the market, "in a state of chronic frustration and anxiety" (Cohn, 1957, p. 59). These groups formed the most unstable element in medieval society, people who had no recognised place, and it was from this population that the millennial groups recruited, in the main, their membership.

Famine, plague, price rises, war, and the Black Death were some of the catastrophes that provided the tipping point of these chronic situations into millennial excitement. It might be said, using psychoanalytic language, that there was a massive failure of containment and paternal authority. The structures of authority and tradition that had been prevalent in the Middle Ages were undercut by socio-economic transition, and by, in the case of the increasingly worldly and rich church, the savage criticism of ascetic preachers and holy men, living in the woods, gathering followers.

"Traditional" medieval society, as the "large group" or organisation, began to fail, undercut both by its own inherent failings and inequalities and by the impetus of new socio-economic forces. This produced a fragmentation and dislocation, and a surplus of displaced and impoverished people, estranged from traditional social bonds, rituals, and identifications.

Cohn makes the important point that millennial movements were part of a larger world of social unrest and political turbulence, in which containing social structures were breaking down. Such movements evolved out of conditions of real injustice and sometimes of unimaginable hardship. If the members of such movements had a grievance then the grievance had some justice. They were, however, qualitatively different from movements of the poor to improve their situation through potentially realisable political and economic reforms, concessions, and even through political revolution. Instead:

> It is characteristic of this kind of movement that its aims and premises are boundless. A social struggle is not seen as a struggle for specific limited objectives, but as an event of unique importance, different in kind from all other struggles known to history, a cataclysm from which the world is to emerge totally transformed and redeemed.
>
> (1957, p. 281)

Cohn's account of the rise of millennialism is an important starting point for the understanding of malignant narcissism in social groups; millennial fantasies start off in conditions of real injustice, insecurity, and oppression; they are fuel to which further suffering and martyrdom can be added. Such suffering and martyrdom can be induced, knowingly at times, by behavioural provocation. Such movements, though they start from a position of real injustice, and are infused with class resentment, are very different from those movements which seek political and socio-economic change, which in other words have limited, potentially achievable aims. Millennial movements instead have an apocalyptic character, and envisage ritualistic and violent purging of badness (the unrighteous) and the idea of an endless blissful state of purity and satiation.

Such millennial movements and fantasies can be seen as infused with narcissistic components: there is a grievance and sense of injustice (which may be historically justified), there is the primitive splitting of the world into good and bad, the righteous and the unrighteousness. There is the primitive emphasis on purity and asceticism, which can tend to break down into its opposite, an orgy of self-righteous violence, and into hedonistic excess. There is a behavioural provocation which tends to actualise the unconscious fantasies and projections, inducing violent retaliations from the authorities, bestowing further victimhood, martyring, suffering, and further fueling self-righteous fantasies of revenge.

In the millennial movements as described by Cohn paternal authority is not real and substantial, the product of actual developmental achievement and identification, but is literally "pseudo" or fraudulent; many of these leaders being imposters, or frankly deluded, or, more simply, not who they claimed to be. There appears to have been a shared identification with these leaders, so that normal behavioural constraints are lost, and there is a regression towards acts of cruelty and aggression, a historical example of Freud's view (1921c) of the projection of the superego into the leader and the collapse of civilised behaviour that can occur in large groups. In the absence of real paternal authority, there is a wish for fusion with the maternal object, identified with a state of bounty and endless satiation in the new millennium. In order for there to be this state of prelapsarian bliss there is a need for the annihilation of the unworthy.

In such a situation it is easy to see the operation, too, of primitive splitting mechanisms, idealisation of the godly, denigration of the ungodly, grandiosity, and infantile omnipotence. These groups appear to meet the descriptions offered by Kernberg of a paranoid group led by a malignantly narcissistic leader.

There is a caveat, however, to this grim picture; Freud and the psychoanalytic tradition tended to inherit a liberal-conservative view of the crowd or group as potential or actual "mob"; such a view is perhaps strengthened by a reading of Cohn. However, the crowd can easily be projected into and attract all sorts of negative attributions. At a more everyday contemporary social level such attitudes can be seen in some of the responses to football crowd violence. Millions of people attend football matches every weekend in large groups. There is very little violence and the overwhelming majority of supporters neither cause nor are involved in any kind of trouble. Those comparatively rare examples of violence that do occur can be seized upon, however, in some quarters, as proof positive of the primitive and boorish mentality of the fans, rather than as evidence, in their exception to the general rule, in fact, of the opposite.

George Rude, in his study of *The Crowd in History* (1964), provided a useful corrective of what might be seen as the politically conservative assumptions and implications implicit in psychoanalytic group theory and the more general liberal fear of the mob. The crowd was often a progressive force in human history, voicing demands for which, in the absence of democratic and accountable structures of power, there could be no other means of expression. Such crowds may have, at times, behaved in a pathologically violent way, but more often they exhibited some degree of restraint, attacking property and symbols of power, rather than people. They often had coherent political objectives, and limited aims. Some leaders may have been demagogic, others tended to cast off their leadership role, or be reluctant heroes. This more positive picture has been clearly evident in, for example, the popular uprisings in the Middle East that characterised the beginning, if not the end, of the "Arab Spring".

What seems important to emphasise is that there are real injustices and grievances. The question is what these groups in their fantasy, ideology, and actual behaviours do with these real grievances. Cohn draws an essential, though perhaps difficult to make in practice, distinction between millennial groups, and those of successful collective movements for social reform and justice, organised by ordinary people, that did manage to secure material and political concessions and gains during the Middle Ages. He suggests that the apocalyptic and unrealisable demands of the millennial groups made them qualitatively different from contemporary reformist or even revolutionary groupings. The millennial groups grew out of periods of instability, turbulence, and social change, and used these conditions as fuel for their essentially destructive purposes. They had no interest in constructively engaging with reality in any normal sense; they had rather more interest in destroying it. This distinction is one in which the pathological element is not aggression, or revolutionary impulses in themselves, but the use of real grievances to fuel omnipotent, unrealisable, and ultimately nihilistic purposes. This is a distinction to which we will return in the next chapter.

The contemporary resonance of Cohn's analysis involves, I have suggested, the relationship between certain forms of social dislocation, and the emergence of pathologically destructive individuals and social movements. Such movements have to be distinguished in their millennial character and objectives from those movements seeking social change or revolution but which have limited and potentially realisable objectives. From a psychoanalytic perspective millennial movements are infused by regressive emotional wishes: the notion of blissful union with a maternal object, the denigration of objective authority, and the adoption of a pseudo paternal authority. Such movements involve simultaneously the splitting off of inadmissible degraded aspects of the self into others, who can then become subject to denigration and attack.

Cohn's analysis (1957) suggests that in terms of the conditions that create these movements it is not poverty itself that is the defining factor, though it may be contributory, but the breaking of "traditional" bonds, the rupturing of established social identifications and relationships, creating conditions of socio-economic *and* psychic insecurity. This is not to suggest that such movements can *only* be created by such conditions – there may be many potential paths – but that there is a link. His analysis, whilst pessimistic in some regards, also offers a repost to those who view the crowd, the mob, and the masses, the populists in contemporary terms, as irredeemably irrational, violent, capricious, and destructive. History suggests that though there is some truth to this pessimistic picture it is true that the large group can operate in a goal-driven, reality-based, restrained and proportionate way, and can become a force for progress. The psychoanalytic emphasis on regressive processes requires to be balanced with attention to contingent historical factors – the underlying socio-economics, the balance of class and political forces, the quality of leadership, and so on. A destructive or regressive outcome is not inevitable.

In the next chapter I return to more recent history. In his *Warrant for Genocide: the Myth of Jewish World Conspiracy and the Protocols of the Elders of Zion* Cohn (1967) relates the close relationship between the fantasies of millennial groups and those of the Nazis. He parallels, too, how these fantasies come to prominence amid conditions of mass insecurity. As he says in his revised conclusion to his study of the former, "the parallels and indeed the continuity are incontestable" (Cohn, 1957, p. 285). It is to this subject, and the rise of nationalist identifications, that I now turn.

Chapter 6

Imagined communities
A historicised psychoanalytic perspective on the rise of nationalism

The coastline around St Mary's island, from Curry's point to Seaton Sluice, just north of Whitley Bay, eleven or so miles to the east of Newcastle upon Tyne in north-east England is one of the most important geological sites in the country. The last ice age, 10,000 years ago, deposited unstable and crumbling layers of mud, rubble, and pebbles, glacial debris, that now characterises the eroding and subsiding cliffs and coastal paths that make up the area. Further down, towards the North Sea, are shore platforms, sandstone rocks, coves, and stacks marooned on the beach. Underneath relatively more recent layers, and exposed by years of erosion, weathering, and the undercutting action of the sea, are ancient coal seams, and the geological fault-lines of the landscape. The coal seams themselves were laid down as rotting tropical vegetation when the whole land-mass was located somewhere near the equator. They later formed the raw material of the once thriving Northumbria coalfield, some of the working seams going far out under the North Sea.

It is only because we see the natural world through human timescales, rather than geological ones, that we see the Alps, the Pyrenees, the Himalayas, as unchanging structures. Such is the nature of geological time. Dynamic movement stretches out under aeons. Under subterranean and hidden processes of pressure and earth movement, rocks have been folded into ridges and valleys, exposing earlier levels of strata as they do. Under the irresistible force of these unseen pressures whole blocks of solid strata split and move relative to one another, along the vertical or horizontal planes. In such ways the fault-lines and clefts of these apparently solid land-masses are exposed and visible.

Geological and topographic structures, pressures, movements, ebbs and flows, have been used in everyday life as spatial metaphors for the depths, complexity, dynamism, periods of quiescence and instability of the human personality. These terms are readily used in the metaphors of ordinary language, "deep feeling", "at the back of my mind", "on the edge", and so on, "feeling in pieces". The fault-lines of the landscape might also serve as images of the fractures and fissures of the human psyche. Cities and civilisations, as emanations of the human mind, also serve to give concrete embodiment to mental processes. In *Civilization and its*

Discontents (Freud, 1930a) memorably used Rome, "the eternal city", as a poetic metaphor for the intermingling of past and present in the human psyche:

> an entity, that is to say, in which nothing that once come into existence will have passed away and all the earlier phases of development continue to exist alongside the latest ones. Where the Coliseum now stands we could at the same time admire Nero's vanished golden house. On the Piazza of the Pantheon we should find not only the Pantheon of to-day, as it was bequeathed to us by Hadrian, but, on the same site, the original edifice erected by Agrippa; indeed the same piece of ground would be supporting the church of Santa Maria sopra Minerva and the ancient temple over which it was built.
>
> (1930, p. 70)

If, for Freud, Rome was the place that poetically embodied the topography of the human mind since antiquity, then surely in early twentieth-century Europe it was Berlin that represented the apotheosis of industrial progress, where it was possible to see these transformative forces of modernity and the outcrops of older eras juxtaposed together in an unstable and dynamic mix. Alexandra Richie's history of Berlin (1998) traces the way in which a provincial outpost, a former military garrison town of Frederick the Great, situated in an expanse of flat marshlands, a remote provincial town of 6,000, was transformed by the 1920s into the third largest city in the world behind New York and London, an imperial capital of four and a half million people.

The Berlin of the 1930s was in part an imperial city of neo-classical pomp, and in part a city of bourgeois parks and gardens, some of it semi-rural in atmosphere. Forests, lakes, rivers, and parks covered 135 of its 339 square miles, particularly in the west. But, most of all, 1930s Berlin, like London, or New York today, was a microcosm of the modern world and the dynamic processes of capitalism and modernity, a living testament to Marx's view of a revolutionary totalising process in which "[a]ll that is solid melts into air" (Marx & Engels, 1848, p. 6). Like London, New York, and other modern metropolis its people came from all corners of the world. The ancestors of the Berlin population had been Dutch builders, farmers, and engineers; Jewish businessmen, bankers, and thinkers; French Huguenots and other Protestant refugees from Poland, Italy, and other southern German states; soldiers from Switzerland and Sweden; Jacobite rebels from Scotland and poor immigrants from all over eastern Europe. Richie (1998) outlines the American-inspired technological utopianism that threatened, or promised, depending on your point of view, to transform urban life into a rationalist and limitless pleasure dome, set free from ordinary constraints. Like London and New York today it was a city in the process of constant change and regeneration. There were massive new technologically advanced factories, like the giant Siemens electrical plant, and the Borsing heavy engineering works. Technological innovation, Fordism, and rampant consumerism created a heady urban landscape, a place to be for all ambitious intellectuals and scientists, for social and artistic aspirants of various hues.

The cultural and literary achievements of the Weimar period are well-known, for example, the cabaret culture and formal experimentation in the arts. Bauhaus architects, such as Walter Gropius and Bruno Taut, were designing horseshoe-shaped housing estates for the workers, including "comfortable rooms and lavish gardens, light, open space, centralised heating, hot water systems, community centres, even piped-in radio" (Richie, 1998, p. 336). However, whilst Richie presents avant-garde Berlin as a creative, talented maelstrom of cross-fertilising activity, a heady intoxicating mix of modernity and the "new objectivity", she also sees it as a narcissistic talking-shop, with a fashionable, somewhat apolitical cynicism ruling the roost; with a counter-cultural and transgressive avant-garde taking pot-shots at authority and the republic, presenting the Nazis and Hitler as risible figures of fun, concentrating their ire on social democratic "fascists" rather than engaging with and recognising the real threat of nihilistic and destructive political movement in their midst.

There are, I would suggest, contemporary parallels with this situation, in a "progressive" milieu in which the term "fascist" is used indiscriminately and ahistorically, often as a means of demonising opponents, and where there is a tendency to conflate populism with right-wing extremism. Meanwhile, the historical reality that fascism became dominant in a technologically advanced and culturally sophisticated society, of which Berlin was the apotheosis, has contributed to a view in which Nazism was the culmination of those rationalist forces unleashed by the bourgeois enlightenment, of those ideals of instrumentalist progress and administrative efficiency. My own view is that this is mistaken and goes against the historical evidence.

One thing is agreed by most historians: it is impossible to view Nazism outside of the historical context of the rise of virulent ethnic nationalism amidst the collapse of the old multi-ethnic empires of Europe. Here we have to briefly return to the Enlightenment, industrialisation, and the impact of modernity. In response to the mechanistic and dehumanising nature of "the age of reason" and the new industrial society, romantic artists asserted a more organic view of nature, and of life. There was a spirit throughout nature, everything was linked. Reality could be appraised poetically and imaginatively, rather than through deadening and objectifying reason. Here we have the major historical root of contemporary subjectivism.

The great radical poet and artist William Blake had been one of the first to see the materialist rationalist heart of the new market society, and its links with the more "satanic" and dehumanising aspects of the new industrialisation. Thus armed, he turned his sword of burnished steel towards the rationalism and complacency and inequality of the new world. The late historian E. P. Thompson (1993, cited in Britton, 1998) has linked Blake to certain radical dissenting lower-class Protestant traditions, particularly those of the Gnostics, claiming as they did a special and direct knowledge of the spiritual world, and existing within the wider tradition of anti-establishment apocalyptic Antinomian sects.

In Blake's own complex and very personal cosmology the human imagination, identified with God or the "divine self", creates a visionary world, the restoration of Eden or a lost paradise, in the place of the material world, of objective morality, and things. The "good object" was the "divine" self. The powerful bad object, in Blake's case, was the new mercantilist-early capitalist bourgeois state with its rationalist and scientific ideology of progress. Blake thus gave primacy to the human imagination, and the products of the self, and for him the danger was other men's minds. Ron Britton has coined the term "epistemic narcissism" (1998, p. 179) to describe this belief in extreme subjectivity: the primal unity of the self, in which truth can only be known through personal revelation. Thus, whilst Blake could be seen as a great critic of the spiritually impoverishing aspects of the new bourgeois society, and its material consequences, he also stood, as Britton has noted, as an early expression of, "[t]he voice of subjectivism, which today finds expression in self-psychology and the advocacy of the authentic, and in which the pathological risk is seen to be false compliance with a powerful object" (1998, p. 166).

If for Blake, and other romantics, it was the pure individual against external reality, in romantic nationalism this purity was projected into the "*volk*", or people. The first wave of romantic nationalists were, in the main, genuine well-meaning intellectuals, who assembled ballads and oral traditions into national literatures. Thus armed with pencil and paper they set off for the villages and "invented a nation". They inhabited the romantic idea of an autonomous, intimate, authentic "community" or tradition that had to be protected from the old regimes of Europe, psychologically the "bad objects" against which the pure self, identified with the authentic organic community, seeks liberation. In the tradition of nineteenth-century romantic nationalism the "Volk" was a dynamic organisation, subject to laws of development, language being the key to these traditions, and a crucial role was played by intellectuals as historians, lexicographers, and, sometimes, revolutionary leaders. Their aim was for the Volk to achieve self-consciousness through literacy and cultural identity, and ultimately through the establishment of the nation state.

Seen in these terms modern nationalism arose as apparently progressive liberationist movements against the old authoritarian order, the oppressive ancient regimes of Europe. In class terms it arose out of a split in the revolutionary movement, and was underpinned by the lesser landowners or gentry and the emergence of a national middle class and lower middle class, the spokesmen for which were professional intellectuals. Indeed nationalism was initially largely expressed by the middle classes rather than the mass of the population, many of whom were in any case illiterate, and who had a distinct regional identity and dialect – if anything their identification was based on religion rather than race. It was the uprooting of peoples, emigration and immigration, that changed these local traditions.

There have been many studies of nationalism, but most theorists (for example, Gellner, 1983) appear to agree that nationalism in the form of the nation-state only really emerged during the period of industrialisation, and indeed was perhaps an inevitable political expression of the concomitant need for a common language, administrative structures, and so on. In its most benign liberal version nationalism spoke of a civic state in which liberal constitutional rights were guaranteed to all of its citizens. There are rights and responsibilities, and the state offers protection of the inalienable rights of its citizens if they in turn agree to subscribe to the state's requirements. Such a state is progressive, liberal, and tolerant of minorities, secular, increasingly democratic, and based on continued material progress together with the requisite social reform. In this sense the nation-state promises a continuation of the rational secular values of the Enlightenment. Such was the case, as a whole, for example, with the revolutionary traditions of Republican France.

At another extreme, some of the forms of emerging nationalism were less rationalistic than the more benign liberal models: more xenophobic, based on an assertion of common identity, birth, and on mystical notions of race. These nationalist ideologies, rather than as in the liberal model promoting inclusivity and citizenship, were either implicitly or explicitly hostile towards perceived difference. The nation was seen as an organic whole, the state had to be identified with the supposed national culture of the majority, and this was defined through language, ritual, and culture.

The problem was that most of the emerging states in Europe in the nineteenth century contained many different groups, and in fact were ethnically and culturally heterogeneous. A further complication was that the old regimes of Europe and the east were *not* uniformly oppressive. Although the old Ottoman and Austro-Hungarian empires, for example, were autocratic and in some ways inefficient and corrupt, they also showed a certain degree of tolerance to the many minority groups that lived within their borders. In Salonika, for example, Ottoman Turks, Sufi, eastern Orthodox Greeks, Sephardic Jews, Bulgars, and Armenians had lived together for generations.

The novelist Joseph Roth, a prime exemplar of the lost world of assimilated Jewish "Mitteleuropa", has been criticised in some quarters for being a romantic apologist for the old Austro-Hungarian Empire. His portrayal of this world in the short story "Strawberries" (1929), though focusing, as it periodically does, on a small Galician town on a "great and sparsely inhabited plain" (1929, p. 134) in what is now eastern Poland, is scarcely idealised. It is a "somewhat rascally" place, poor, remote, but full of talented people, with its park with its chestnut trees and a soda pavilion "run by a beautiful statuesque blond woman" (1929, p. 149). It has around ten thousand inhabitants, "three thousands of them insane if not dangerously so" (1929, p. 134). It is a diverse place, many languages are spoken, but peaceful, "only near neighbours are enemies", and "no distinctions were made between people of different nationalities, because everyone spoke different languages". The Jews, though, did, Roth writes, stand out, and occasionally there were "little pogroms" but these were "soon forgotten" (1929, p. 136).

In the short story "The Bust of the Emperor" (1935) Roth conveys the ramshackle tolerance of the old dual-monarchy Hapsburg Empire, as seen by the eccentric, austere, and solitary figure of Count Franz Xaver Morstin. Although the scion of an old Polish family, which had in fact come from Italy in the sixteenth century, the Count thought of himself as "a man beyond nationality", a true aristocrat travelling all over the world, and speaking many languages. He lives in his ideal place:

> Like every Austrian of that time Morstin was in love with the constant in the midst of change, the familiar in the variable, the dependable in the midst of the unaccustomed. In this way what was foreign came to be homely, without losing its timbre, and home had the reliable charm of the exotic.
>
> (Roth, 1935, p. 237)

Thus, everywhere throughout the lands of the empire were different songs, different clothes, and different languages, and yet, "all over were the same coffee houses, with vaulted, smoky ceilings, with dark niches where chess players sat hunkered like alert fowls, with bars full of multi-coloured bottles and sparkling glasses, presided over by bosomy, blonde barmaids" (1935, p. 237).

In Roth's short story the old world, together with the Austro-Hungarian Empire and Emperor Franz Joseph himself, dies with the Great War. The count, for his part, goes on to a dying exile in the south of France, and at the end of his life bemoans, once again, modern nationalism:

> I hate nations and nation states. My former home, the Monarchy, was different, it was a large house, with many doors and many rooms for many different kinds of people. This house has been divided, broken up, ruined. I have no business with what is there now. I am used to living in a house, not in cabins.
>
> (1935, p. 258)

For Roth, writing with a mixture of leftist class consciousness and old world conservative disdain, the new nationalists were mediocre bourgeois, lacking talent, embittered, holding a grudge, "tooth surgeons who never made it up to be dentists" (1935, p. 241); would-be artists who never got into the academy. Thus for Roth, narcissistic wounds, a sense of inferiority and of entitlement, underpin the psychology of bourgeois nationalism, with the self now identified with the grandiose and purified nation-state. As the sardonic narrator of Roth's tale notes, "for it had been discovered in the course of the nineteenth century that every individual had to be a member of a particular race or nation, if he was to be a fully rounded bourgeois individual" (1935, p. 241). The Count (and Roth, I think it can be safely assumed) saw this new bourgeois nationalism as a stepping-stone towards bestiality.

Benedict Anderson (1983) argued that the nation was a socially constructed, "imagined" community. Eric Hobsbawm (1997) has demonstrated that "traditional" ways of life celebrated by romantic nationalists were usually idealised, ahistorical reconstructions evoked to serve contemporary and not always honourable purposes. Myth and counter-myth underpinned political conflict, and the rise of the nineteenth-century nation-state; for example, in Turkey and Armenia, Greece and Macedonia, where fictional events, particularly those held to involve victimhood and martyrdom, were co-opted into "national" narratives as objective truth, and came, over the years, to be uncritically accepted as such.

Such a view is supported by the historian Oliver Zimmer (2003) who suggests that the nationalist ideal had always represented, in its purest form, a people worshipping themselves (Breuilly, 1993), sanctified by martyrdom, sacrifice, a community no longer imagined but of collective experience and sentiment, "the nation as an extended family, and the promise of transcendence" (Zimmer, 2003, p. 43). Such a process, motivated by emotional factors, was in the end indifferent, or positively antagonistic, to the claims of external reality and objective truth, outside of wish-fulfilment.

In the European borderlands, the Baltic republics, western provinces of Belorussia, Ukraine, and Moldova, however, there was relatively little conflict before the First World War, in part because Russian and Austrian imperial policies were aimed at maintaining stability. Although concerned with control they were also concerned with reform and modernisation. How, then, to explain in historical terms the rise of a more malign, xenophobic form of nationalism? Historians have argued that there is no one single factor that in isolation can explain this rise, reaching a crescendo at the end of the nineteenth century and the early part of the twentieth. However, there are factors that do seem to be well-established as central to any historical understanding. Zimmer lists these as:

> rapid industrialisation, increased geographic and social mobility, the extension of democratic rights, state induced programs of cultural assimilation, increased inter-state competition, the breakdown of institutions and redrawing of state boundaries, the quest for political and cultural recognition of stateless nationalities.
>
> (Zimmer, 2003, p. 122)

It was the end of the old multicultural empires and the growth of nationalism that led, though perhaps not inexorably, to the genocidal ethnic conflict of the twentieth century. With the outbreak of the First World War, in particular, there was a focus on nationalism as a means of galvanising communities. Relations between Polish landowners and Lithuanian peasants, Poles and Ukrainians, Baltic people and the Germans, and all of these and the Jews collapsed into rivalry and mistrust. At the end of the war ethnic groups competed for resources and control of territories, leading to pogroms, massacres, reprisals, and so on. These were often carried on by local people, and were institutionalised in the form of state politics with the creation of the new states of Poland, Czechoslovakia, and the Baltic republics (Prusin, 2010).

How does Nazism fit into this picture? The Fascism that emerged in Germany in the 1920s and 1930s, from a small political party into a mass movement, was different from more old-fashioned right-wing or conservative authoritarianism (for example, from Franco's Spain, or Salazar's Portugal) that had become dominant elsewhere in Europe, partly, as in Germany, as a response to the "threat" from the political left. It was also substantially different in the extent of its xenophobic murderousness from Mussolini's fascists in Italy. As Kershaw (1987) notes, the National Socialist Workers

Party (Nazi Party) was an anti-socialist counter-revolutionary mass movement whose very name ("National Socialist") spoke of an attempt to steal some of the clothes of left-wing parties and to co-opt class resentment and social anomie into the direction, not of socialism and internationalism, but of the "organicist" community based on "race", and nationalism. Their resource to rallies and mass mobilisation echoed the Bolshevik revolution. The party was a mass movement "from below", bypassing traditional institutions by resource to new forms of direct communication with the masses, antagonistic to the old conservative elites as well as to the forces of liberalism, socialism, and Marxism.

Although the Marxist and socialist movements were also hostile to capitalism (though parliamentary Socialist parties had long supported liberal democratic institutions) these parties shared the same intellectual heritage in the bourgeois Enlightenment and the principles of the French Revolution. Marx saw the scientific and innovative aspects of productive capitalism as part of human progress – though not the end point. The Fascist movement, on the other hand, was decidedly not part of the Enlightenment process, and indeed was wholly antagonistic to it. Fascism, as it emerged in Germany, was hostile not just to constitutional liberal government (freely elected governments, rights to assembly, the rule of law, citizens' rights and liberties such as freedom of speech and right of assembly) but to the basic humanistic and rationalist tenets of liberal civilisation itself.

Hobsbawm (1994) points out, further, that, unlike other anti-modernist and anti-liberal conservative and reactionary movements of the time, the Nazi party was not fighting for the protection of at least partially real traditions and ways of life. Rather, they seized on a farrago of disparate and discreditable racial theories pertaining to the purity of "Nordic" races (an inchoate concept that wasn't invented until the late nineteenth century) and mixed these with a reductive version of social Darwinism and "the survival of the fittest".

It took a socio-economic crisis, however, for a worrying social trend to become the dominant trait. Eric Hobsbawm notes (1994) that the rise of Fascism would most likely not have taken place had it not been for the Wall Street Crash and the Great Slump. The Nazi party was reduced to a small electoral rump after the economic upturn of 1924, well behind the liberal, social democratic, and Communist parties, but by 1932, in the midst of an economic crash, it secured thirty-seven per cent of the national vote. These are important historical realities in the context of contemporary discourse on the subject, a discourse that can throw around the term "fascist" with ahistorical abandon, and which can present populism as a step towards fascism.

To further explore this subject, I want to turn next to Oliver Hirschbiegel's 2004 film *Downfall* (*Der Untergang*) set in Berlin in 1945 and based on the memoirs of Adolf Hitler's private secretary Traudl Junge (Junge, 2004). The film provides a compelling account of the last days of the Third Reich but also illustrates the often conflicting contemporary understandings of this period in human history, and, at a more fundamental level still, of the nature of human destructiveness.

Chapter 7

The downfall of destructive narcissism

Downfall focuses on the chaotic denouement to the war, and Hitler's last few days in the *Führerbunker* underneath the Reichstag, during the final days of the Third Reich, as the Red army gradually encircles Berlin. It juxtaposes scenes underground, in the bunker, with life outside, as the battle for Berlin takes place, with its carnage amongst the tenement streets and courtyards of Berlin. For, if this was an imperial city of places and parks, a city of the avant-garde and of technological innovation, it was also an urban landscape of working-class housing, *Mietskaserne* (dark tenements and barracks) in unbroken hollow squares, with inner courtyards linked by dark tunnels of archways, surrounded by railways, good yards, factories, municipal slaughterhouses, and miles of industrial canals.

Downfall is framed by footage of the real Traudl Junge, now an old lady looking back on her life, filmed shortly before her death. She says that she was never an enthusiastic Nazi, and that fate had taken her to a place that she would never have (consciously) chosen. The film ends with another interview with Junge, recorded shortly before her death, where she tries to explain, but not to justify, her years of enthusiastic loyalty to the system and her apparent unawareness, or turning of a blind eye to, or disavowal of, the atrocities that were going on.

The "real action" of the film opens with a file of attractive young women apprehensively and excitedly moving through a military zone for a job interview. However, this is not any old secretarial job, but that of Hitler's personal secretary. The Hitler that emerges to meet the aspiring secretaries is a stooping, frail-looking, perhaps somewhat diminished figure, and is apparently charming, paternal, and kindly. He quickly chooses Traudl: "A Munich girl!" he murmurs in approval, and tolerantly overlooks her initial nervousness. "He gave me a job!" she excitedly exclaims to the unsuccessful applicants, who bravely manage to put enough of their own disappointment and jealousy aside to congratulate her warmly. This sets up one of the main themes of the film: feelings and situations, emotional responses and behaviours that would be normal, charming, heart-warming even, become, by dint of a deeply abnormal situation that can only be consciously or unconsciously split-off from awareness, instead perverse.

It is clear that there is a kind of bond between Traudl and Hitler. Hitler is charming, despite his unprepossessing, stooped, prematurely aged physical appearance, and the trembling arm caused by his advancing Parkinsonism. Much of the critical attention following the release of the film focused on this characterisation of Hitler, as played by Bruno Granz. The performance was praised by the Hitler historian and biographer Ian Kershaw as the most convincing film representation of the dictator to date. Some people, though, objected to the "humanising" aspect of Bruno Ganz's portrayal: how could such a monster be made human? So, in *Downfall* we see that Hitler is a vegetarian who loves his dogs and is kind and courteous, to the last, to Traudl. But of course evil usually comes not wrapped up in monstrosity but in charm or banality (Arendt, 1963), in the humdrum, and in contradiction. It is too easy to present monstrous people simply as monsters.

The scene having been set, time is flash forwarded to April 1945, to the underground bunker during the last days of the Reich, the endgame, the denouement, the "downfall". The film quickly juxtaposes two worlds, two different topographical spaces. There is the claustrophobic world of the underground bunker, where we see Hitler holed up with hand-picked Schutzstaffel (SS) guards and his senior officials, Goebbels, Bormann, Kreb, Bugdorf, Wiedling, and other Nazi operatives and functionaries, trying to assert their will even as reality breaks into their enclosed world, with the sounds of bombs and Russian artillery overhead. Then there is the reality of the world outside, on the streets of Berlin. Here we quickly learn that the Red Army, the denigrated "Asiatic" and "Bolshevik hordes", as Hitler saw them, have encircled the city, that fighting is now going on in the outer suburbs. Vigilante and revenge mobs are shooting "deserters" and settling old scores with opponents of the regime, children are being drafted into the army, and food is running out, the city's population of three million, many with no electricity, no gas, no water, and no food, is sheltering in cellars and subway stations. Conflicts rage between the professional soldiers of the *Wehrmacht* under General Weidling and the "people's militia", the *Volkssturm*, commanded by Goebbels. Horrific and arbitrary murders are inflicted by roaming fascist vigilante groups exercising summary and wholly arbitrary "justice" on an already traumatised and exhausted population.

Whilst in the streets of Berlin people, for the most, try to survive as best they can, in the *Führerbunker* another reality holds sway, increasingly disconnected from the outside world, even as the telephone lines are cut. We are shown a situation where the Führer is lost to reality, moving devastated and surrounded divisions that now only exist on a map. We see the Nazi organisation breaking down, under massive external pressure from the inescapable reality of the Red Army and the Allied advance. Hitler becomes weak, capricious, contradictory, and prone to mood swings, euphoria, and despair. There are manic flights away from reality, an assertion of the will against an encroaching inescapable reality; we see Hitler and his generals gathered round the map, on which the movement of the Red Army is being tracked. Here reality has its verdict, and we see Hitler move from states of utter despair and raging impotence and demoralisation, into manic grandiosity and states of unreality. "We will drive back the Soviet Units in the north and the east!", "Steiner's division will attack from the north and unite with the ninth!",

"Have Wenck support them with the Twelfth Army!" Hitler exclaims: "Wenck will come!"

We see Hitler declaring "Clausewitz", and ordering Berlin to become a "front line" city. There will be no evacuation of civilians. As the reality of defeat against the "Asiatic hordes" of the Red army looms, we see Hitler turn on his "betrayers", the German people; they, not him, are responsible for the downfall, along with colleagues, the army, the generals –anybody, in fact, other than himself. And the German people are not his responsibility, even though he spoke in their name, of the "*Volk*" or the "Aryan race". Hitler makes it clear that he has no feelings for people who have proved themselves "too weak" – "If my own people fail this test, I will shed not one tear for them. They deserve nothing else. It is their own destiny. They themselves are to blame."

Meanwhile, elsewhere inside the bunker the various factions of the Nazi party are beginning to jostle for power, to look towards protecting their own skins, the gangster organisation beginning to implode under pressure, the corrupt and para-sitical nature of the "loyalty" to the organisation more fully apparent, now that the end is in sight. We learn that Heinrich Himmler and Herman Göring have both been jostling for power behind Hitler's back, and see Eva Braun's brother in-law Herman Fegelein murdered by the SS as a consequence of internecine machina-tions within "the brotherhood". Other factions decide that it might be better to "use politics" rather than war and terror. Their grandiosity and cynicism betraying their loss of contact with reality, they imagine that they might be able to sue for peace with Eisenhower and Churchill as a western bulwark against the Soviet Russia, as if they had something to bargain with. Later they try, with equal lack of success, to dictate peace terms with Marshall Zhukov of the Red Army, on the grounds that both nations have suffered equally.

In direct contrast to this we are introduced to Captain Schenck, an SS man who tries heroically and selflessly to mobilise hospital and civic resources for the civil-ians left in Berlin. We are witness to the struggles of a working-class couple and their young son, Peter Krantz, who, inspired by romantic ideas of heroism, self-sacrifice, and romantic martyrdom, volunteers, against his father's wishes, for the doomed job of fighting off the might of the Red Army. The father implores him: "It's over, can't you see?"

On occasions there are temporary excursions out from the underground world. April 1945 finds a Berlin spring with Traudl Junge and Eva Braun emerging briefly from the underground bunker to take the air in the Reichstag gardens. On film this creates an oddly quiet and peaceful moment where somehow flowers are blooming and birds singing in the linden trees, a momentary lull from the dull thud of the shelling. The haunting poignancy of this scene is that it provides a glimpse of an alternative or virtual history, of how things might have been. The scene is powerful also for invoking the restorative powers of the natural world when, in the near distance, we see glimpses of blackened ruins tinged red with the glow of firestorms, shell craters, brick, rubble, and the dead bodies of men and animals. We know that there is heavy street-fighting nearby. We see Hitler emerge briefly from the bunker, for the last time, into the Reichstag gardens to give a medal to Peter Krantz, his shaking hand held behind his back.

For the most part *Downfall* shows Hitler's acolytes and functionaries under a malign spell, struggling and sometimes unable to break out of the closed space of the bunker, even as the prospect of personal survival seems to dictate that they should try to make the escape. We see people breaking down when Hitler cannot provide the leadership and direction they want, when he cannot sustain their illusions with promises of ultimate victory. At the same time we also see the strength of these libidinal ties of loyalty to the leader, ties that go beyond the grave and lead to suicide, in identification with Hitler, even against all claims of normal self-preservation. Hitler and Eva Braun marry and shortly afterwards commit suicide. Many of the other regime functionaries also choose the same path. They never escape the bunker. Most shockingly of all Magda Goebbels poisons her own children rather than leave them in "a world without national socialism".

Traudl manages to bring herself to leave the bunker, and to avoid the pull of killing herself, though not without evident internal conflict. She has to be persuaded to attempt to walk out from the darkness of the bunker, and back into the apocalyptic world outside. The Russian troops have arrived, and large groups of soldiers are everywhere. Some are singing and dancing. Campfires have been lit. There is still confusion, with groups of SS men carrying on fighting in a show of nihilistic defiance, whilst others have accepted that the game is up. Many give themselves up and are taken prisoner by the Red Army (interestingly the credits of the film show that many of them in fact survive and return to Germany in the 1950s). Traudl becomes separated from some of her friends as she risks walking through the Russian lines. In her escape she also meets up with Peter Krantz, the bereaved young boy whose parents we have seen randomly murdered by fascist thugs, and, uneasily, heads down, avoiding doing anything that might bring them to attention, they are somehow able to walk unchallenged through the Russian ranks to the outskirts of the city. In the last scenes of *Downfall* we see a young girl and a younger boy leave an apocalyptic blasted city behind them, cycling through the countryside, as if they are beginning to emerge from a terrible nightmare into the fresh air.

The film appears to make no attempt (at least overtly) to explain Hitler, and the rise of German Fascism. Rather, it sets out to faithfully represent, in a rather old-fashioned realist way, what actually happened during the last days of the regime, in Hitler's bunker, and in the besieged Berlin above. Well-researched historical characters feature, events that really happened are represented, although in condensed form. A meeting that may have taken place over a few days is compressed into a few minutes, for example, the regime's grandiose attempt to sue for peace with the Soviet General Zhukov. The film is formally conservative, being realist in its form, seeking to represent things as they happened and to let the audience reach their own conclusions.

Although critically lauded, *Downfall*'s realism, its account of "what really happened", is, of course, also a selective artifice, and has not been without its controversies nor its critics. Mention has already been made of the – in my view tendentious – criticism of Bruno Granz's portrayal of Hitler. Perhaps the more serious criticism was that *Downfall*, although critical of Nazism, was part of a revisionist view of history that adds the German civilian population to the list of depoliticised "victim groups" of generalised "tyranny"; the same German population large swathes of which actively supported the Nazis, and who at best turned a blind eye to the reality of the atrocities carried out in their name.

In his review in the *Times Literary Supplement* of *The Third Reich at War 1939–1945* by Richard Evans (2005), Nicholas Stargardt (2008) notes that the German biographer of Hitler, Joachim Fest, was the man responsible for the book on which the script (by Bernd Eichinger (2004)) of *Downfall* was based, alongside Traudl Junge's diaries. Stargardt comments that in his book Richard Evans takes issue with Fest, accusing him of a form of neo-conservative romanticism, one which highlights Hitler's pathological irrationality, and makes the German people appear "as both his dupes and his final victims" (Stargardt, 2008, p. 8).

Downfall too, was accused of distinguishing between the fanatical hardcore inner circle of the Nazi party, holed up in the bunker, and the old-fashioned professional *Wehrmacht* on the streets of Berlin, doing a job that had to be done but without entirely losing their humanity, and without giving vent to sadistic violence. Further, in the film the SS Captain, Ernst-Gunter Schenk (another real person about whose actual role there remains some controversy), in particular, is presented as being a "good German", a doctor, rational, humane, trying to attend to a civilian population whilst Hitler and his coterie argue amongst themselves, invent imaginary armies on a map, and more or less abandon the Berliners to their fate. The ordinary Berliners become, in the film, as much the victims of Hitler's "insane" refusal to concede the reality of defeat as of the Red Army; a traumatised population reduced to sheltering in subways and cellars without electricity, water, and food, prey to random violent reprisals by roaming groups of disaffected fascist vigilantes for their "defeatism" if they seek to surrender.

In *The Third Reich at War* Evans (2008) points out the brutality of the German campaign in the east, in Poland and Russia in particular, in which the local populations were treated as sub-humans, and that this was conducted not simply by the Nazi party, or even the military state, but also by much of German society. He also points out that, though they might have been carried out in the service of a deeply irrational cause, Hitler's military interventions were not in themselves irrational, that is, judged purely as military strategy. Hitler's pathological irrationality can be exaggerated and this preoccupation may serve to get away from a more disturbing reality, the nature of willful destructiveness.

I want to try here to tentatively develop this subject matter by returning to Herbert Rosenfeld's ideas (1971) about "destructive narcissism". Of course, Rosenfeld, himself a Jewish refugee from Nazi Germany, was ostensibly writing about the internal emotional world of individual patients (and to an extent of all human beings) rather than a complex socio-political organisation or structure such as the Nazi party. Concepts derived from the study of the individual personality and its psychopathologies cannot be simply "transferred" across to understanding complex multi-determined social phenomena such as the rise of Fascism. However, whilst psychoanalytic understandings cannot replace historical analysis they can complement it.

Rosenfeld's analogy of the destructive parts of the personality with a mafia gang has become famous in psychoanalytic literature, and central to most psychoanalytically informed understandings and treatments of a particular group of very disturbed patients, who present clinically with a picture of extreme self-destructiveness and/or destructiveness, symbolic and real, towards others:

> the destructive omnipotent way of living … often appears highly organized, as if one were dealing with a powerful gang dominated by a leader, who controls all the members of the gang to see that they support one another in making the criminal destructive work more effective and powerful.
>
> (Rosenfeld, 1971, p. 174)

Rosenfeld was describing metaphorically the dominance of "bad" parts of the self, over a more vulnerable, dependent, and needy part of the personality that might wish to engage with reality and with ordinary human relationships. This "bad" part of the self could be idealised, as the solutions it offers seem to provide a refuge from normal human pain and vulnerability. In Rosenfeld's vivid metaphor these "bad" aspects of the self are personified as a ruthless gang or organisation, imprisoning more vulnerable and constructive "good" parts of the self. He was describing an internal set of relationships between different parts of the personality, and between different unconscious identifications. His analogy helps to understand "negative therapeutic reactions" in which the patient, appearing to have made progress (made more contact with the therapist and with life), suddenly regresses or deteriorates, with increased self-harm, suicidality, and attacks on treatment – and on life. It is as if there has been a serious "betrayal", as Rosenfeld suggests, and that what follows are violent reprisals against the more healthy part of the self (and indirectly against the source of help). Such a pathological organisation of the personality can thus be represented as an internal mafia gang.

As *Downfall* makes clear, Hitler and the Nazis underground have insulated themselves from internal and external reality, and as this reality inescapably impinges, in the shape of the encircling Red Army, then it has to be ever more desperately and manically denied. This doesn't work, and internal collapse into despair ensues, followed by further manic activity and escape – but only for a while. The air of manic unreality is represented by the figure of Eva Braun and her cheery admonitions; "Come on, kids!", "Have some fun!", apparently playing the good sport until the bitter end, organising a swinging party (until a bomb disrupts proceedings). In a more reflective moment she says to Traudl: "It's all so unreal, you want to wake up and you can't". There is a mood of empty hedonism as whatever moral code remaining in these circumstances begins to break down into drunken debauchery.

The verdict of reality finally trumps the application of the will. Much as the Nazis might wish to believe that it is otherwise, Berlin is fallen, and the game is up for the regime. The outcome of this, reflecting the nihilism and emptiness that seems to have lurked not too far beneath the surface of Nazism, is death; for the bunker is a kind of last resting place, below the ground, literally insulated from the external reality it has helped to create but violently hates; an unmetabolised destructive core, a malignant narcissism, which in its essence, in its hatred of life and idealisation of death, comes close to a historical embodiment of Freud's controversial notion of a "pure culture of the death instinct" (Freud, 1923b, p. 53). Normally the destructive aspects of the psyche are fused with libidinal ones; in some situations, however, these are present in "purer" form. That the presiding spirit of the bunker is death, rather even than the self-interested and elemental urge to survive, is made clear, and the film represents the struggle of many of the subordinates – unsuccessful in many cases – to free themselves, as Eva Braun could not do, from this spell, even after the death of Hitler.

Although there is no overt analysis of character and motive, some characters in the film are shown to be totally under the sway of a destructive organisation, internally and externally (identified organisationally with the Nazi party, and by the underground reality of the bunker). This is even to the extent of overriding the normal instinctual desire for self-preservation. Others are shown as influenced by this destructiveness but not wholly in thrall to it, as struggling, themselves, to escape the bunker, and sometimes helping others to do so. They range from apparent political innocents, such as Traudl herself; to some of the old *Wehrmacht* professional soldiers and officers "just doing a job", but not themselves sadists; to the highly ambiguous figure of Albert Speer, who tries to moderate the destructiveness of Hitler and Goebbels, the two characters who are most fully identified in a conflict-free way with the omnipotent destructive organisation. Albert Speer tries to talk to Hitler, and tries to convince Magda Goebbels not to kill her own children – to no avail.

Above ground, in the reality of the besieged Berlin, on the other hand, we are introduced to a number of characters who try to relieve and help the trapped population, and whose realistic engagement with life and death are shown to be in stark contrast with what goes on underground – the main figure being SS Captain Schenk, shown risking life and limb, disobeying orders, trying to organise humane relief for the dying and ill. Peter Krantz's parents are a working-class couple who have been shown as exemplary people of social conscience, engaged with the reality of the situation, trying to keep their son away from the pull of romantic self-destruction. These characters "above ground" – whatever the accusation on political grounds of sanitisation and revisionism – serve an important structural function in the film. They represent some kind of tainted ordinariness, some degree of (albeit self-interested and morally compromised) normality, some degree of engagement with reality; that is, they try to ask, and answer, normal questions. How might I get out of here alive? How might we help the wounded? These characters represent the motivation towards something reconstructive, engagement with life at an ordinary realistic level, a reparative movement. In short, these figures represent some kind of normal human values and functioning.

By contrast to the more constructive attempts at help seen above ground, what goes on in the bunker – a place that also externalises in a concrete way a particular state of mind – does not involve, by any approximation, realistic engagement with life. Nonexistent armies are moved about on the maps. Hitler's character, like the other characters in the film, is not shown by interiority but through topography and events. Everything is on the outside, in disturbance, chaos, and destruction. Inside, the film implies, is emptiness – the banal heart of radical evil.

Hitler's grandiosity is represented by a scene in which he luxuriates in the magnificent models of the proposed Third Reich, the Berlin designed by Albert Speer, a pompous overblown neo-classical triumphalist and kitsch capital of wide boulevards and monuments. This model might stand as a three-dimensional representation of a grandiose self, one conspicuously lacking in anything human; instead, a sterile monumentality, the empty self, identified with the neo-classical buildings. The film shows that Hitler never had any real link to or real interest in "the German people". What has been driving him on is some other force, not that of human relating. His relationship with the German people is shown to be not with real people but with some idealised aspect of himself, as represented by the grandiose models of Albert Speer, in short, a narcissistic relationship, with underlying hatred never far beneath the surface, now increasingly emerging. He makes it clear that he has no time for the "weakness" of compassion or sentimentality: "If the war is lost, then it is of no concern to me if the people perish in it. I still would not shed a single tear for them; because they did not deserve any better."

Downfall suggests that processes equivalent to the dominance by a "bad" part of the self, by an omnipotent destructive narcissistic organisation, can also apply, with some translation, at a socio-cultural and political level. Indeed, the film could be seen in part as a direct external representation of the internal scenarios Rosenfeld identified. It does this through its representation of the characters and their different levels of identification with, and imprisonment by, an external and internal destructive organisation, and the extent and limits of their capacities to influence each other. It does this, too, by the formal juxtaposition of the world of the bunker (a fortified underground insulation against reality) and the external reality of besieged Berlin.

Downfall does, however, end in a spirit of qualified hope, as it shows that some characters are able to escape from the internal and external shackles of this organisation, to emerge, literally and metaphorically, from the underground bunker. Indeed, the closing scenes of the film, with Traudl and Peter Krantz cycling through the German countryside, have the feel of emergence from a delusional state, a nightmare, into reality. This may also be an image of a reborn Germany, which, after all, did not perish in the bunker with Hitler, which somehow survived – and prospered. This has produced some objections, as noted earlier, that *Downfall* is an example of revisionist history, sanitising the moral complicity of the "ordinary people" of Berlin, and the country as a whole.

In order to consider these objections further it might be helpful to look more closely at the role in the film of Traudl Junge, on whose memoirs the film is partially based, and who, in her real-life person, frames the beginning and end of the film with her thoughts and recollections. The events are relayed in part through her consciousness, in particular as registered in her expressive, open face. This gives the audience a framework within which to place the extraordinary events of the last days of Hitler and the Third Reich. In this sense Junge becomes, through the structure of the film, the voice and vulnerably attractive and innocent face of "ordinary Germans" seeking to explain what has happened; and to explain and, perhaps, to justify their own involvement, and the questions she apparently never asked at the time: How can she be judged, or judge herself?

As Hitler dictates his last testament to her, Traudl, head down, seems to struggle to suppress her shock and astonishment at the virulence of Hitler's anti-Semitism – with the rather unlikely implication, it seems to me, that she has not heard this before. Here the viewers, in identification with Traudl's shocked "sane" bewilderment, are made to listen to the pathological, paranoid madness at the heart of Nazi ideology; pathological grievance at the defeat and emasculation engendered by Germany's defeat in the Great War, and the humiliating conditions that followed. I think that the effect, and, perhaps, the intent, of this scene, conscious or otherwise, is to increase the distance between the site of pathology, Hitler, and its ordinary witness, Traudl, and, by extension, from the ordinary audience.

At the same time, however, the film demonstrates the more disturbing reality that in Germany at this time the deeply pathological and the "ordinary" were inextricably interlinked. Traudl was, after all, Hitler's stenographer.

Perhaps the most disturbing aspect of *Downfall*, then, is that it dramatises the connection between the apparently ordinary Traudl Junge, and the deeply pathological or "radically evil" Hitler. This might serve as a metaphor for the link between the Nazi party as a destructive organisation, or mafia gang made real, and the masses of the ordinary German people. Although *Downfall* shows Traudl as able to escape, literally and metaphorically, the clutches of the organisation, it does not, and cannot, explain satisfactorily how and why she got involved in the first place. And people like Traudl may have simultaneously both known and not known about the real destructiveness going on. And by choosing not to see, or to know, by turning a blind eye, they themselves are caught up in a perverse scenario. The same might be said, historically, of a substantial portion, though of course by no means all, of the German people at that time.

It is also necessary, however, to remind ourselves that although we have seen that Richie (1998) punctures some of the more romantic urban myths associated with "Red Berlin", it was, nevertheless, the case that there was strong Communist and socialist opposition to the Nazis in some of the working-class areas. It remains the case that in 1932 almost three out of four Berliners had voted against the Nazis. Even in the election of March 1933, with most political opponents locked up and proscribed, the Nazis gained less than a third of the total votes.

Chapter 8

Historical and psychoanalytic perspectives on Nazism

The late Tony Judt (2007) has described Western post-war Europe as "an imposing edifice resting atop an unspeakable past" (2007, p. 3). W. G. Sebald, in his posthumously released non-fictional work *On the Natural History of Destruction* (2003), states what is implied and dramatised in his fiction, that in Germany, "the national humiliation felt by millions in the last years of the war had never really found verbal expression and those directly affected by the experience neither shared it with others nor passed it on to the next generation" (p. viii).

I not sure, though, whether the situation described by Judt and Sebald still pertains. Memoirs, books, films, monuments, memorials, and museums abound. The subject of the Second World War – Nazism and the Holocaust – is endlessly invoked and discussed. The question may no longer be whether such things are publically remembered – they surely are – but how they are remembered and to what purpose. Many of these memorials, and many works of literature and historical recollection, are extremely powerful and moving. However, there are also darker trends. In egregious examples of contemporary post-truth politics, history has been relativised and exploited, particularly by forces in those countries of Eastern Europe that have at times sought to present themselves, with varying degrees of historical inaccuracy, if not downright lies, as mostly passive victims of the "equally bad" tyrannies of Nazism and Stalinism.

Vilnius, the capital of Lithuania, was known as the Jerusalem of the north; in Kaunas, the country's second city and former capital, there was an integrated and cultivated Jewish community, which had long since escaped the shackles of the literal and metaphorical ghetto on the other side of the river. Yet it is also an indisputable and incontrovertible historical reality that the destruction of this culture was more complete in the Baltic States than anywhere else in Europe, with over ninety per cent of the pre-war Jewish population wiped out. It is also an incontrovertible historical reality that the genocidal massacres started before the Nazis arrived, and that, when they did arrive, they found many willing accomplices. That there were also citizens who, at great risk, tried to help their Jewish neighbours, colleagues, and friends does not alter this reality.

This reality would not be apparent, though, if you visited the Ninth Fort on the edge of Kaunas, part of a historically evocative ring of Napoleonic-era forts and barracks, and where some of the worst atrocities took place. Here, as in the Museum of Terror and Occupation in Vilnius, history has been relativised and, whilst Nazi genocide of the Jews is recognised and marked, the Lithuania role is underplayed; rather, the country and its citizens become the innocent victims of the equally bad totalitarian tyrannies of Communism and Fascism. In fact, this is not quite true, as it becomes clearer with further research that in this mindset the primary evil was that of Bolshevism against which Fascism, including the Fascism of some Lithuanian citizens, partisans, and national heroes was a response.

Lithuania declared independence in 1918 and became a democratic republic, a heroic struggle in which many of the country's Jewish population participated. During the lead up to the outbreak of the war, and during the time of the cynical Soviet-Nazi pact, the county was once more occupied by the Russian. The removal of the country's intellectual classes, during this and the post-war era, has been in some quarters reconceptualised as a genocide on par with the massacre of the Jews, enabling historical revisionists to present the country as a victim. The actions of the Soviets deserve to be highlighted and condemned, but this relativisation is an intellectual sleight of hand that absolves the country from the necessity of really facing its past.

One of the reasons proffered for the hostility and rank murderousness of sections of the population towards the Jewish population was that some of the latter had been Communists, or of the left, and, in the murky tumult of the times, it was believed they had been in collaboration with the Russians. In this sense anti-Jewish sentiment has been re-contextualised and rationalised as (misplaced) patriotic anti-Bolshevism.

That these attitudes die hard was brought home by the treatment meted out to elderly Jewish anti-Nazi partisans in 2008 (Ginaite, 2008). Looking to obtain some redress for their experience of persecution and violence at the hands of war criminals yet to be brought to account, they found themselves under investigation for war crimes and pro-Bolshevism and threatened with court proceedings. That these were eventually rescinded shows that there was some sanity at work, but hardly counts as historical redress.

The relativisation of history has not been confined to the Baltic States. Similar forms of historical revisionism have been observed in other parts of Eastern Europe, in, for example, Hungary and the Ukraine – though they have also, as in Lithuania, been met with opposition. These are the countries that have joined, or are seeking to join, the European Union, in part as proof positive of their move to liberal modernity, in part as their wish to move out of the sphere of influence of President Putin's Russia. That the proclivities of the latter may offer itself as a ready and perhaps justified focus of historic anti-Russian sentiment does not diminish the uncomfortable reality that a desire for the benefits of capitalism, the free market, and Western individualism may also be accompanied by illiberal and authoritarian impulses.

This points to a curious aspect of our current political discourse – for whilst in the UK much attention has been devoted to alleged anti-Semitism within the

Labour party (for which there appears unclear actual evidence) and the alleged "Little Englander" xenophobia of those that voted to leave the European Union, the situation in mainland Europe has been much less commented on. However, it is within Europe – held in these discourses as the acme of liberal pluralism and tolerance – where there appears to be a disturbing rise in the far right, and the resurgence, in some murky quarters, of those pathological anti-Semitic tropes that see Jewish conspiracy behind both international Communism and international capitalism. The question, to which I will return later, is whether these movements are being fueled by the very forces of liberal globalisation and supranational politics that are held in current progressive discourse as offering the solution.

However, we also need to maintain a sense of proportion. It might be argued that Lithuania and the other Eastern European countries are slowly but, overall, successfully, working through their traumatic histories towards pluralistic societies, and that the process is inevitably an uneven one, and subject to periodic regression. Is the glass half empty or half full? It depends on your point of view.

This is important because in the contemporary denigration of populism there is the assertion, frequently made, that Fascism was popular, and that, indeed, in Germany was voted into power democratically. Thus, in these accounts, there are warnings of the "slippery slope" that leads from "right-wing" or "authoritarian" populism, the vote for Brexit and the election of Donald Trump, to Fascism. I believe that such an analysis, though seductive, is based on a misreading, both of the contemporary situation and of history.

Contrary to these claims (which have as their implicit subtext a profound distrust of the "masses") German Fascism, though it had support throughout German society, particularly amongst the lower middle class, the déclassé, and students, was not in any meaningful way freely democratically elected. It came to power in the context of economic crisis, enfeebled central authority, and a rampant violence and intimidation. At the time of the 1932 election many of the Nazi's opponents were in prison. The Nazis were helped in their bid for power by the hapless miscalculations of the old ruling classes, who thought that they could control Hitler if they invited the Nazis into the political establishment, and by the catastrophic split amongst the left. For although socialists, Communists, and trade unionists were in the vanguard of opposition to Fascism (and were amongst its earliest targets) under instruction from Moscow the official Communist line had been to attack the Social Democratic Party rather than form a united front against Fascism. More widely, as Richie (1998) has outlined, it became fashionable in "radical" circles to direct contempt and ire as much towards social democrats and conservatives as towards the Nazis.

There *is* here an uncomfortable parallel with what is happening now, in that sections of the liberal left have retreated from Enlightenment universalism to fighting cultural wars with the socially conservative, rather than really engaging with the macro-economic issues of inequality: the crisis of wages and productivity, how to effectively respond to civil war, societal implosion, population displacement, and the refugee crisis; issues with which of course they, like all of us, are inevitably implicated. Nor have they really engaged with the issue of how best to understand and respond to the presence of real fascist organisations in our midst – ISIS, or so-called Islamic State, and other related death cults. These are subjects to which I will return in later chapters.

In the meantime, though, there has been an understandable view amongst scholars that when confronted with the enormity of the destructiveness of Nazi Germany, a form of destructiveness that is linked not to impulsive violence or self-preservative aggression but to advanced technology and "rational" planning, historical analysis can only take us so far. As the noted historian and biographer of Hitler, Ian Kershaw (1985) has written: "In Nazism we have a phenomenon which seems scarcely capable of subjection to rational analysis" (1993, p. 3). He adds: "faced with Auschwitz, the explanatory powers of the historian seem puny indeed" (1993, pp. 3–4). As Primo Levi wrote in *The Truce* (1963): "In short it was more than a sack; it was the genius of destruction, of anti-creation, here as at Auschwitz; it was the mystique of barrenness, beyond all demands of war, or impulse for booty" (1963, p. 295). Such comments would suggest that historical analysis needs to be combined with a study of the emotional and psychological factors at work.

The psychoanalytically influenced Frankfurt School of social critics linked the rise of Fascism to the "authoritarian" family structure of pre-war Germany (Adorno et al., 1950*)* and the inculcation of rigid and unthinking discipline through a harshly paternal family structure, lending itself to the mindless following of orders. However as Christopher Lasch (1977) has argued, this analysis does not, looked at again, seem a persuasive one. The predominant libidinal ties of Fascism (and of later neo-fascist, terrorist, and fundamentalist groups) seem to be less those of the bourgeois patriarchal family and rather more the "homo-social" band of blood-brothers. As Hobsbawm (1994) points out, one of the key factors in the formation and membership of the Nazi party was a large disaffected pool of ex-servicemen for whom "the lowlands" of ordinary civilian and family life were of little appeal compared to the "mountain peaks" of military service in the Great War, with its opportunities for personal achievement and bloody camaraderie. This was a significant group, as it was in the formation of the Italian fascist party: "for whom the experience of fighting, even under the conditions of 1914–1918, was central and inspirational; for whom uniform and discipline, sacrifice – of self and others – and blood, arms and power were what made masculine life worth living" (Hobsbawm, 1994, p. 125). A further recruiting factor was the frustration of those younger men who had missed their first chance of heroism, and became enthusiastic Nazi foot soldiers, hoping to make up for lost opportunities.

The late psychoanalyst Janine Chasseguet-Smirgel (1990), who lost many of her own family in the Holocaust, has suggested that it was not the overt ideological content of Nazism that was important – the intellectual content of which was, in any case, as Hobsbawm has suggested, contradictory and risible – but the deeper unconscious fantasies underpinning this. For all the talk of the "Führer", Nazi ideology may have involved a killing off of, rather than a mature identification with, the oedipal father, and a fantasy of a merged union with the maternal object, symbolised by nature, or the "*volk*". In this fantasy the "impurities" of the self, which may prevent this idealised narcissistic state of bliss, were identified with the city, the forces of modernity, and, particularly, with the Jewish race, and also with other "outsider groups", the Roma, homosexuals, and the mentally ill: denigrated and relatively powerless populations, suitable receptacles for the projection of unwanted aspects of the self.

Chasseguet-Smirgel's suggestion (1990) of an underlying unconscious fantasy of a union with a maternal object represented by the "*volk*", and the denigration of real, as opposed to "pseudo", paternal authority, echoes Cohn's (1957) analysis of the fantasies of millennial groups. Mindless routine and affectless violence, she suggests, can only be explained by deobjectalisation, the anal universe in which good is perverted by bad, and everything is turned in the unconscious to faeces. Chasseguet-Smirgel (1985, 1990) relates these propensities, above all, to the universal human conflict between accepting reality (things as they are, separation, loss, and disappointment) and wish fulfilment in which frustration and disappointment, separateness, and the oedipal order can be circumvented.

Chasseguet-Smirgel linked the emergence of this perverse pathology to certain pre-existing traditions in German romantic nationalism, typically expressing a wish and fantasy of a return to nature, traditions that tended to idealise nature and death, demand a strong leader mystically "at one" with the German people, and denigrate the "decadence" of liberal modernity and of the city. It was an anti-democratic tradition, which historians (Evans, 2005, 2008; Kershaw, 1985, 1987) have shown already existed before the rise of the Nazi party, and which was given added impetus by the real derelictions and deprivations of German society of the 1920s and 1930s, and the evident weakness of the pluralist political establishment to resolve socio-economic crisis. Thus German Fascism sought to by-pass reason as it by-passed traditional political institutions, and to appeal directly to gut emotion, to feelings of victimhood, and the desire for apocalyptic regeneration of the self, identified with the purified nation.

An integration of psychoanalytic ideas with historical research (Evans, 2005, 2008; Kershaw, 1985, 1987) appears to confirm Kernberg's view that there are very direct parallels between the paranoid and the narcissistic features of political organisations and mass movements, and the processes of projective identification, denial, pathological splitting, and omnipotent control seen clinically in severely personality-disordered individuals. This picture of the catastrophic coming together of regressive social processes and gross narcissistic individual psychopathology also chimes with Chasseguet-Smirgel's description (1990) of the triumph of an "anal universe" in which the world is turned upside down, and the capacity for differentiation and separateness, inherent in logical thought and reasoned analysis, standing also for mature paternal functioning, is violently attacked, in a fantasy of fusion with the maternal body. The actual coming to power of a mass political movement embodying these sorts of propensities in the Germany of the 1930s can be at least partially understood as the catastrophic coming together of certain specific socio-cultural traditions and "structures of feeling" (particularly those related to romantic nationalism), as a crisis within pluralist political institutions and of weak paternal authority. As Kernberg has suggested, this created a situation of regressive large-group instability in a whole society, exacerbated by certain kinds of destructively narcissistic psychopathologies in key individuals with a gift for the exploitation of channels of mass communication.

Richie (1988) and other historians have had no doubt that Hitler and the Nazis possessed a certain kind of genius in touching and exploiting these subterranean currents in the emotional life of the German nation, in setting in motion already existing structures of feeling. The Nazi party rejoiced in overturning the oedipal order, so that children were invited and encouraged to spy on their own parents. Moreover, in the Weimar Republic of Berlin the state was weak, the paternal authority figures senile, enfeebled, corrupt, lacking inner conviction, and offering no paternal containment or potent authority against the rising force.

In this situation the destructively narcissistic personalities of key leaders of the Nazi party, as portrayed in *Downfall*, might be seen as inhabiting an already existing tradition of romantic nationalism, in which there was a narcissistic identification of self with a resurgent nation state or "*volk*", under the influence of a powerful omnipotent leader. Underpinning this can be discerned a sense of pathological grievance and victimhood, concretely associated with the lost lands and financial demands of the post-First World War treaty of Versailles – a concretised motif of national shame and narcissistic humiliation. The individual and the collective working through of these inadmissible feelings was circumvented by an omnipotent assertion of the will: the world as it was wished to be, rather than as it was. A state of destructive narcissism came to predominate – one that idealised omnipotent violent solutions, in which weakness and vulnerability was seen as an object of contempt, and in which unacceptable parts of the self were projectively identified with denigrated scapegoats and "outsiders". Here, belief is treated as knowledge, and, in Freud's terms, illusion triumphed over reality.

However, a note of caution is in order. Most psychoanalytically orientated authors, like most historians, rightly acknowledge that the particularly virulent form of destructiveness of the Nazi regime resists full explanation, that the features they describe may be *necessary* to understand the rise and ascendancy of German Fascism, but they are not *sufficient*. Janine Chasseguet-Smirgel (1990) put forward some of the most convincing attempts at elucidation but also cautioned: "For it will doubtless remain as unfathomable as the navel of a dream, and though we may continually take soundings, we may never be able to plumb the full depths of its black heart" (p. 175).

Chapter 9

From the post-war settlement to the end of history

The immediate years of post-war Europe and the USA were of utter desolation, and of emotional and physical exhaustion – "photographs and documentary films of the time show pitiful streams of helpless civilians trekking through a blasted landscape of broken cities and barren fields" (Judt, 2007, p. 31). Rationing and austerity followed, but then came a period of economic expansion, especially from 1952 onwards. This boom was to last for some twenty-five years, only ending after the oil price rise accompanying the 1973 Arab-Israeli war. The result was technological, and material progress and an unprecedented rise in living standards and life opportunities for many people.

These transformations were not confined to the West; Hobsbawm (1994) reminds us that, despite all the failures and brutal enforcements of the Eastern bloc, "the major and lasting impact of the regimes inspired by the October revolution in Russia was as a powerful accelerator of the modernization of backward agrarian countries", so that, by the 1980s, "socialist Bulgaria and non-socialist Ecuador had more in common than either had with the Bulgaria and Ecuador of the 1930s" (1994, p. 9).

Although in part a consequence of the naturally occurring cycles of boom and bust within capitalism, the unprecedented post-war boom was also the consequence of a determination, in both Eastern and Western Europe, though expressed in very different ways, not to return to the insecurities of the 1930s: a resolve to establish the normalisation of prosperity, optimism, and peace – to not go back to the economic instabilities and deprivations from which the utter ruinations of Fascism and the Second World War had emerged.

In the United States, although some of the more radical aspects of the New Deal did not survive the war, there was nevertheless, in the post-war years, a heavily state-managed mixed economy; with innovation and scientific management usurping the role of the individual entrepreneur, and a relative decline in the power of finance capital. It was this basic project of reconstruction that enabled the transition from wartime to peacetime, and this formed the basis too for the reconstruction of Western Europe and Japan. Trade was liberalised. Private and public investment in infrastructure and industry and increased overseas trade, with low-cost imports and high-cost exports, led, in historical terms, to unusually high growth rates in major European countries. Demand was managed in order to sustain growth, and this led to increased technological innovation. Such policies were also a response to the demands of trade unions and organised labour, the wish, evident in the 1945 election in the UK, which returned Clement Atlee's reformist Labour government, for a new start, for a welfare state, union recognition, and full employment. Governments increased expenditure and budgets, rather than cutting them as they had done in the 1930s.

There were also, of course, international dimensions to this. Tony Judt (2007) has calculated that some forty million workers moved within countries, between countries, and into Europe from overseas. They were an unorganised, cheap, and plentiful source of labour; coming predominately from the older rural areas of Europe; Portugal, Italy, Spain, Turkey, Greece, and, further afield, the old European colonies and dependencies; existing for the most on low wages and meagre employment rights, and without whom the post-war boom would have not been possible.

Meanwhile in the post-war era, Nazi Germany and the Soviet Union under Stalin were seen as paradigmatic examples of totalitarianism; a viewpoint increasingly influenced by the complex and rich work of Hannah Arendt (1951). For Arendt, such states had, within their own terms, an internally consistent and coherent ideology, based around the organising principles of, respectively, race and class, from which flowed congruent structures. In tyrannical states there is a total destruction of the public realm. Totalitarian states, however, went further, by destroying this realm from within – the invasion by the state of the subjective mind, the permeation of ideology into the inner life of the individual.

In such societies there is the dominance of a single unifying idea – an explanation for everything – rather than thinking that is pluralistic and acknowledges complexity. The masses consist, in the main, of hitherto rather atomised, lonely, and apolitical individuals rather than classes or smaller organisations drawn together for specific purposes. Propaganda is ubiquitous and terror is routinely employed as an end in itself. Such states are characterised by the abolition of civil and political rights, political violence, and intimidation, and the collapse of private and civic society. Politically they are characterised by a utopian ideology and total mobilisation of the population, and absolute intolerance of dissent. The totalitarian state seeks the isolation and expulsion, at worst the annihilation, of those seen as the enemy. Subjects of the state are made complicit in this process through ideological compulsion, manufactured plebiscites, and the like. They are, themselves, meanwhile, in an insecure position, in the knowledge that they too might soon be viewed as the enemy.

Political theories of totalitarianism were also, however, themselves in part a product of the cold war era, contrasting liberal democracies, civil rights, pluralist cultures, and open markets with oppressive and monolithic terroristic or authoritarian regimes. Thus, on the one side, free markets; on the other protectionism; on the one side, individual autonomy – increasingly the autonomy and primacy of individual desire set free from oppressive constraints; on the other, restriction and closure. There was much that was true in this picture. However, increasingly democratic liberal pluralist societies ran alongside a fundamentalist version of free-market capitalism that was itself totalising, and which, when pursued without adequate framework and restraint, undermined the psychic and social affiliations, identifications, and traditions necessary for such a society to function. It is to this shift that I now turn.

By the 1960s the vast majority of people were much better off and healthier, and better educated, than their grandparents' and parents' generations. There was a degree of social mobility, and of aspiration for the next generation. Judt (2007) points out that throughout recorded history, and well into the 1950s, most people had very little disposable income, once essentials had been purchased. In the conditions of the post-war boom, due to rising wages, mass consumerism became increasingly characteristic of Western Europe and the USA. For the first time, workers had extra spending money in their pockets, with a consolidated era of higher wages and low inflation, high employment rates, and strong unions.

Underlying and gradually undermining the post-war consensus in the West and in the United States, was a gradual shift from a society based on industrial production to consumption, from one based on making things, to one based on buying. There was a gradual but pervasive decrease in skilled manual work, accompanying the decline of coal, steel, textiles, shipbuilding, and other heavy industries, although this was not obvious until the 1960s. There was also a parallel decline of "traditional" working-class solidarities and institutions.

Dating back to the 1950s, this was the beginning of what has been termed late capitalism. Such a world was characterised by new forms of business organisations (multinationals and transnationals) expanding beyond national borders, and, as a concomitant, the internationalisation of business. It was a world where corporations and multinationals appeared larger and to have more power than the nation state. The business of making things was outsourced from the old centres of manufacturing to parts of the world where production costs and wages were lower, amid the growing globalisation of the economy. The economic decline of these areas was increasingly accompanied by a cultural denigration of their hitherto idealised social traditions. This was accompanied by changes in what Raymond Williams (1968) termed the "the structure of feeling" in everyday life; the growth of individualism, the replacement of citizenship with consumer identity, the growing penetration of the language of market and commodity into everyday relationships, the relative decline of collective identity, association, and affiliation.

Meanwhile there was, as a concomitant of these processes, a turning away from the state towards the individual, and towards the market. Ideologically there had long been a growing interest in more individualist free market libertarian thinkers; Paul Mason (2010) notes the popularity of Ayn Rand, an emigré Russian living in the USA, whose 1950s novels and writings trumpet individualism, self-interest, entrepreneurship, untrammeled free markets, and self-reliance, against the alleged corruptions, blandishments, and inefficiencies of the state and collective endeavours. Later, economists such as Friedrich Hayek and Milton Friedman and the Chicago school argued that private property and the market were the corner-stones of political freedom. Such ideas had, from the start, a fundamentalist and utopian caste. Adam Smith had evolved the modern conception of the market as an autonomous sphere of human activity, and which therefore might be subject to scientific laws and knowledge. He was also a social moralist and was anxious about the consequences of unfettered self-interest (Metcalf, 2017). By contrast, Hayek's was "a total worldview: a way of structuring all reality on the model of economic competition" (2017, p. 30). In this mindset it is the liberated market that determines real value and what is really important, and which protects against totalitarianism. Unlike in classic liberal laissez-faire economics, the function of the state is not to keep well clear but to support the free market, providing a fixed legal framework for its unfettered operation. The market is an end in itself, an ultimate determinant of worth, and is not subsidiary to other social goals.

As the crisis of the post-war settlement gathered, these ideas moved from the fringes to the mainstream. The marker for the move of these ideas into the political centre stage was President Nixon's abandonment of a fixed exchange rate and impo-sition of wage controls, in the face of rising inflation and lower growth. And after the 1976 International Monetary Fund (IMF) bailout in the UK the Labour government cut spending and raised taxes. The Carter administration faced inflation of eighteen and a half per cent, raised interest rates, and forced banks to hold more money. The oil price rises of 1973 had exposed an underlying crisis of productivity, only par-tially disguised by the rise of consumerism, and leading to inflation and slow growth in Western societies. Meanwhile, the all too evident failings of "actually existing socialism" in Eastern Europe provided a convincing rationale for the idealisation of the market, even allowing for the fact that the semi-feudal, poorly developed Tsarist Russia was hardly what Marx had had in mind as a testing ground for Communism. The opponents of socialism, indeed of moderate social democracy, could usefully conflate all forms of socialist interventionism with the failures of Soviet Socialism, and the xenophobic paranoia and brutality of the years of Stalinist terror.

Although radical free-market ideas were gaining increased traction, such a mov-ing away from the post-war social democratic consensus was not confined to the right. Mason (2010) has also suggested that the downside of the post-war, mixed-state, welfare-economy consensus was a certain stultifying conservatism, and, from the point of view of a younger generation, the primacy of "family values" and social convention over the individual, together with the continued existence of racism and prejudice against minorities. The individualism and libertarianism of the counter-culture in the sixties *appeared* at times to be "revolutionary" and cloaked itself in the language of the left. These trends, themselves also in part a product of consumerism and the commodification of "youth", were, in my experi-ence of growing up in Tyneside in the seventies, still a potent cultural influence. The link between the radical counter-culture and free-market capitalism was later made clear by the subsequent career trajectories of many counter-culture luminar-ies. Revolution based on generational difference and the battle between "youth" and elders always had a clearly limited revolutionary shelf life.

At the same time, across sections of the left there was also, as we have seen, a crisis of confidence in the universalist rationalism of the bourgeois Enlightenment. How was it that a country that was steeped in such traditions, Germany, the acme of technological modernity, as Ritchie has pointed out, could have descended into such unfathomable barbarism? Perhaps the endpoint of such traditions was not progress but states of pathological certainty, in other words, in totalitarian states of mind. Such questions were raised by Horkheimer and Adorno in 1944 in their *Dialectic of Enlightenment* (2002) and have been echoed by later writers, for example, Zygmunt Bauman (1989).

More widely, there was a cultural shift amongst sections of the left – or what held itself as the left: a growing antipathy to all meta-narratives and claims to knowledge, and to the very notion of truth itself. For where the "traditional" left responded to the social changes and dislocations, and the creative destruction of free-market capitalism through the universalising language of class and internationalism, underpinned by a tradition of rationalist analysis dating from the European Enlightenment, counter-strands of progressive opinion had a very different perspective. The proponents of liberal-left "anti-imperialism" and identity politics increasingly saw these values – ideas of reason, progress, humanism, universalism, and the scientific exploration of reality – as merely part of a dominant ideology of the West. Indeed, this was only part, in some quarters, of a more fundamental antagonism to established canons of thought and, at the postmodernist and social constructivist extremes, of opposition to the Enlightenment ideal of rationality itself; to the idea of historical and natural truths, independent of, rather than created by, "discourse". There was, rather, a suspicion directed towards all claims to objective knowledge, unmasked as the disguised and oppressive ideology of vested interests.

The danger, need it be said, of a world of competing narratives of victimhood and antipathy towards the notion of objective truth was that of the assertion of subjective truth without a foundation in external reality. Historically, of course, the narratives of the powerful, held up as objective reality, tends to trump those of the victims. There were, and are, real injustices to be marked, and marginalised histories to reclaim, not least those related to the onerous history of Western imperialism and its relationship to racist ideology and practice. However, history also tells us that it was emotionally driven identity politics and claims to righteous victimhood that underpinned the rise of xenophobic nationalism at the end of the nineteenth century, amid the collapse of the old multi-ethnic empires of Europe, a process reaching its apogee in Nazi Germany. As Hobsbawm (1997) has written:

> For nations are historically novel entities pretending to exist for a very long time. Inevitably the nationalist version of their history consists of anachronism, omission, de-contextualisation and, in extreme cases, lies. To a lesser extent this is true for all forms of identity history, old or new.
>
> (1997, p. 357)

Self-designated labels proclaiming progressivity had, though, as now, to be taken with at best a pinch of salt, at worst as manifestations of a self-serving, class-based, pseudo-radicalism. As Judt (2007) pointed out, things were not as they seemed:

> Whereas the humanist of an earlier generation had been drawn to Marx and Hegel, the self-doubting Seventies were seduced by an altogether darker strain in German thought. Michel Foucault's radical skepticism was in large measure an adaption of Nietzsche. Other influential French authors, notably the literary critic Jacque Derrida, looked instead to Martin Heidegger for their critique of human agency and their "de-construction", as it was becoming known, of the cognitive human subject and his textual subject matter.
>
> (2007, p. 480)

Thus we were seeing the beginnings of the move away from the traditional left preoccupations with the universal of class, socio-economic equality, and justice, to those of "theory", language, and culture – and increasingly the waging of cultural wars with socially conservative groups. As Judt suggests, the "narcissistic obscurantism" of much of the language with which these battles were being expressed was "very much of its time, its detachment from daily reality bearing unconscious witness to the exhaustion of an intellectual tradition" (2007, p. 481).

I want to end this chapter by briefly summarising five convergent, interrelating socio-economic and emotional trends, crossing the political and socio-cultural divide, which, I believe, have contributed to the evolution of that intensely subjectivist, narcissistically driven "post-truth" culture, which is the subject of this book. The first was the economic shift from the post-war broadly Keynesian social democratic settlement, to a Hayekian free-market fundamentalism. Here the workings of the market became an end in themselves, and we saw a world where, without the necessary checks and balances, market values and the forces of commodification colonised and undercut social traditions and institutions, and permeated social relationships and transactions. Indeed, notwithstanding the reality that there is always a degree of resistance, in nature and in human beings, to commodification, it might be said, for better or worse, that free-market capitalism had entered human subjectivity more fully than Communist ideology had ever done in the days of Stalin.

The second trend involved those changes in "traditional" working-class industries and communities incurred through globalised late capitalism. These processes were reflected in the international division of labour, with new work forces overseas, and the relocation or "outsourcing" of production from the West to relatively advanced "third world" countries; the corollary of which was, and continues to be, de-industrialisation and a crisis of "traditional" labour and its associational and cultural institutions – subject to either continued decline on the one hand, or gentrification, a process from which most of the original community is excluded, on the other. At the same time, such communities were increasingly subject to cultural opprobrium, not least from sections of the population that were the beneficiaries of change. This inevitably made the necessary adjustment to such social dislocations and losses more difficult. A denigrated past cannot easily be mourned, and, in psychoanalytic terms, internalised. There were, and are, of course, many such beneficiaries, and, more widely, many of the changes incurred through a liberalised global economy are real and for the better. The picture though is intrinsically unequal, uneven, and one's view of these processes may be dependent upon where one is situated.

The third factor was the moving away by sections of liberal, progressive, and radical opinion from Enlightenment rationalism and from the universalist socio-economic focus of the traditional left towards the politics of identity, a process that has only intensified in recent years. I make clear here that to question the contemporary identity politics of the "progressive left" – now being mirrored in a more malignant form by the populist right – is not to argue against the need for continuous struggles against prejudice, and the absolute centrality to any progressive project of the fight for a more tolerant and pluralist culture. It is rather to note that amongst sections of "progressive" opinion there has been a notable shift from a capacity to relate to "people as people" in an ordinary way, irrespective of ethnic background, sexuality, and so on, to a much more impersonal and politicised adherence to often exclusivist identity politics. Such a mindset, especially when allied to a culture of victimhood and the cultivation of offence, actually serves to keep people, in an essentialist way, separate. It is also to note that this has been accompanied, too frequently and too indiscriminately, by a denigration of a putative "white working class", particularly the male working class, vilified variously in recent time as "xenophobes", "deplorables", "white supremacists", and the like. It should scarcely need pointing out that these characterisations, simultaneously divisive and self-perpetuating, display the very illiberal and intolerant caste of mind held that is being attacked.

In making these comments I make the distinction between those struggles for civil and minority rights, against prejudice and discrimination, that remain central to any progressive movement, and a trend towards intense subjectivism, and the splitting of social groups in polarised ways into victims and oppressors; a process that becomes self-reinforcing, and also, as we have seen, involves a hostility to all meta-narratives and claims of expertise. I shall suggest, later, that this position represents the ideological manifestation of thin-skinned narcissism, of a mindset in which the only people capable of understanding your experience are members of your own selective group, this group increasingly being constituted over electronic media, a situation that renders people vulnerable to prompt deletion if they have the temerity to take a different perspective.

The fourth factor, linked to the above, was a more general shift in the relation to history. For Frederic Jameson (1991), writing of the postmodern cultural logic of late capitalism, there had been a weakening of the relationship to public history This had involved, he suggested, immersion in a concrete and unrelated present, and the breakdown of signification (or, in psychoanalytic terms, symbolic functioning, reflective thought in depth) into what he termed the experience of pure material signifiers. There was no "outside" of ideology or textuality. Daily life, cultural language, psychic experience were dominated by categories of space rather than time. This was embodied by two-dimensional screens, flat skyscrapers full of reflecting mirrors, a reality of multiple surfaces – archetypal of which was the Westin Bonaventure Hotel in Los Angeles (Jameson, 1991). These changes represented, in Jameson's view, the total victory of commodification over all aspects of life.

As a correlate of these shifts, in a therapeutic, or, it might be argued pseudo-therapeutic culture, in the West, there was no shortage of studies of individual loss and the grieving process, or of trauma and victimhood in the narratives of identity politics; those more collective social losses, associated with the decline of "traditional" manufacturing and its accompanying associational life and civic culture were largely unacknowledged; their landmarks destroyed, their hollowed out communities denigrated as the repositories of outmoded patriarchy, of racism, intolerance, and xenophobia, of, in current political parlance, the angry white man. Such a characterisation appeared to be made in total ignorance of the rich intellectual and self-educating traditions of the British working class (Rose, 2002).

This, though, was only one aspect of a deeper alienation from a shared sense of the past. The fashion for cultural nostalgia and pastiche excepted, the public remembrance of things past became something of a forgotten art, and D-Day and the other war memorials were poignant because they were exceptions to this trend of forgetting; events in which the intersection of the private and public lives of people were formally acknowledged and given expression:

> the destruction of the past, or rather of the social mechanisms that link one's contemporary experience to that of earlier generations, is one of the most characteristic and eerie phenomena of the late twentieth century. Many young men and women at the century's end grow up in a sort of permanent present lacking any organic relation to the public past of the times they live in.
>
> (Hobsbawm, 1994, p. 3)

It was not only the young that were so estranged. During the 1990s I worked for a period in a psychiatric day hospital in the old London Docklands. Although the service was for working-age adults, one afternoon a week was set aside for elderly people with dementia. They were very likeable people. The intact social skills, charm, stoicism, and residual glint in the eye disguised, though, what were in some cases quite profound levels of memory loss. The dislocation, confusion, and the beginnings of a fragmentation of the personality were, of course, linked to organic pathologies, to changes in brain function, associated with Alzheimer's disease, or cardio-vascular degenerative processes. However, it always struck me that no one appeared to have considered how the external landscape of these people's lives had contributed to their sense of dislocation.

Buildings matter. So do statues, ruins, and even stretches of vacant land. Buildings provide shelter for human activities, but it is the activities, not the shelter, that make structure and spaces important to human beings trying to define their place on this earth. Buildings and monuments are also the visible remnants of the past: they often outlast the human beings who created them. How these structures are seen, treated, and remembered sheds light on a collective identity that is more felt than articulated.

(Ladd, 1997, p. 2)

It is to these subjects, and to what Jameson (1991) has described as the two-dimensional world of late capitalism, a world characterised by a sense of living in a timeless present in which the past appears only as nostalgia or pastiche, that I turn in the next part of the book.

Chapter 10

Lost worlds

The unmourned past as a psychic retreat

The late historian of the French Revolution Richard Cobb's "Ixelles" (1998) is an unsurpassable evocation of a commune of Brussels in the immediate post-war years, roughly between 1944, after the liberation, until the mid-1950s; as Cobb puts it, "a framework of a novel that has not been written and that I will not be likely to write" (1998, p190).

Ixelles was a nineteenth century municipality, in essence a small town with its own town hall, the *maison communal*. Cobb's loving evocation of the Ixelles of the post-war years captures a place self-enclosed, with its parks and ponds, its high street and town hall, a small rural town transported to an urban environment, unrevolutionary, ordinary, dominated by diurnal and seasonal routines and predictability. It was a place that perhaps also embodied something of Cobb's internal world and its needs; "an enclosed, protected, gradually discoverable domain of habit, prudent friendship, careful observation" (1998, p. 193). What is distinctive about Cobb, and what separates him from more modern psychogeographers, is his evocation of particular times and places, and his tentative, yet at the same time, profound connection with people. His Ixelles is that of the immediate post-war period, with its demobbed soldiers wandering through the streets of Brussels in the early mornings after a night on the tiles in the Marolles. In the Ixelles he stayed in the underground basement of an anarchic and marginal family and their friends. These were carpenters and toymakers, people with an "admirable" unselfconscious indifference to orthodoxy and convention, immune to social comparisons, to social envy, individualist and eccentric, yet also deeply social, people "joined together by a relative lack of success", undertaking precarious seasonal work, existing on the margins of society, strangers to conventional time and work discipline: people with whom Cobb clearly identified.

I have friends in Brussels, and from my own wanderings I suspect that outwardly the commune of Ixelles has in fact not much changed since Cobb's description. It is still possible to walk past the two ponds, Les etangs d'Ixelles, and visit the bar in the Maison de la Radio, next to the Eglise Sainte-Croix. However, in this case, Cobb is describing not the physical dissolution of an area, as happened with many working-class localities, but the changes that have occurred from the inside of a mixed artisan, petit-bourgeois and bourgeois district;

> The facades of Ixelles are still much the same, but I no longer know what lies beneath them. I can no longer look down through the iron grating of an area, to spy friends in a lighted room below ground. I can only walk alone in streets that were once inhabited by people I knew.
>
> (1998, p. 199)

He searches the streets, and wears out his shoe-leather, to visit "a few scattered witnesses to the warmth, simplicity and generosity of lives once tentatively shared and explored" (1998, p. 199). Cobb's writing is informed by a profound sense of melancholia, of public and private loss, but, as he says, "it is a story which has moved on without consulting me, but still leaving me with a heritage of enrichment, and with the warmth of once shared experience – a great deal of it bizarre, most of it quite outside the ordinary run of things" (1998, p. 199). Cobb's comments might be heard as a comment on life itself, and the tension between allowing engagement and attachment – and therefore also pain and loss – and detachment. Cobb in his writings conveys the impression of having, throughout much of his life, found a half-way house between these positions.

During my time in London I used to make occasional solo forays across to Paris. Cobb's fellow historian and editor, David Gilmour (1998), remarks that like the Belgian crime novelist George Simeon, Cobb was a writer of "[l]oneliness and alienation, of the process of urbanisation in human terms" (1998, p. ix). However, Cobb's France was not that of aromatic herbs and Mediterranean sunshine, but of " the banal, the ordinary, the unheroic, of people and their routines, of tramways and railway stations, of townscapes of mills and brick chimneys and back to back terraced houses"(1998, p. ix).There was, as Gilmour has made clear, a romantic poetry of the outsider in Cobb's evocations of these urban landscapes, an objective correlative of some internal state that could only be expressed poetically, like the vision of the broken-down working-class tenements of northern Paris that I used to eagerly glimpse as the train exited the Gare du Nord:

> You would never find Cobb amongst the immaculate stone villages of the Dordogne or the Luberon. He was a winter man with a taste for harsh geography, for the stark angularity of quaysides and canals, the wide horizons of the Beauce, the blackened brick streets of Roubaix and Lille.
>
> (1998, p. viii)

Cobb's loneliness drew him into routines and timetables, walks, observing other people, and overhearing conversations in cafés and buses. A certain loneliness and detachment, however, also facilitates curiosity, and the pleasurable coming together of the familiar and the unknown. Such a routine serves both as a defence and a means of contact. "Regular itineraries then represent the fragile barriers erected by the timid and fearful, people like me" (1988, p. 106).

His writing was, in part, a hymn of praise to a certain kind of urban life, "geared to the modest aspirations of routine and habit of individuals and individualists; the enemy is loneliness, and the remedy is companionability and verbal exchange" (1998, p. 150): to the night-time world – the attic with the skylight, the rooftop vista of the city, a café ablaze with light, and a promise of chance encounters. Cobb insists that this Bohemian nocturnal world with its endless sociability did exist in the Paris in the 1930s, revived again in the 1940s, but that "it doesn't anymore" (1998, p. 151).

There may be a thin line between situations where a position such as Cobb's allows some creative engagement, albeit under restrictive circumstances, and situations that become more "stuck". My impression is that for Cobb, as for the late architectural critic Ian Nairn (Nairn, 1966), who in a grainy black and white film footage from the 1960s can be seen brilliantly berating architectural vandalism, whilst at the same time looking close to breakdown, in a neglected and ruined northern Church; emotions are displaced on to objects, and in particular on to the resonant but transitory artefacts of earlier eras. In his writing on Ixelles Cobb poetically evokes the sights, sounds, and smells of the world that has been lost, *à la recherche du temps perdu*. Cobb evokes the colours – beige, russet, lime-green, red, and black of this world, of the cottage houses, the lights of the early morning cafés, of parking trams, on the top of the menacing Maison de la Radio. He evokes the smells, fresh coffee, *frites*, chocolate, and cheroots – small cigars – the characteristic "parfum de Bruxelles" (1998, p. 192). He evokes the architecture of the low cottage-type houses and the grander Leopold II style of the more bourgeois enclaves, ornate ironwork and stained glass. He outlines the class and social composition of the area, the cafés and taverns, with their Stella Artois, Gueuze-Lambic, and Bières de la Meuse (1998). This is a world of artisan workshops and establishments, "merceries, pâtisseries, ressemelage, blanchisserie, cordonnerie, papeterie, marchand de journaux" (1998, p. 192).

Cobb's writing on Ixelles might be seen as an example of the work of mourning, the need to revisit and recall, often in tangible material detail, what has been lost, as part of a process whereby the object is relinquished internally and established within the self. It is itself a sensual recreation of a lost world, a world that is at once personal and social. Loss is worked through sensually, through the invocation of objects, colours, and smells. These recollections and recreations also express a particular mode of relating to the world: the very powerful pull to keep on walking down the old streets, to revisit the sometimes derelict and blasted, sometimes gentrified sites of the old connections. There is a pull to pay homage at the sites of the legions of "the missing". However, it may be that what is being missed also relates to more personal losses, and dislocations, and that there is something oddly comfortable and secure in this position.

John Steiner (1993) has written about what he has termed "psychic retreats" – pathological organisations of the personality that "function to help the patient avoid anxiety by avoiding contact with other people and with reality" (1993, p. 2). These type of patients, all individually different and with particular anxieties and complex systems of defence, were, nevertheless, all, to greater or lesser extents, in some way "stuck" developmentally, because of their tendency to retreat in a habitual way to "an area of the mind where reality does not have to be faced, where fantasy and omnipotence can exist unchecked and where anything is permitted" (1993, p. 3). Steiner was writing about individual cases but his description, I suggest, is also paradigmatic of wider socio-cultural trends in late capitalism – including the tendency to project personal loss into the social environment, to projectively identify with relatively marginalised and excluded social groups, and to walk the streets of the unmourned and unacknowledged past, with the wish to find a home or refuge. Such trends gain creative (and immensely poignant) expression in the writings of Ian Nairn; born in Home Counties suburbia Nairn's birth certificate nevertheless records the city of Newcastle upon Tyne, which he regularly visited during the 1960s, as his place of origin.

Another example comes from the film director and author Pier Paulo Pasolini's writings about the proletariat and the subproletariat of Rome, exemplified by the novel *Ragazzi di Vita* (1955), consisting of vernacular vignettes from the Roman underworld of pimps and prostitutes, thieves and vagabonds (Thomson, 2008). Initially Pasolini lived in the slightly claustrophobic and run-down environs of the ancient Jewish ghetto, then moved with his mother into the Roman "*borgata*" (suburban districts), a section of the city described by Thomson as "neither rural nor urban but a midway zone of high rises and fields, often blighted by crime" (2008, p.7). It was into these areas that the new migrants arrived, particularly from the south of the country, with their own distinctive moralities and languages. Many of the old inner-city dwellers, of the old medieval alleyways and squares flattened by Mussolini's modernist rebuilding of the city, were also rehoused here. In this rapidly built housing was that intersection "of the poetic and the squalid", urban detritus amongst the flowers, that fired Pasolini's imagination; amidst junk-yards and rubbish tips lay a rejection of the new consumerism.

The reformed prostitute mother of the film "Mamma Roma" (1962) hopes to move into a more respectable middle-class neighbourhood, to better herself, and provide for her teenage son, Ettore. He, however, as if in reaction to this ideological sell-out, increasingly inhabits a criminal underworld, and when he dies he is framed by the camera as a Christ-like martyr. Such was Pasolini's response to the impact of the consumer revolution of the 1960s on the Roman poor.

Thomson (2008) suggests that Pasolini's attachment to the underclass of Rome was part of an oedipal psychodrama. He was profoundly attached to his mother, Susanna, who had come from a small town in Friuli, near the old Yugoslav border, to where the family returned to live after Pasolini graduated. His first poems were written in the Friulian dialect characteristic of the poor local peasant community. Influenced by Gramsci's ideas about a "popular nationalist literature" incorporating marginalised Italian people and their dialects, Pasolini, Thomson suggests, sought to replace the lives and language of the Friulian poor with those of the

Roman subproletariat. He identified himself with this underclass, itself an extension of his feelings towards his mother.

It seems clear that Pasolini was idealising – and eroticising – a kind of pre-
capitalist netherworld, an island of opposition to the inroads of consumer capitalism, and the conformity that it imposed. As Thomson puts it, "blessed are the
poor for they are exempt from the unholy Trinity of materialism, rationalism, and
property". Ranged against such forces, in profound identification with this underclass, was Pasolini's own unholy trinity of Catholicism, Gramscian Marxism, and
masochistic homoeroticism. And Thomson notes that when his beloved Roman
poor revealed that, like most of us, all they really they wanted was an ordinary
life, Pasolini turned against them.

Pasolini and Cobb were, ostensibly at least, very different. The former was a Catholic Marxist whose life ended in his fifties in sinister circumstances, left for dead,
perhaps after a sexual assignation gone wrong, in one of those transitional zones that
were the subject of his work. The latter could be seen, perhaps, as a Tory or liberal
anarchist, also identifying with those at the margins, but able to secure domestic happiness and dying in old age surrounded by his family. It could be argued, however,
that both were romantic individualists, conservatives in their wish to preserve some
element of tradition and the past. It might be that for both Pasolini and Cobb – as for
some later urban *flâneurs* and self-styled psychogeographers – trailing the desolate
streets of the disappeared was also a component of a psychic retreat from life, and
from the demands of too much closeness. For both, there was a wish, in the face of
fast-flowing change, a need to find a niche, a ledge on the cliff face. Cobb clearly
identified with, and found a temporary home with, the unorthodox and anarchic fam-
ilies of carpenters and toymakers now ejected from a cleaned-up Ixelles. Is this, he
asks, how all transitory human contact, the brief sharing of lives, ends up – does it
simply peter out in emptiness, absence, indifference, and uncertainty?

It is, of course, human nature to see the past, particularly the past of youth, as
more vivid than the present, too see the café lights as having been much brighter
then. However, it would be a great mistake to think that these laments were only
personal, and that they did not have something to say about the nature of historical change and the significance of what was being lost. What Cobb, like Pasolini,
was seeking to evoke, or even to preserve in some way, was a world before a
consumerist revolution, promising endless choice but actually making everything
the same and reducing individuality. Both railed against a bourgeois world fatally
lacking in the imagination, the chain of association, and the richness of the old
civic life. This was not to idealise these pasts:

> What historical interest, and the fascinating jumble of ancient, narrow fronted
> plaster houses, may mean in terms of human misery to their inhabitants, often
> crowded a whole family to a room. The people who live in Rue Volta, the
> only street in Paris with fifteenth century half-timbered houses, would not
> feel themselves particularly privileged.
>
> (Cobb, 1998, p. 136)

Cobb celebrated the old anarchic individualism of revolutionary Paris, set against the massive authoritarianism of Baron Haussmann, as he swept away the old medieval revolutionary city. Not surprisingly Cobb was aghast at the wholesale modern gentrification of increased areas of central Paris, with the expulsion of the original inhabitants to the *bidonvilles* of the outskirts:

> a social revolution so completely cannot fail to alter the character of Paris as a whole, by destroying the neighbourliness of the quartier, the village mentality of those who live above their place of work, depriving the city of much of the wit, the individualism, and the independence of the small artisan and of the violence and playful sexuality of the old population of the Halles.
>
> (1998, p. 139)

Whole districts of urban areas have become dead, or dangerous, or transformed into tourist-trail heritage and middle-class ghettos. "One would be quite hard put to encounter, as one used to, Algerian workers in the small hotels of the rue de Roi-de-Sicile, or Yiddish – or Polish – speaking Jews in and around the rue des Rosiers" (1998, p. 179). These are areas populated by ghosts, sometimes immaculately restored and preserved, but actually marked by absence, by the shadow of something missing, their inhabitants expelled to the ring of high-rise apartments circling the city of Paris, the *grand ensembles*, leaving areas that, for Cobb, remained as empty shells, denuded of reality. He is evoking something important – the loss of an urban environment with a human scale, in which a certain amount of social connectedness is possible. It is not the grand Paris that Cobb celebrates, for example, but the city accessible only to the walker, of tiny courtyards and houses, secret passages, fleeting views of domestic interiors, hidden gardens, small shops, workshops, cafés and restaurants:

> It is no longer a place where people of all conditions may meet regularly, informally, in the endless excitement of a chance encounter. Where would they meet? There is no longer any common ground and much of the old centre has become a single class stronghold, shuttered, selfish, and uninviting.
>
> (1998, p. 151)

Though they may involve a degree of idealisation of the past, Cobb's writings have continued relevance and might be seen as having given early expression to socio-cultural and geographical changes that have only intensified, leading to the removal of swathes of the working and lower middle classes from the centres of cities such as Paris, New York, and London; a process accompanied by the servicing of the new rich, living in a limitless pleasure dome of fine art and world food, by largely immigrant workers, living precariously on poor wages and temporary contracts.

Meanwhile, the most critically acclaimed and perhaps the most original, recent voice of loss, memory and destruction is the late W. G. Sebald. Sebald's narrators (Sebald, 1990, 1992, 1995, 2001) are morose, introspective, uneasy, and prone to the modern version of the vapours – mental and physical breakdown and exhaustion. The "I" of the narrative voice is, from the limited information we get, similar to the "real" Sebald, but is also a character himself, and thus not to be taken at face value. The discursive narrative, travelogues, vignettes, literary allusions and anecdotes, circumstantial detail, grainy photographs that may or may not be "real", which characterise Sebald's writings, might be seen as an attempt to give indirect representation to something that cannot be directly conveyed in words: an absence; at a psychic level, the maternal object perhaps; at a historical level the old polyglot multicultural world of pre-war Europe and its vanished Jewish culture, from which so many of his characters are – sometimes unknowingly – exiles.

This invisible sense of dislocation and loss penetrates into his characters' lives, so that they appear to become increasingly disembodied, desiccated and detached ghosts, even whilst still alive. The suicides of many of his characters is no surprise. At the same time there is good deal of deadpan, possibly unconscious, black humour (redolent, like much of Sebald's work, of Kafka) in the kind of profound existential ennui that results from a gloomy, neurotically fastidious, and solitary high-culture Germanic intellectual visiting a fair-to-middling fish and chip restaurant in Lowestoft (1995). From a psychoanalytic perspective, however, Sebald's work might be seen as a self-consciously knowing representation of the way in which traumatic, verbally unrepresentable experience, of a collapse that is at once personal and cultural, is not available as memory but is instead lived out as a life. His books, particularly *Austerlitz* (2001), represent the necessity of continuing to seek representation of something that can never be expressed, a history that can never be recovered.

As we have seen, Jameson (1991) has described late capitalism as a two-dimensional world without depth, the consequence, he suggested, of the incursion of commodification and marketisation into all aspects of life. The late crime novelist, the urbane and well-travelled Michael Dibdin (2007) captures something of the feeling of the new world through the character of his melancholic Venetian detective Zen:

> For years now, Zen had been living in a world where reality seemed to have been drained of all substance. Once upon a time, and he could still remember that time, authentic experience had been the default position, as unremarkable as gravity or the weather. Now, though, the authentic sounded a melancholy blue note as it receded, a Doppler effect induced by the speed of cultural change, as though sadly waving goodbye.
>
> (2007, p. 143)

This is not a rehash of the tired old hippy distinction between "authenticity" and mass production where "real music" might be contrasted with "artificial" or "mass-produced" pop in a simplistic and patronising way, so that, for example, the "manufactured" but supremely resonant music of Tamla Motown might be adversely contrasted with something called "deep soul". Such arguments were and

are based on a specious distinction between idealised nature and denigrated artifice. Indeed, "authenticity" is by now, in any case, itself an increasingly saleable
commodity, claims to which can be regarded with suspicion. However Dibdin's
remarks do capture something about the contemporary world in which experience
seems flat, thin, "as if", a self-conscious representation of something rather than
the thing itself, in which pre-existing social traditions are either hollowed out and
obsolescent or repackaged and transformed as a product to be bought or sold in
the marketplace. However, as Dibdin's Zen discovers, there are exceptions to this
rule, and some places where – for good or bad – "authenticity was not yet under
serious threat", this being the case on the road south from Rome to Cosenza in the
poor heart of southern Italy. There were, of course, and are, "islands of opposition" to the relentless commodification of experience and social institutions in late
capitalist life.

In recent years much of the most insightful and emotionally powerful popular art eschews the confessional mode but instead plays on the tension between
artifice and emotionality, conveying emotion not through direct expression but
through the creative evocation, at once ironic and loving, of the "anomie deluxe"
(Fagen, 2013) of certain aspects of contemporary life. Here "less is more", emotions are restrained, narrators are not to be wholly trusted, particularly when they
are claiming righteous sincerity; rather, emotional expression is through stylisa-
tion and the skillful evocation of the artefacts and forms of previous eras. Such
a sensibility can be seen in phenomena as varied as the non-naturalistic plays of
the late Dennis Potter (1978, 1986), in which characters burst into popular song,
in the English group Roxy Music's combination of glamour, futurism, and nostalgia, and the American group Steely Dan's invocation of a lost jazz age. Such a
sensibility is evident, too, in the loving attention to surface detail, photography,
and music in the films of Woody Allen, and in the television series *The Sopranos*
(Chase, 1999–2007). Here we see the ironic juxtaposition of sordid behaviour,
seedy locales, violent action, corrupted family life, with emotionally resonant
popular music – perhaps most memorably in the use of Frank Sinatra's 1965 version of "It was a very good year" (Drake, 1961) during the opening of the first
episode of the second season, "Guy walks into a psychiatrist's office".

The Sopranos, amongst many other things, might be a portrayal of a seductive perversion of family life, and of psychotherapy, by criminality and corruption, and of the consequences of the repeated turning of a blind eye. The song
against which this is juxtaposed belongs to a different register; it is an elegy
to a life well lived, but also to transience and passing time, a marker both for
the existential realities of life, the pain of attachment and loss, and also of the
rapid changes and social dislocations of late capitalist life; the sense of fash-
ions, styles, movements emerging and disappearing in the blink of an eye. In
the timeless present it is the instantly nostalgic invocations of the transient and
creative artefacts, styles, and art of mass culture that are perhaps the nearest we
get to collective social mourning, to the marking of losses that are simultaneously deeply personal and universal.

In this chapter I have focused on the experience of the individual in the face of rapid changes and dislocations. It has often been the alienated and déclassé individual, caught between classes and systems, who is at the best vantage point. As a case in point, the acutely observed long-running British television comedy of the 1970s, *Whatever Happened to the Likely Lads?* (Clement & La Frenais, 1973–74), first conceived by two then little-known, lower middle-class writers, Dick Clement and Ian La Frenais, had as its subjects social changes in North East England that occurred as shipbuilding, mining, and other heavy industries declined, slum clearances changed the face of parts of Newcastle, and the old associational working-class life was hollowed out. The eponymous likely lads, old friends, Terry and Bob, have very different identifications and aspirations. The former is in melancholic resistance to these changes, and risks being washed up by the tides of history, the latter is conflicted by the tension between his personal and class loyalty to his friend on the one hand, and his bourgeois aspirations, represented by his fiancé, Thelma, on the other.

The mode of the series is comedy, in particular, social comedy. However, like many other of the classic television comedies of the time the underlying mode is tragic; what is conveyed through all the humour is an immense sadness, connected most of all with the passing of time. For these are meditations not simply on social change but on the personal associations and vulnerabilities that accompany these changes; the passing of youth, the fraying and endurance of friendships, the loss of ideals, doomed class aspiration, and the failure to achieve potential. On the other hand, the characters are sharp, witty, and fundamentally well-disposed. Even Thelma, beautifully played by the actress Brigit Forsyth, has a heart, is really a good egg.

The series is also, then, a celebration of good times, of bonhomie, solidarity, and humour. Change offers opportunity and it is, paradoxically, the recognition that something valuable *has* been lost that mitigates against the pull of narcissistic immersion in the past as a form of identity, as in part represented in the series by the character of Terry, and allows the possibility of engaging more creatively with the present. In this sense, Terry and Bob may be personifications of the two halves that exist, to greater and lesser extents, in all of us.

I have turned in the last part of this chapter towards the area of popular culture. This is because it is in this arena that more collective responses to the changes and dislocations I have been addressing in this book are most clearly expressed. In the next chapter I remain in North East England, and turn to the subject of professional football, and its place in the changing psychic and real economy of the area. It is one of the long-standing jokes of *Whatever Happened to the Likely Lads* that it goes without comment that Bob goes to bed each night wearing a Newcastle United football top. Football has long been a source of collective identification but, I suggest, in the context of de-industrialisation and the social changes that occurred following the collapse of Communism and the ascendancy of neo-liberalism, it began to carry an emotional weight it could no longer manage. At the same time, the traditions of the sport – representing at best an outlet for creativity, spontaneity, and creativity often denied in an increasingly rationalised society – were undermined by the incursion of the market and of commodity on the one hand, and by incessant cultural opprobrium, on the other. I suggest that these processes were microcosmic of larger socio-cultural shifts, and, in particular, of the increasing denigration of the working class and its traditions, at the point of its relative decline.

Chapter 11

Problems with the defence

On Thursday 4 November 1994, the frigate HMS *Richmond* sailed down the slipway at the Swan Hunter shipyard in Wallsend into the River Tyne in North East England. The frigate, small compared with its more famous predecessors but replete with state-of-the-art technology, was delivered on time and in perfect order, in what could be fairly said to be "adverse circumstances"; for with the order books empty this was the last, of 2,700 ships built over 130 years. James Bedigan, engineering team manager, recalled his last working day: "they told us to put all our property, overalls and safety gear into a big cardboard box – after seventeen years working at Swan Hunters they didn't seem to trust you, as if you'd go round smashing things up" (Campbell, 1994).

The shipyards and the cranes were part of an evocative and historically resonant urban landscape – the site of the yard was the location of over two thousand years of industrial history. Next to the company entrance was Segedunum, a Roman fort built at the eastern end of Hadrian's Wall, the northern frontier of the Roman Empire. Where now the remaining Geordie welders and fitters toiled there had once laboured exiled Tigris boatmen. There had been shipbuilding at Wallsend from the 1850s, and the site that was to become Swan Hunter's was acquired in 1873. The company, a complex amalgam of several different concerns, moved from the building of colliers and barges ferrying coal from the Northumberland and Durham mines to London, to the construction of large ocean liners. In 1898 the *Utonia* was launched, and in the next five years twenty more liners were built. The most famous of all was the *Mauretania*, a transatlantic ocean liner launched in 1906. The ship, 790 feet long, with a beam of eighty-eight feet and a tonnage of 31,938, had the capacity to carry 2,000 passengers. For twenty successive years it won the annual award for the fastest crossing of the Atlantic.

The slow decline in British shipbuilding, running in parallel with that of mining and steel-making, was, of course, linked to changes in market demands and the emergence of cheaper overseas competitors with lower wage costs. Swan Hunter, though, managed to survive, through investment and modernisation – it had one of the most up-to-date dry-dock steel-making facilities in the world – but also because of the renowned innovation of its designs, and the reliability and skill of its workforce. The company developed a strong relationship with the Royal Navy and built over four hundred naval vessels, many also for other nations, including the aircraft carriers *Illustrious* and *Ark Royal*. By the early 1990s, however, government orders for warships were declining, such contracts as were available being awarded on "best value" criteria to cheaper competitors, whilst the firm was being effectively excluded from merchant markets.

Change was of course inevitable, and loss had to be faced, but this did not mean that the irreplaceable engineering traditions which had sustained the yard could not be put to good use. Swan Hunter had a highly skilled design team and workforce, whose experience and skills would have been eagerly sought out elsewhere in the world, and there were credible plans for diversification. Such plans, though, cut little ice with free market ideologists, for whom "bailing out" struggling industries was merely throwing good money after bad.

Meanwhile, if there was marked hostility on the free-market right towards the old centres of manufacturing, some sections of what became the self-styled "progressive left" gave the distinct impression that the decline of the old industries and their attendant communities was to be welcomed. Once the object of idealisation, such places were reconstituted as cultural wastelands, patriarchal, monolithic, and closed. Such attitudes found their concrete expression in the fate of the old dockland areas of our major cities;

> By the late 1980's, almost the only evidence that there had ever been a dock in Poplar, in Millwall, in Blackwall, in Silvertown, in North Woolwich, was to be found on the name plaques of luxury developments, inhabited by bankers, which cynically proclaimed their authenticity by calling themselves Cinnamon Wharf or Ivory Dock. A few of the older warehouses and custom houses and dock masters' houses were preserved, but whole areas of the docks became deserted, post-industrial wastelands scoured by the westerly's that blew in from the city.
>
> (McGrath, 2003, pp. 227–278)

Back in the north east, the loss of a manufacturing base to the economy was not simply felt in terms of loss of jobs, or the depletion of skills, though this was bad enough, but also at a deeper level of communal and personal identity. The shipyard served as a good symbol of a wider process of loss, as a ship was a creative and highly visible and concrete product of labour (as in the clichéd but still powerful old photographs of the old liners dwarfing the terraced street). In order to build a ship properly there was a requirement for teamwork, and those essential Conradian virtues of craftsmanship and integrity. Certainly for many on Tyneside, shipbuilding had represented a potent form of identification and of pride, in hailing from an area where, to further invoke Joseph Conrad, some real work was going on.

More practically there was a loss of developmental opportunity. The apprenticeship system in the shipyards, for example, represented a transitional phase for young boys who were not traditionally academic, from adolescence into adulthood, and provided opportunity for identification with the older workers. What would be the new source of pride and identification in the void left by the shipyard, in a situation in which, in that part of Tyneside in 1994, there was already twenty-six per cent male unemployment?

However, if there was gloom about the shipyards and the fate of manufacturing industry, the clichéd "grim up north" scenarios that the closure of the shipyards might have evoked did not entirely ring true. Despite economic recession, high unemployment, and the inactivity of the iconic cranes, Newcastle on a Friday night, or a Saturday night, did not look or feel like a city in the throes of depletion or loss. Rather the reverse; the mood was exciting, euphoric, and full of possibilities. Newcastle in fact had – and has – what has been described as one of the most vigorous popular cultures in Western Europe; one that centred very much on youth, consumption, and basic good-time, largely good-natured, hedonism. Perhaps this should not have been so surprising. The city of Newcastle upon Tyne itself was historically a centre of consumption and administration rather than of industrial production (Colls &Lancaster, 1992).

In 1994 though, there was another reason for a sense of well-being. As the sun set over the yards the famous but underachieving football team were stirring again. Newcastle United had been a famous old club, steeped in romantic history, but had fallen on hard times. During the 1950s, in the days of the famous Jackie Milburn, scion of the rich culture of the Northumberland coalfields, the club won the famous FA Cup three times. The only trophy they had won in recent years, though, was the European Inter-City Fairs Cup – in 1969, at the time I was first old enough to register my support, famously parading down the Danube after beating "crack" Hungarian favourites Újpesti Dózsa. Overall though, the club remained an underachieving giant with a huge potential support and with the endless capacity to raise hopes and dash them again. There had been an unmistakable gradual decline, culminating in relegation to the old second division. Crowds were down and the famous city centre stadium, St James' Park, though still atmospheric and evocative, was, like the team, in need of renewal and investment.

The state of affairs eventually led, as it did throughout the higher levels of professional football, to a boardroom class revolution. Out went the old guard, the languid patrician directors, scions of the old professional and moneyed classes on Tyneside, seen, however charming, as aloof and paternalistic figures; and in came another "Geordie messiah" – the self-made entrepreneur and property developer Sir John Hall, a populist local boy made good, all folksy wisdom, regional pride, and a certain degree of class consciousness imbued with a free-market individualist ethic. Bought in 1989 by Hall, for three million ponds, the football club gradually became part of a rhetoric of regional regeneration featuring cultural projects, high tech businesses, tourism, and shopping – and, of course, football.

As the new manager, the ex-player Kevin Keegan was in this sense the right man in the right place at the right time – or the wrong man, depending upon your point of view. Another self-made man with a penchant for folksy rhetoric and a capacity for inspiring devotion, conviction, and self-belief, Keegan had arrived when the club had been on the verge of relegation to the old third division. From the onset he inspired belief in players hitherto lacking in confidence. The club was saved, and in the next season he made a number of particularly astute, not to say inspired, buys, most of them modest outlays. Keegan was strong on adrenalin, inspiration, a sense of "can do", drama, getting the best out of hitherto underperforming or underrated players: he could make people believe in themselves. At an emotional level he connected with the players and with the fans. There was a quasi-religious fervour about this. In 1992–1993 Newcastle United gained promotion, winning the first ten games of the season.

By 1994 there was a mood of euphoria, and the first hints of triumphalism. The team was now playing in front of all-ticket capacity crowds, in a spectacularly replenished stadium, St James' Park, challenging for the premier league championship, soon to qualify for Europe. We began to see the now common, but then slightly disconcerting, phenomena of middle-aged men in Newcastle United football tops pushing shopping trolleys around out-of-town hypermarkets. That this transformation was at least partially the responsibility of the contradictory figure of the chairman, property developer, arch-Thatcherite, miner's son, and paternalist capitalist with a conscience, Sir John Hall (also responsible for the development of the Gateshead MetroCentre Shopping Centre), was a reminder that, to paraphrase Walter Benjamin, there is no monument to civilisation – St James' Park – that is not also a monument to barbarity – in this case the aforementioned MetroCentre.

Football serves many functions for a community, but one of the most important functions of the team was as a source of local identification, for Newcastle and its traditions. This was not simply with the team itself, but also with a certain way of playing, embodying attacking principles, commitment to the cause, skill, flair, and a certain big-hearted swagger, not to say arrogance. The crowd's idols had always been players who embodied these qualities, and if they had quirks or all too human temperamental flaws then the crowd loved them even more. As a succession of exasperated managers of the pragmatic school were to find out, the St James' crowd did not care for "percentage football" and, if the team were perceived as too defensive, the admonition "Attack, attack, attack!" rained down from the terraces. And in bygone days, when more progressive managers tried to adopt a more nuanced "continental" passing game, with the emphasis on retaining possession of the ball rather than all-out attack, the phrase, at least until a few years ago, "None of yer tappy-lappy, get stuck in!", could be heard emanating from the stands.

The team represented how the area would like to be seen – as its own slightly idealised view of itself. The stylishness and brio, the sharpness, the generosity, and the entertainment, expressed, too, the character of the Saturday night out, at least at its best. This was exemplified by the team's joyful supporters, the self-styled "Toon Army" (a night on the town, "toon" in Geordie, making the link with the wider culture clear), who, by and large, were generous-spirited, and life-affirming. They could be a bit rough round the edges perhaps, but were fundamentally decent, capable of self-mockery, although likely to stand no nonsense when goaded beyond a certain point of reasonableness.

Kevin Keegan, a Doncaster miner's son, a player who had not been blessed with the greatest natural talent or physical attributes, but who, through dedication and motivation, had made himself into a genuinely great footballer, somehow had what group analysts called a "valency" (an innate propensity to accept a certain kind of projection of feeling from others) for the part, for the role being asked of him.

As other sources of identity appeared to be under attack, particularly for young males – the loss of manufacturing, apprenticeships, the economic base – so the football club became ever more important as a source of local identity. And football remained, after all, the working-class sport par excellence, something which, in spite of Lord Justice Taylor's otherwise exemplary report, all seating stadia, and attempts to make football just another family leisure pursuit, still had an edge of unrespectability.

How secure though, was it, to hitch your wagons psychically to the fortunes of a football team, no matter how talented and entertaining they may be? And how much did the activities on Tyneside and the much-vaunted "popular culture" represent real resilience, real strength and resource, a genuine vigour – or a manic defence against depression, against those seemingly inexorable forces of loss and depletion evident in the decline of the shipyards? If the new reality at Newcastle was a heady, exciting one, it also seemed clear that the old atmospheric "Saturday afternoon" culture of football, and of city life, was disappearing fast. One by one they all went; the old football stadiums, moved to out of town localities (though not, thanks to Sir John, in Newcastle); the old pubs with their snooks and snugs; the city centre newspaper offices; the Saturday evening football "Pink", with its miraculous full match report printed, apparently, before the match you had just been watching had finished; the eccentric taverns full of even more eccentric market traders and seventy-five-year-old barrow boys; even the old sporting Saturday with its full fixture list and the excitement of the half time scores: all going, going, gone.

The disappearance of the cranes from the Tyneside skyline was, thus, only part of a wider process; the public libraries and associations, the city centre cinemas, the old greasy spoon cafés, the independent shops, and the social, communal, more public aspects of the working- and middle-class life, associated with an earlier stage of industrial capitalism (and having roots in pre-capitalist structures) – were now little more than obsolete outcrops in the smooth manicured lawns, business parks, and out-of-town shopping malls of late consumer capitalism. We were in a world of theme parks, theme pubs, enterprise zones, and yachting marinas. Cities and town centres increasingly became homogenised, with identikit and largely bland retail, office, and housing developments replacing older public spaces; erasing the industrial histories of the older forms of productive capitalism, and the more collective forms of institutional and social life from history. If they returned it was only as packaged and ersatz heritage "experience".

I lived, during the 1990s, within a stone's throw of the wide loop of the river Thames as it passed between the Isle of Dogs and East Greenwich. The industrial heritage of the old London docks, "the pool of London" as it had been called, was not simply no more but had been almost completely erased from history and from the visual landscape. This left only the fascinating but increasingly des-iccated visage of *London's Lost Riverscape* (Ellmers & Werner, 1988), as two local authors entitled their book of photographs of the Thames: a melancholically beautiful evocation of a "then" in which it had once been possible to walk across the packed lighters from one bank of the Thames to the other, as opposed to a "now" of a quiet and sometimes near-empty river populated only by pleasure craft. When I first came to London, it had still been possible, walking along the famous dockside street, Shad Thames, to detect, after it had rained, the smell of exotic spice emanating from the brickwork of the old Hanoverian and Victorian warehouses; now increasingly derelict and ripe for demolition, or for transforma-tion into mainly upper-class housing developments. In 1994 in Greenwich there were still areas, as you headed further east, where there were working boatyards and public access to a lively riverside life, human in scale. When I returned there recently the public right of way had been closed off, and the boatyards replaced by housing.

On Tyneside, further up the river from Wallsend, near the old shipbuilding area of Walker, there was a yachting marina where there used to be a shipyard; all cra-vats and neckerchiefs, as it were, and admittedly a pleasant place to while away a Sunday morning. But nothing happened there – another example of sanitised dockside places where, as Ed Glinert wrote of the docklands transformation of Wapping and Limehouse in London, there was "no discernible traces of com-munity or of life" (2000, p.252). The new consumer-based life, in which leisure and pleasure, buying and selling, replaced the old arts of making things, seemed to be summed up in microcosm by these new marinas and their like, built in identikit style on old industrial riversides throughout the country. It was as if these new structures, born out of the ruins of the old docksides and warehouses, encapsulated something of a larger socio-economic and cultural shift within the country as a whole. Neat, tidy, striving not to create offence on the basis of perceived difference, socially inclusive – and to that extent an unobjectionable "good thing" – but lacking in depth and resonance, bland, and with a more hidden privatised exclusivity based on money, gated housing developments, and inacces-sible riverside vistas.

It was no wonder we all had to get to the match.

Newcastle United for their part were now challenging for the premiership title. Somewhere along the way, however, Kevin Keegan, a mercurial and volatile fig-ure, and the crowd, got carried away with something manic and grandiose; buying new players at a time when the team was slightly wobbling but still well set at the top of the league, disrupting the shape of the team at a vital moment. There were already some worrying signs; whilst there was a boom, increased ticket prices, and replica shirts, there was a lack of investment in infrastructure, the youth acad-emy, and training facilities. Meanwhile, Keegan had simultaneously scrapped the reserve and youth sides, thus putting all his eggs in one basket, going for glory with a first team of "stars". Increasingly, the relentless search for big names – something that played into the grandiose big club fantasies of the chairman, Sir John Hall, and an increasingly large section of the fans – meant that local players, or promising signings from the lower leagues, or the squads of other clubs, would rarely get a look in, except as bit part players. This process – later to have a serious impact on the quality of the national team – was also happening at other big clubs in the premier league.

The rest is well known. A twelve point lead was lost. Keegan famously "lost it" in a post-match interview when, wild-eyed and ranting, stabbing a finger at the camera, he shouted that he would "love it" if Newcastle beat Manchester United to the title. We knew at that time that he *had* lost it, and that Newcastle United would not win the premiership title. Afterwards, the football played by the team was still of unparalleled swagger and attacking brio, and the achievement of Keegan in terms of entertainment can never be forgotten. Nevertheless, there *was* something manic about it all, and if Newcastle had an Achilles heel it was connected to a problem with the defence – best exemplified by a famous game at Anfield, held to be one of the best in Premier League history, in which the side, after a heroic come-back, ended up losing four-three to Liverpool after conceding an injury time goal.

The defensive weakness of Newcastle United must be seen structurally and systemically, as a symptom of something more than the deficiencies of individual players. The idea, perennially popular amongst supporters, that the problem could be solved by buying a better class of "star" defender was just a fantasy, and doomed to failure. Just as in group therapy, when, to the apparent relief of all, a "difficult" group member leaves, and the prospect of a quiet life begins to appeal to the beleaguered and long-suffering group therapist, another, hitherto "quiet", patient will take up the "difficult" mantle and begin to cudgel the group, so Newcastle United's defensive problems survived all changes in personnel. For, as Freud remarked, that which is not remembered, or understood, is doomed to be repeated like an unlaid ghost. The defence, and the club, was carrying too much weight of expectation and emotional investment.

It had, of course, long been the case that, in the face of the decline of manufacturing, the football team, in Newcastle and elsewhere, became an increasingly important source of local identification. The difference now, though, was that it was becoming, as the shipyards closed and the old associational sites demolished, one of the *only* sources of identification. Ian Jack (2011) has made the point that in Glasgow the twin football citadels of Ibrox (home of Rangers) and Parkhead (home of Celtic) existed as part of a huge urban landscape, of housing, warehouses, factories, shipyards, churches, pubs, clubs, and associations. They were part of a wider pattern of social identification. Now they stood concretely, on their own, and they carried too much baggage. They could not, like Newcastle's notoriously porous defence of that era, bear the emotional strain of the displaced expectations and feelings that were being projected into them.

At the same time football, like other sports, was becoming a microcosm of wider socio-cultural shifts. For Christopher Lasch (1979), at its best, professional sport represent a creative form of play, in which the artificial conditions and the equality of all players before the rules allow for the emergence of uncertainty, risk, daring: elements of play increasingly denied in a rationalised society. There is a partially unconscious "social contract" between sportsmen and fans, in which an ostensibly trivial activity is invested with high seriousness. The crowd and the team have some common understanding of the art of the sport, of standards of conduct and excellence, and an appreciation of its finer nuances, and there is a complex process of identification between the supporter and the team. For the spectator, therefore, the sporting experience is far more than one of the passive consumption of a spectacle. These traditions, though, were under increasing attack, and were beginning to buckle under a weight of expectations, moral injunctions, and emotional investments that could not possibly be met.

Lasch had noted the intrusion of television into sport in America in the 1970s, diluting, and in some cases destroying, these links between spectator and team, in the commodification and management of the experience. He argued that what corrupts sport is not increased professionalism, more money, or the spirit of competition (as some "radical" critics might have it) but the breakdown of the sports' conventions when ritual and public festivity is transformed into self-conscious "spectacle", into, in other words, a commodified product. At the same time, it becomes subject to liberal concerns and preoccupations with inclusivity and identity. Sportsmen and women are entreated to become role models, sport to become a means of moral improvement. Such a development was inherently problematic, as sport represents a prime example of autonomous social traditions that carry their own implicit values and codes of conduct.

In the UK, football and the premiership increasingly became a product to be honed and invested in, and football fans were no longer supporters but consumers. This, together with the introduction of all-seating stadiums, and all-ticket entry, led to a change in the dynamic and the feel of going to a football match. At one level there were massive gains – improved facilities, a decline in crowd violence, and the evolution of what was unquestionably one of the most exciting leagues in the world. However, at another level the sport became a more passive spectator experience, with many of the fans – though not all – sitting back in their seats and waiting to be entertained, and to be brought success. This has led to what, in my experience, has been a diminishing of the spontaneous and unpredictable nature of the occasion, the humorous and lively (rarely physically violent in my experience of watching many years of football at Newcastle) engagement of rival sets of fans. In fact, such away support as there was tended to be given tickets high up in tier seven, row Z, that is, somewhere in the gods. The only times this changed was for FA-cup ties, which continued to have a different and more generous mode of ticket distribution, and consequently tended to produce a much more vibrant and lively atmosphere.

The crowd became paying customers, not fans, expectant of success and impatiently critical of frustration. The good-humoured and slightly self-mocking bonhomie of the early years of Keegan gave way, gradually, to a rather crabbed joyless obsession with success, and with evermore big name players. Meanwhile, if, amongst some sections of the liberal intelligentsia, football was the people's game and was capable of poetic beauty and high drama, for more people, football was a game played by overpaid working-class upstarts with vulgar tastes, watched by sexist, racist, homophobic thugs. That there was little real evidence for such a view mattered little and those comparatively rare incidents when players, managers, or fans did conform to these attributions were eagerly seized on as proof positive of a more general underlying reality.

I could speak, as a lifelong football fan myself, from my own experience. When in the 1980s and early 1990s the British National Party (BNP) and other racist organisations attempted to target and recruit supporters from Newcastle United they were strongly resisted and repulsed by a combination of fans, local anti-racist organisations, and key members of the club itself, including the manager Kevin Keegan, under the banner "Geordies are black and white!" (the team's famous colours). This was a highly successful campaign. This is not to say that there did not remain racists in the crowd, or to minimise the appalling casual racism that was very much part of the 1970s and 1980s, but to note that there were strong countervailing tendencies, in the crowd as there are in individuals. Such distinctions, such discrimination in a positive sense of the word, became increasingly lost in a certain liberal-left narrative, which instead chose to accentuate the negative and eliminate the positive, and did not care to mess with mister in-between. Thus football became a form of proxy cultural war, the attacks on the sport and its supporters being a primary example of the denigration of the "patriarchal" world of the British working classes.

What could be more a symbol of commodification and marketisation than the current English Premier League, with its bloated salaries and tales of corrupt practices? However, it is also, of course, part of the continued attraction of football that it also expresses a form of resistance to these very same processes, and can never quite be subsumed to them – as gloriously highlighted by unfashionable and humble Leicester City beating all the big moneybag clubs to win the English premiership title in 2016. The fans, too, never fully accede to the identification of a consumer of a product; they remain supporters. And it could be argued that the multiracial make-up of most football teams makes the sport perhaps the major site of integration in contemporary life. As for the crowd – unlike in some parts of continental Europe there is little tolerance for racism and prejudice.

Football, though, continues to serve as a microcosm for larger socio-economic and cultural shifts. One shift is the incursion of market and commodity value into every aspect of life, and social relationships, a process that is also subject to resistance. Another shift is the struggle of sections of the left to find a response to a process in which they are implicated, indeed from which they may also be beneficiaries, instead, as a form of displacement activity, turning their ire on the presumed reactionary thuggishness of the masses. Such a mindset is only one manifestation, though, of what the late historian Raphael Samuel (1998) described as:

> a new imaginative complex in which militant masculinity is seen as the villain of the piece, an Arnoldian contempt for the narrowness of provincial life

and a corresponding certainty that the culture of the metropolis – defined these days as lifestyle rather than classical education is a very emblem of sweetness and light.

(1998, p. 161)

How had such a new imaginative complex come about? In order to begin to look at this question we need to return the end of the post-war settlement, and the vicissitudes, following the collapse of Communism, of progressive and radical opinion – or that which held itself as such.

Chapter 12

Subjectivism, postmodernism, and identity politics

After the fall of Communism, the territories of the old Soviet Union went through a period of extreme free-market "gangster capitalism", in which radical privatisation arose triumphant, unaccompanied by any kind of accountability, or legislative and civil framework. Whilst some thought that this was a necessary transitional phase to a more functioning market economy, the immediate consequences were that although some people got very rich very quickly, overall life expectancy declined and the economy imploded. The phrase, derived from Nietzsche, "everything is permitted", also a key theme in Dostoevsky's great novel on the theme of patricide, *The Brothers Karamazov* (1880), became a popular way in Russia of describing those immediate post-Communist years.

The impact of the fall of Communism, however, went far beyond the territories of the old Soviet Union; for it was not simply that Communism appeared to have been pushed out of history, but that socialism, indeed the whole post-war social democratic settlement, seemed likely to be pulled down into the whirlpool with it. Increasingly, the state was seen as a lumbering behemoth pressing down on individual initiative and private enterprise, whilst the market, revered in quasi-religious terms, was no longer a mechanism in the exchange and selling of goods and services, best operated under appropriate regulation, but was instead a force of divine providence. As a political corollary, the civic freedoms and material gains associated with pluralist liberal democracies were not so much the product of long political struggle and popular pressure but the inevitable concomitant of a neo-liberal economic system. The invocation of political freedom against tyranny on behalf of the "free world" became indivisible from a clamour for the omnipresence of free markets.

As a cultural correlate of these changes, postmodernist and social constructivist ideology privileged culture over nature, in a fantasy of endless Protean self-invention; multiple selves in a technologically utopian landscape, freed from human needs and wants, in an endless present split off from any historical context. It was, of course, a seductive vision, made more so by technological innovations that appeared to make real the triumph over nature and reality. The appeal of this position, in the era of the end of history, was that it appeared to offer a world without limits, in which the limitations of external reality, and of nature, could be ignored. The world became a playpen of different identities and limitless possibilities.

Such processes were not without their contradictions. In the United Kingdom the Conservative Party struggled – as it has done ever since – with the contradictory position of supporting free-market individualism, which was at the same time undercutting the very "traditional" ways of life and social bonds that the party had been brought into existence to protect. Conservative commentators and intellectuals bemoaned the social and moral outcomes of their own policies. It was thus historically fortuitous that they were able to lay the blame on the postmodernist left, on groups whose values were not of the traditional left at all but were rather of a murky strain of German romanticism, and whose relativism was entirely consistent with free-market ideology, with a world where everything was permitted, and, increasingly, restrictions did not apply – unless you stopped to read the small print.

By the early 1990s in the UK the idealisation of the market and of consumer values came from both sides of the political divide, to such an extent that for a time the apparent conflict between right and left, in this regard, increasingly resembled what Freud termed "the narcissism of minor difference", and party politics degenerated into the competing claims of individual personalities, rather than the clarification of genuine political choice. Such choices as could be made were no longer easily categorised in terms of conventional political labels. As the late historian Tony Judt (2007) has pointed out, to be on the "right" (certainly on the free-market right) during this time was, from one perspective, to promote radical change; whereas to identify yourself as "old left" was to express a wish to conserve older traditions and ways of life in the face of a system in which, as Marx and Engels (1848) famously put it, "[a]ll that is solid melts into air" (p. 6).

In the last chapter I considered the way in which the resurgence of Newcastle United may have served as part of a social defence against the full experience of the psychosocial dislocations attendant upon de-industrialisation. It is, of course, of limited value to sentimentalise the past. Mark Mazower (2004) poignantly describes the loss of the old chaotic polytheistic city of Salonika in Greece as its labyrinthine alleys and courtyards were buried under the linear street grids of the late-nineteenth-century bourgeois nation state. He also comments that no city can become a museum to its past, and change is, of course, the essence of urban life. However, the neglect and denigration of the manufacturing heritage of the country was one of the more curious and self-defeating aspects of the Anglo-Saxon version of neo-liberalism. For while competitor countries such as Germany protected, invested in, and developed their manufacturing skills and technology, the UK became increasingly reliant on an economy based on financial services and a housing and credit boom – and, as it turned out, very little else. The outcome – a chronic imbalance between imports and exports, a balance of payments crisis, low productivity, and stagnant wages – was finally exposed by the economic meltdown that followed the credit crunch; a situation from which, despite nascent economic recovery based in part on the reignition of a house price and credit boom, the country has yet to recover.

As we have seen, for some sections of the right, but also for sections of the liberal and progressive left in the years following the collapse of Communism, the market was idealised, and the state denigrated. There are compelling reasons for believing that markets form a central place in any functioning society. However, thinking in terms of Britton's (1998) notion of pathological splitting, the Hayekian market was imbued with "divine" qualities: the pure, uncorrupted individual was writ large; the unfettered workings of the market would somehow lead to the general good; the state was seen as having the denigrated characteristics of neediness, dependency, and the dead hand of the oppressive object. I am suggesting that emotional factors were at work, that the wish was father to the thought, and that thinking on the issue had become concrete and fundamentalist. Britton writes about states of pathological certainty, the proponents becoming convinced not only of their own righteousness but that they represent the truth: "Belief rests on probability not certainty, and yet it produces the emotional state that goes with certainty" (1998, p. 8).

However, such beliefs also serve particular interests and it is important to retain a political perspective. In the old-fashioned but perhaps still conceptually useful Marxist sense of the term, an ideology is a way of seeing the world, held all the more powerfully at an implicit and preconscious level, and is related in complex ways to particular socio-economic systems and class configurations. An ideology, in this sense of the term, tends to legitimise particular ways of doing things as simply, and naturally, "how things are". The idealisation of the market, the denigration of manufacturing, might be seen in political terms as part an ideology rationalising a rebalancing of power away from the centres of collective labour to those of capital. As Thomas Frank (2002) has noted:

> Once Americans imagined that economic democracy meant a reasonable standard of living for all – that freedom was only meaningful once poverty and powerlessness had been overcome. Today, however, American opinion leaders seem generally convinced that democracy and the free market are simply identical. There is precious little that is new about this idea, either: for nearly a century, equating the market with democracy was the familiar defense of any corporation in trouble with Union or government; it was the standard-issue patter of corporate lobbyists like the National Association of Manufacturers. What is "new" is this idea's triumph over all of its rivals; the determination of American leaders to extend it to all the world; the general belief among opinion makers that there is something natural, something divine, something inherently democratic about markets.
>
> (Frank, 2002, p. 336)

Such a mindset, though, went far beyond the free-market right. The American liberal political scientist Mark Lilla (2014) argues that, in historical terms, there has been a new cultural outlook amongst educated urban elites – the primacy of individual self-determination over traditional social ties, lack of concern in regard to differences in religion and sex, and an a priori obligation to tolerate others. This was accompanied, in most cases, by an unreflective belief in the cost-free benefits of free trade, deregulation, and foreign investment.

This mindset, strengthened by the fall of Communism, became something of a default position. It became, in the absence of meaningful opposition, complacent and blind to its own contradictions and limitations. As we see only too clearly today, democracy was insecurely established, or under attack, in many places, with new oligarchies, clans and sectarian groups, theocratic rulers, and forms of despotic mercantilism. Within capitalist liberal democracies wishes inevitably conflicted – between people, and, one might add from a psychoanalytic perspective, within people. Lilla makes the important point that although people may rightly believe that liberal democracy represents the best way of escaping poverty, oppression, and ignorance, this may not include an adherence to the individualism that comes with it, nor an agreement with those combinations of libertarianism and market forces that serve to undercut "traditional" values such as piety, deference to the past, commitment to place, and generational obligations and proprieties.

In a classic paper Tom Main (1967) described how a creative innovation in a residential therapeutic community treatment programme at the Cassel Hospital in London, relating to patients being free to choose their weekend activities and leave, became over time rather stultified and a matter of mindless routine: "A kind of moralism had crept into the procedures" (1967, p. 65):

> A fixed procedure had emerged out of a flexible technique, and an idea had become a morality. What had begun as a free ego-choice had grown into a fixed discipline … it had become either *good* or *bad*, a matter of conformance and not thought, an affair of the nurse's superego and not her ego.
>
> (1967, p. 66)

Main saw this in generational terms, as what he called "the hierarchical promotion of ideas" (p. 66), "moving from the experimental and thinking areas of the ego of one generation into the fixed morality areas of the ego ideal and superego of the next". This generational process of knowledge, as it passes from the ego to the superego, helps to explain how ideas, even good ideas, can become emotional objects. What was once an insight becomes a moralistically tinged article of faith, of belief rather than thought. Certain ideas were held on to because they seemed morally right, and desirable, and the question of whether they were actually true became less important than the emotional pressure that they *should* be. As Main (1967) puts it, ideas become emotional objects, used for emotional purposes, and a source of individual and group identification.

Lilla (2014) regards contemporary liberalism as essentially dogmatic, in that it allows ignorance of the world, and lack of curiosity as to its impact. He suggests that though it starts with the sanctity of the individual, the centrality of individual freedom, distrust of authority, general tolerance, and the ubiquity and general good of markets, it goes no further. It has "no taste for reality"; for understanding its antecedents, or acknowledgment of the necessary tension between individual and collective purposes. In this sense it is not classically liberal as the founding fathers of that movement would have recognised. It is more akin to a faith, or an idea that has moved, in Tom Main's terms (1967) from the ego of one generation to the superego of the next. It is a "mentality, a mood, a presumption" (Lilla, 2014) that can attract because of its simplicity and lack of curiosity about its own contradictions and conflicts, and widely divergent adherents. By contrast, an ideology, in Lilla's non-Marxist sense of the term, requires work, revision, testing out against reality. It invites and allows the possibility of refutation. For Lilla (2014), however, the libertarian age, by contrast, "is an illegible age": it lacks the vocabulary and intellectual framework within which it can recognise, understand, and attend to, its own contradictions and problems.

Lilla is here talking most centrally about the USA, but his analysis has wider implication. In the UK, the Thatcherite response to the crisis of the post-war consensus had been the blitzkrieg of large swathes of British industry, disproportionately located in the Labour-voting industrial heartlands of the north, in favour of small business, and the financial and service sectors located primarily in the south. This appeared, however, less a geographical phenomenon and more a question of an old-fashioned battle for power, a war waged against an increasingly denigrated industrial working class and its more collective institutions. The petit-bourgeois individualism of Margaret Thatcher and her supporters in the UK went further than constitutional antipathy to the state or socialism, as for them there was, famously, "no such thing as society". Thus, "there is no alternative" to free-market capitalism. Such beliefs, and the policies that flowed from them – leading to the industrial and cultural fragmentation of the "traditional" working classes and their social solidarities and institutions – ruthless as they were, found a resonance with many members of the public, especially with swathes of the upper working and lower middle classes. Here Thatcher's views resonated because they connected with people's experiences, or rather with their gut emotions; where traditions of individual hard work, self-improvement, and self-reliance, under the pressure of economic insecurity, moved into distrust and resentment of those "uneconomic" individuals and organisations who, perceived as lacking these values, existed on "handouts" and state subsidies.

The metaphors of the Thatcherites about "not spending beyond your means" had their spiritual and ideological roots in lower middle-class non-conformism, and resonated with people's experience of household economising; as the more counter-intuitive neo-Keynesianism of spending your way out of a recession did (and perhaps still for some do) not. They also found resonance because those upper working-class and lower middle-class sections of the population, alienated both from established interests and from the trade union and collectivist traditions of industrial labour, were feeling insecure, financially and in terms of class status, as the post-war boom ended.

Across sections of the left there was an intense dislike of the new conservatism without any real engagement with what it was that might be making these policies resonate with people's experience. Growing up in an upper working-class/lower middle-class area on the residential coastal fringe of industrial – or post-industrial – Tyneside, I bowed to no one in my dislike of Thatcherite policies; but I sometimes felt that the almost de rigueur visceral hatred towards the woman – "Thatcher!" – and all her works, carried a distinct tone of social snobbery, of inherent aristo-cratic disdain for petit bourgeois individualism and social aspiration. And if the old sepia-toned working-class communities could still be idealised in their decline into apolitical and ahistorical "heritage", then the same was not true of the new houses and estates of the upper working classes and lower middle classes, who had deserted Labour for Thatcher. Here "left-wing" disparagement and disdain increased, apparently unencumbered by any political engagement with, or even knowledge of, most people's everyday socio-economic concerns.

From one point of view, the wish of the "New Labour" theorists to be congru-ent with the reality of socio-cultural change seemed reasonable and intellectually hard-headed, when set against these regressive trends on the left. It was undoubt-edly the case that the left was in danger of becoming moribund and irrelevant to people's concerns, unless it changed, and addressed the concerns of the majority in the UK. However, New Labour tended to idealise the process of modernisation and change, and to underestimate people's attachment to community and tradi-tion. They appeared happier challenging conservatism and vested interests within their own ranks than the real seats of power. In the face of the irreducible conflict, their default position was to split the difference: thus, the mantra "tough on crime, tough on the causes of crime"; thus the inherent tensions between capital and labour could be reconciled without an "either/or" allocation of resources. The rich could have tax cuts, the economy could be deregulated, and the market allowed free reign without the stranglehold of the state; the proceeds of this could be used to fund welfare and welfare reform. Conflict could be "triangulated", in what proved to be a (temporary) triumph of wishful thinking ("all must have prizes") over reality.

Looking at it now, the substantial successes of the "third way" approach lent too much credence to a form of wishful thinking, in which the inherent ten-sions between capital and labour could be reconciled without pain to either side. The result, as Larry Elliot and Dan Atkinson (2016) have pointed out, was that, although there were real achievements, New Labour left an economy in which, despite surface appearances, the foundations were weak; with a depleted manu-facturing base and too much reliance on housing and consumer credit. Insufficient regulation of the financial sector and the neglect of industry and investment, and their apparent indifference to the old art of making things, came back to haunt the party during the crisis of 2007–2008.

Free-market fundamentalists and New Labour theorists seemed alike in their indifference, running to outright hostility, towards the engineering and manufac-turing traditions of the country. The difference in policy was not about fundamen-tals – the inevitable decline and rundown of manufacturing – but the speed and manner of the way in which this process was managed. Indeed, for some sections of progressive opinion, the fracturing and disappearance of the old associational world of "traditional manufacturing" was to be welcomed. This world, once idealised, was now denigrated as the epitome of oppression and xenophobia: "The mining communities are here seen as the relics of patriarchy. Politically they are one of the original heartlands of that "old Labour" from which Mr Blair is seeking to extricate his party" (Samuel 1998, p.155).

Clearly the antipathy towards the old centres of manufacturing and their associations and institutions could not wholly be explained by economics. There was a political imperative at work; for the free-market right there was a perception, actualised by the miners' strike, that they needed to take on and defeat the diminishing but still potent power base of organised industrial labour, now reconceptualised as "the enemy within", and mainly, though not exclusively, centred in the industrial heartlands of the north. The hostility could then be seen in class terms, as a rolling back of what remained of the post-war social democratic consensus, a rebalancing of power back from labour to capital. However, if in this sense the hostility from the free-market right might have been expected, it was also evident, as we have seen, from sections of a self-designated progressive liberal-left. Here the old centres of industry were now viewed as ecological nightmares and socio-cultural wastelands, monolithic and closed, antagonistic to women, and sexual and racial minorities (Samuel, 1998).

How do we understand this shift? At one level, these attitudes reflected underlying changes in class. Samuel's essay "The SDP and the new middle class", originally published in *New Society* in 1982, and reprinted in *Island Stories* (1998), was an early foray, almost eerily prescient, into the split, so apparent today (not least in the polarisation over Brexit in the UK, and in the USA around the election of Donald Trump), between what has been termed "liberal elites" and the "masses".

In the UK the substantial post-war governmental achievements of the Labour party would not have been possible – and will not be possible in the future – without an alliance between the majority of the working class and sections of the liberal middle class. The significant post-war achievements of the party were both socio-economic and civic, social and liberal; from the creation of the NHS and a welfare state, to the liberal reforms under Roy Jenkins.

Samuel charts, however, a change in the middle classes, and the evolution of a new political class who, though still heralding themselves as progressive, were, nevertheless, in, their preoccupations and values, "unmistakably hostile to the working class" (1998, p. 265), to the point, in some quarters, of denying that such a class still existed. This new political group, though occupationally diverse, were in some sense more unified than the older, stratified middle classes, more outward-looking, less beset by social snobbery and anxieties about place, status, and social decorum. Culturally discerning, tending towards the exhibition of conspicuous good taste, tolerant of difference, and often owing their place as much to education and professional achievement as to an "accident of birth", they were developing, as a class, according to Samuel, "a different emotional economy" (1998, p. 259) than their essentially pre-war predecessors; open and relaxed, they tended to view themselves as reasonable, civilised, clear thinking, opposed to atavistic appeals to tradition and unthinking adherence to authority. In other words, this subsection of the new middle class, the beneficiaries of social change, were deeply opposed both to the Conservative party and, notwithstanding a commitment to an abstracted equality, to a working class held as sectionalist, class- rather than issue-bound, and closed; "under any of these optics, the people become objects of disgust, at best yokels and buffoons, at worst hooligans and wreckers" (1998, p. 161).

The Social Democratic Party (SDP), for their part, might be seen as a political expression of these shifts, with the SDP as the imaginative " 'modernizers', taking on the national equivalent of a rundown street" (1998, p. 264). In such a mindset the working class is "the cynosure of all that is backward-looking – 'tribal' in its allegiances, insular in its preferences, suspicious of progress and change" (1998, p. 265). The relevance and continuity of Samuel's analysis to contemporary politics isn't hard to see. In the early days of the SDP their largest branch was located in Richmond and Twickenham; the electoral locality that had the highest number of votes for Remain in the 2016 European referendum.

The SDP, of course, could not sustain their initially spectacular electoral success and fell into decline. However, by the 1990s the Labour Party was reiterating its debt to Methodism rather than Marxism. It was burying Clause IV of its constitution, its "historically anachronistic" commitment to nationalisation and state ownership, in a bid for renewal and reinvention; even if this policy commitment had long been more symbolic than real. The emerging modernists and reformers of "New Labour" argued, plausibly to many, that the party needed to make themselves electable, to engage with Middle England, in order to create what became called a "progressive alliance"; rather than withdraw into self-indulgent internecine ideological squabbling. Indeed the modernisers had a point: some people on the self-styled "hard left", at that time full of sectarian division and various forms of infantilism, seemed to prefer permanent opposition to permanent revolution.

Meanwhile, in wide sections of a metropolitan left and middle-class bohemia that had themselves benefited from the increased social mobility of the "golden age" of post-war capitalism, there was a replacement of the old-left focus on socio-economics with a new moralism, manifest in self-consciously "correct" attitudes. These positions were held with such a degree of belief and certainty as to their inherent self-evident progressivity that it became very difficult to question their assumptions without being attacked as a reactionary. Yet, looked at more closely, many of these positions were not as progressive as they seemed – the political correctness of "political correctness" could not be taken as read.

As we have seen, for sections of the progressive left the politics of identity and victimhood were replacing the old universalist questions of class, economics, and socio-economic justice. I want to make it very clear here that, in making this point, I am not falling into the position that the "real" issues are socio-economic, and that the struggle for civil and minority rights are somehow secondary to this.

These struggles are ultimately indivisible, and any genuinely progressive move-ment for socio-economic justice must also have the necessary fight against preju-dice and for equality on issues of race, gender, and sexuality at its heart. What I am highlighting, and challenging, however, is the evolution, within certain sec-tors of "progressive" opinion, of a culture dominated by competing notions of exclusivist identity buttressed by states of emotional certainty, and in which there is a hypersensitive intolerance of a different perspective. There is a huge differ-ence between a cosmopolitan, liberal, and pluralist society, where there is recog-nition of difference and the inevitability of conflict, and a liberally authoritarian and intolerant society in which there is a polarised split between victims and vic-timisers, the enlightened and the prejudicial, a split that is in part motivated by emotional factors, and which is sustained and exacerbated by class differentials and projective processes. As Lilla remarks, the "omnipotent rhetoric of identity" (2016) that now constitutes much of what terms itself progressive opinion, tends to reproduce itself.

In the UK the attacks on football and its supporters as irredeemably patriar-chal, prejudiced, and so on, was indicative of this shift. This was really a proxy attack on the "traditional" male working class. There was, of course, some truth to this picture, and evidence could always be found for the prosecution. Brutalism, oppression, and prejudice exist to varying degrees in all communities, including those of liberal elites. What was striking, though, was not the need to highlight and combat these tendencies where they existed, but a highly critical mindset where the beliefs and actions of single individuals and/or small fringe groups were held to be characteristic of the latent attitudes and views of the majority; this, when there was a strong argument to say, by contrast, that the actual situation was something much more complex and mixed, a gradual coming together of a more pluralist world, though not without islands of opposition.

The corollary of this denigration of the reactionary masses was an uncritical celebration of the shocking and the outrageous. Culturally, as Slavoj Žižek (2006) has suggested, transgression became something of a default position – or an easy way of asserting an "edgy", morally relativistic radicalism without doing any-thing that might harm career prospects or really challenge a "system" in which outrageous activity and outré viewpoints were the lingua franca and profitable currency. For, although increasingly culture and art became a site of rebellion, as Jameson's famous article (1991) on post-modernity as the cultural logic of late capitalism has suggested, such activities were entirely at one with the values of a culture that traded on schlock and kitsch; in which there had been a breakdown of the distinction between "low" and high" art. Indeed transgression was integral to the functioning of such a culture.

Turning to the emotionally charged questions of race, what picture do we see when the subject is removed from the distorting lens of contemporary identity politics? As the biologist Steven Jones remarks, "[i]ndividuals – not nations and races – are the main repository of the human variation of functional genes. A race, as defined by skin colour, is no more a biological entity than is a nation, whose identity depends only on a brief shared history" (Jones, 1993, p. 263). From a psychoanalytic perspective it is the very meaninglessness of race as a category that makes it a suitable vehicle for projection of unwanted and degraded parts of the self (Rustin, 1991, p. 62): there is no reality or external object to think about. What is clear is that it is most often bad inadmissible aspects of the self that are projected into the other group, often in the language of physical and sexual repulsion and disgust, couched in the basic language of the body and of bodily and/or sexual functions – a debased and degraded other.

Rustin goes on to suggest (1991, p. 59) that very young children are pretty indifferent to such racial differences, relating to adults in terms of proximity and friendliness rather than superficial bodily characteristics. It is at the period of latency, when children are more preoccupied with fitting into their social milieu that racial patterns emerge in thinking and behaviour. This forms the basis for understanding that racism might be understood psychoanalytically as the projection of bad parts of the self, in a process of pathological splitting, identified with out-groups. This is usually balanced out, however, by a growing awareness of the universal aspects of experience, and a more secure sense of personal identification.

As Julian Lousada (2006) has argued, "fear of the stranger", however, is likely a latent aspect of the human psyche, a fault-line likely to be activated in certain psychic and social conditions, and countered, optimally, by a sense of universalism, grounded in the local, of common human predicaments and vulnerability. The question, however, of whether this fear leads to racist or fascist ideology is dependent upon the complex interplay of specific individual, group, and sociopolitical factors.

Whilst it is essential to continually highlight and challenge racism, some forms of contemporary antiracism perpetuate the empty categories of the racist (Rustin, 1991) by foregrounding racialised analysis and dialogue at the expense of other factors. Frequently in this dialogue racism is attributed to prejudice and cultural factors, rather than it being seen that these are matters inseparable from economics and politics. Prejudice and racism are, in these discourses, routinely attributed, as we have seen, to those very "indigenous" working-class communities that have, in many cases, long been living, often in straightened circumstances, with difference. As Slavoj Žižek (2016) has suggested, cultural discourse becomes, in this context, a way of not talking about, or of mystifying, politics. Such discourse neglects – or rather purposefully obscures – the connection between marginalisation and economics, a situation that is also inseparable from class factors, and which requires socio-economic and political attention.

Thus there is a danger of the insights of one generation becoming, in Main's terms, the superego-driven moralism of the next. Thus the mantra, heard in some anti-racist trainings, of a universal "unconscious racism", an attribution that can neither be denied nor confirmed, but the denial of which is sometimes treated as proof positive of guilt. Whether or not this formulation – ultimately unprovable – is correct, there is a significant difference between situations, in groups and societies, where racism becomes an ideology and a dominant trend, and those where it does not. If we are to consider the psychosocial conditions from which racism arises, we also have to acknowledge that throughout history there have, and continue to be, many places

> where countries, communities, allegiances, affinities, and roots bump uncomfortably up against each other – where cosmopolitanism is not so much an identity as the normal condition of life. Such places once abounded. Well into the twentieth century there were many cities comprising multiple communities and languages – often mutually antagonistic, occasionally clashing, but somehow coexisting. Sarajevo was one, Alexandria another, Tangiers, Salonica, Odessa, Beirut, and Istanbul all qualified – as did smaller towns like Chernovitz and Uzhhorod.
>
> (Judt, 2010, p. 206)

As Keenan Malik (1996) argues, some forms of contemporary anti-racism, by contrast, appear to have foundations in the very anti-universalist mindset that created the notion of race. As mentioned earlier, certain strands of liberal-left "anti-imperialism" influenced the view that the intellectual principles underpinning the bourgeois Enlightenment and the industrial revolution (ideas of reason, progress, humanism and universalism, scientific exploration of reality) were merely part of a dominant ideology of the West. Enlightenment universalism came be seen as the imposition of Euro-American ideas of rationality and objectivity on other non-European peoples, imposing uniformity on diversity and difference. Such a dichotomous picture, though, does not stand up to historical scrutiny; the Caribbean writer C. L. R. James, for example, wrote very clearly in the tradition, born out of the renaissance and the Enlightenment, of reason, progress, humanism and universalism, scientific method, and democratic politics. These "Western" traditions themselves incorporated traditions of Islamic scholarship and learning, in mathematics, astronomy, and so on. The important point here, as Malik emphasises, is not to fall prey to an assumption that these are essentialist Western ideas simply because of their contingent historical and geographical location. Truth is not dependent on perspective.

As a corollary of the shifts noted above the notion of multiculturalism has been held up as a badge of progressiveness, opposition to which can be marked out as reactionary and racist. A historical perspective, though, is required here also. Multicultural societies had, as we have already seen, a long history before "multiculturalism": the ramshackle, authoritarian but benignly tolerant Austro-Hungarian empire of Franz Joseph II as chronicled by Joseph Roth; the Sarajevo that had a mosque, a synagogue, and an eastern Orthodox cathedral in the same street; the Salonika of the Ottoman Empire where Ukrainians, Bulgarians, Serbs, Vlachs, Albanians, Sufis, Whirling Dervishes, Greek shopkeepers, Armenian shipping magnates, and Jewish dockworkers intermingled in a multi-confessional polyglot city for centuries – before its transition into "an ethnically and linguistically homogenized bastion of the twentieth century nation state" (Mazower, 2004, p.11). These truly were the infinitely rich, infinitely varied, worlds we have, for the most part, lost.

However, some contemporary versions of multiculturalism have a different ideological inheritance and seemed to involve a retreat into a regressive kind of state-sponsored ethnic identity politics, in which what is emphasised is the difference between people, rather than what potentially unites them as human beings. Malik (2001) has described the way in which, in a Bradford faced with growing militancy, the local council drew up equal opportunity statements, establishing race-relations units and funding black organisations. Bradford was to be a "multi-racial, multi-cultural city" in which "every section of the community has an equal right to maintain its own identity, culture, language, religion and customs" (2001).

The focus changed from wider universalist political issues (racial inequality, political disaffection, social deprivation, unemployment) to religious and cultural issues (the demand for Muslim schools and separate education for girls). Moreover, the council was funding and setting up religious umbrella groups representing different parts of the community, Sikh and Hindu as well as Islamic. Well-meaning as the policy was, the effect was to increase tension and division between different parts of the Asian community, as each fought for council funding. People looked inwards towards religion, ethnicity, and community as badges of identity; different parts of the community increasingly lived "parallel lives", in different areas, going to different schools, and organised by different institutions. Communities in effect became segregated and

> in areas where there was a sharp division between Asian and white communities, and where both communities suffer disproportionately from unemployment and social deprivation, the two groups began to view these problems through the lens of cultural and racial differences, blaming each other for their problems.
>
> (Malik, 2001)

From this perspective, rather than embodying the more universalistic views of the Enlightenment, some forms of postmodern multiculturalism instead see people, in historic terms, not as being at different stages of development and integration, but as permanently different, and appear pessimistic, if not nihilistic, about the possibility of social development and progress. The proponents of such a view concentrate on divisions between people rather than what they have in common, not least their vulnerability in the face of the existential facts of life, as I described earlier:

> The multicultural approach appears to be a sensitive response to the needs of black communities. In fact, it is underpinned by the same assumption that has dogged the debate about race relations from the start; the idea that black people are in some way fundamentally different from "British" people and that the problem of race relations is about how to accommodate those "differences".
>
> (Malik 2001)

An old-fashioned class perspective is required. Whilst a tolerant attitude towards race has become a leitmotif of progressivity, there is sometimes a hidden element of social exclusivity in such positioning, particularly when this is combined with an excoriation of the presumed racism of other social groups. There was always a significant difference between those expressions of pluralism and multiculturalism arising from those existing within an economically protected environment (in which the biggest personal impact of large-scale immigration, for example, might be a larger choice of restaurants at which to eat and markets at which to shop) and those arising out of the more atavistic struggle for housing and work, characteristic of old working-class communities, whether in some northern mill towns or areas such as Dagenham in East London.

When I lived in London I was familiar with Spitalfields, home to successive waves of French Huguenot, Irish, Eastern European Jewish, and then Bengali immigration. The "indigenous" white population had been leaving for Essex since the 1960s. They were replaced by artists and craftsmen, the artistic avant-garde and urban bohemians, and conservationists; bravely ploughing a furrow in a hitherto decaying immigrant area where no one had wanted to live. They were quickly, however, followed by estate agents and financiers who, in time-honoured fashion, set about transforming the undoubted character and potential of the area into a saleable product. "Spitalfields" became a commodity to be sold; imbued with Georgian heritage and multicultural ambience, it became desirable, as the east London chronicler Patrick Wright (2009) noted, as "a reclaimable area of beautiful houses and exotic contrasts that had survived the levelling embrace of the welfare state" (2009, p. 114). As an area, it had "the characteristic romance of the zone of transition where different worlds rub up against one another, languages intersect on every corner, and psychotics jabber in the street" (2009, p. 116). New arrivals could congratulate themselves for living in such an alive, "edgy" locale, but as Wright mordantly put it;

> Older waves of gentrification were sometimes justified on the grounds that they helped upgrade whole areas, but in Spitalfields the visible signs of what used to be deplored as "inequality" are re-established as cultural exotica – a diverting performance in the retinal theatre of the incoming *flâneur*.
>
> (Wright, 2009, p. 124)

Meanwhile, the old decaying industrial heartlands, semi-derelict mill towns, and decaying seaside resorts of the country were targeted by far right groups intent on capitalising on alienation, anomie, economic decline, and the collapse of older socialist alternatives against the incursions of the market. Here the BNP were obtaining council seats, though still very much a minority and facing fierce local resistances and campaigning. The extremely limited success of the BNP tended, however, to feed into the left liberal narrative of a degraded indigenous working-class population, excoriated for their presumed racism, thus creating the conditions for a self-fulfilling prophecy: the ensuing siege mentality, together with the reluctance of the left to address the more universal issues that were affecting all people of every ethnic background, of class and economics, actually only pushed people further into extremist corners.

Those residual hollowed-out communities of the old industrial heartlands, once the idealised site of heroic labour, now had to contend with cultural denigration as well as social dislocation. In his outlining of this "play of ancient tropes" (1998, p. 161) Samuel notes the vilification of "sink estates" as a repeat of the old fear of the animal-like "lumpen-proletariat" who Charles Booth in *Life and Labour of the People of London* (1892–1897) labelled as the vicious poor, now applied to the contemporary indigenous "underclass". At a wider level:

> The very qualities which had recommended it to the "new wave" writers and filmmakers now served as talismans of narrowness. The rich associational life, such as that of the workingmen's clubs, was seen not as supportive but as excluding, a way in which the natives could keep newcomers and strangers at bay. Likewise pubs, though warm and friendly places to the regulars, took on a quite different perspective when viewed from the perspective of health food fanatics and associated with the horrors of beer gut. The solidarities of the workplace were reconceptualized as a species of male bonding, a license for the subjugation of women; while the smokestack industries which had been the pride of the North now appeared, retrospectively, as ecological nightmares.
>
> (Samuel, 1998, p. 166)

This echoed the way in which some "progressives" in the USA patronised the "backwoods" hinterland of the Bible belt and social conservatives, the pro-life, gun lobby, and the creationist right – as if it went without saying that these people and their views were automatically ignorant, misguided, credulous, wrong, and their own views innately enlightened, tolerant, right, and progressive.

Such pathological splitting, the creation of idealised and denigrated polarities, distorted reality and also tended to create self-fulfilling prophecies. The late psychoanalyst, Hanna Segal, (1997) argued that the USA and the Soviet Union needed each other during the Cold War period; needed to set the other up as a foe to its fundamental way of life, and to exaggerate the threat involved, in a mutually collusive defensive system. A kind of deadly equilibrium, achieved at the cost of the threat of mutual nuclear destruction, was achieved. Within these, for Segal, clearly "mad" limitations, the system was stable, and met the mutual needs of both societies. It was easier to unite against a common enemy, an external and essentially unknown other, into whose mystery and menace all the disavowed "bad" aspects of each society could be projected, than look at problems and conflicts within each political system.

Whether there is agreement or not with Segal's specific formulation, it does seem true that political positions which are apparently polarised and diametric opposites, often reveal themselves as mirror images of each other, each projecting on to the other what is inadmissible in its own self-image. This process was exemplified in the liberal reaction to George W Bush being re-elected as American president in 2004. For some, this was a fundamental split of seismic proportions. Some liberals had woken up and found themselves in an alien country, about to float off from New York and California into the Atlantic and Pacific oceans. They took on the mien of an embattled civilised minority, occupying literally and meta-phorically "the coastal fringes" of a great continent, hanging on to the ledges of civilisation and pluralism; as a great alien occupying force conquered the prairies, the wheat-fields, the suburban hinterlands, the executive estates, and the out-of-town shopping malls. This process seemed as inexorable and sinister as the arrival of the alien pods in *The Invasion of the Body Snatchers* (Siegel, 1956).

Liberal commentators bemoaned a change in the nature of the Western world, the triumph of a new right, as alien to them in their illiberal fundamentalism as the Muslim fundamentalists who were blowing American soldiers – and Iraqi civil-ians – into little pieces with roadside bombs and detonated cars. American Bush-haters in the UK held placards saying "Sorry!" In actual fact it was the social conservatism of this apparent swathe of America, rather than nihilistic terrorism that earned the most opprobrium from what had by now become the self-styled "liberal left".

The USA was now represented by a right-wing Christian fundamentalist heart-land, the interior; protecting your own, at home and abroad, were the dominant values. In such a narrative these irredeemably conservative voters were for low taxes and against government spending, for traditional marriage and against abor-tion, for the war on terror and against "being soft" on miscreants. Living in the outer suburbs and heartlands of the interior, they sanctified belief, and conviction, rather than scientific and objective appraisal of the facts; some were creation-ists. The response of left liberals in the USA, and, increasingly the UK, was, in a mirror-image of the certainty of the fundamentalist right, to bellicosely assert their tolerant, rationalist, secular, Enlightenment values, and their social progres-siveness – contrasting their own tolerance with the narrow-mindedness of the conservative heartlands.

There was, of course, a degree of truth to these attributions; there were, and are, reactionary swathes of opinion, intolerance, and prejudice, running the gauntlet from the "tea party" conservatives to pathological right-wing extremism. These forces existed and have come to light again in the form of the "Alt Right", and they require vigorous and unflagging opposition. This is not, though, the cen-tral issue. The problem was that in some liberal narratives the mass of ordinary "conservative" people tended to be tainted with the same brush as the extremists, and their concerns and values minimised and denigrated, dismissed as merely the product of prejudice and/or ignorance. It has been said that the "neo-cons" had to create and exaggerate the threat of Islamic fundamentalism, in order to create a raison d'être for their own existence, and to cement their power. It might be said that some left liberals have also exaggerated the power of the neo-cons and Chris-tian fundamentalists to cement theirs, in the absence of a robust ideology of their own, and in the face of their own adherence to the individualist orthodoxies of market capitalism, orthodoxies that themselves have a consequence of producing greater social inequality; in other words, of producing the very circumstances that fuel right-wing extremism in the first place.

The reality was that this "embattled" left-liberal position was both narcissistically self-serving, and from the perspective of pragmatic politics, counter-productive. That is, this fear tended to become a self-fulfilling prophecy. Moralistically tinged attacks on the values of Middle America, substituting for a more universal socio-economic critique of consumer capitalism and economic individualism, tended to provoke, in turn, a besieged and defensive response. The difference between the Democratic and Republican states was as much about class, economics, land use and ownership, the tension between the city, its hinterlands and the countryside, as it was about the cultural attitudes over which "cultural wars" took place. Moreover, the fatuous and patronising nature of some "progressive left" characterisation of ordinary Americans as irredeemably reactionary and racist, and so on, was exposed in 2009; Barack Obama could only have been elected by receiving substantial support from across all the geographical, class, and racial sections of American society – as occurred again with his re-election. The election of Donald Trump in 2016 demonstrates the salutary reality that these situations are dynamic, and are influenced by contingent historical factors and, particularly, by the quality of available political analysis and leadership.

In this chapter I have offered a psychoanalytically informed political personal view of the vicissitudes of the left and of progressive opinion after the fall of Communism. My analysis only refers to certain trends and does not attempt to provide a total picture – there were, and are, many more adaptive responses. Nevertheless, there is little doubt that the fall of Communism also brought to a head a crisis of the social democratic left. The abandoning, amongst some sections of radical opinion, of the universalist socio-economic traditions of the left, and the critical rationalist epistemology derived from the bourgeois Enlightenment, for the subjectivist politics of identity, was a major symptom of this crisis.

In the next part of the book I look at this move towards subjectivism. I begin with the psychological correlate of this shift: the emergence, and increasing dominance, in the West, of what Christopher Lasch has famously termed a "culture of narcissism".

Chapter 13

A culture of narcissism?

We have seen earlier that personality and character arise out of the infinitely complex interaction of temperament and environment, the internalisation of the interpersonal and socio-cultural environment not necessarily simply as it is but under the influence of powerful emotions and projective processes. Whilst it is essential to look at the interplay of specific intrapsychic and intrapersonal dynamics there are also wider socio-cultural and ideological considerations.

Christopher Lasch (1977, 1979) contended that studies from cultural anthropologists, sociologists, and psychoanalysts, regarding the impact of culture on personality show that "every culture works out distinctive patterns of child rearing and socialization, with the effect of producing a distinctive personality type suited to the requirements of that culture" (1979, p. 238). In the early era of "high capitalism", the dominant and most adaptive character type was that associated with thrift, living within your means, modesty, sobriety, and planning for the future. These were puritan values associated with living in a state of grace in relation to a more personal God, a process that was individualised and unmediated by collective institutions:

> The Protestant concept of the calling not only dignified worldly life, it insisted on the moral value of work, and legitimized prudent calculation and provision for the future, it also upheld the spiritual dignity of marriage and domesticity … The new style of domestic life created psychological conditions favorable to the emergence of a new type of inner-directed, self-reliant personality–the family's deepest contribution to the needs of a market society based on competition, individualism, postponement of gratification, rational foresight, and the accumulation of worldly goods.
>
> (1977, p. 4)

In psychoanalytic terms, the dominant character structure in such societies was therefore centred on repression, socialisation within the family, and the internalisation of strong moral values, discipline, responsibility, the capacity for delaying gratification, and so on – also useful values in the workplace. However, in the late capitalist world in the West, productive work was being increasingly outsourced to less expensive locations. And, whereas in the past, personality had been formed upon a temperamental substrate, through a complex series of largely unconscious identifications within the family, these structures were now under attack. Technological change and the incursions of commodity value rendered local traditions obsolete. At the same time there was an undercutting of traditional paternal authority. Lasch noted that the role of the father was under threat of instant obsolescence, not only within the family but also within the everyday social and work milieu:

> The deeper psychological significance of paternal training lies in its capacity to temper the child's fantasies with practical experience, softening the early experience of an omnipotent, wrathful, and punitive father. If the son is to overcome his jealous hatred of the father, the terrifying figure of the father has to be reduced by daily contact, in the course of which the father establishes himself in his son's affections by his mastery of the skills and techniques the son also needs to master. The modern father finds it difficult to provide this information. Such skills as he possesses becomes technologically obsolete in his own lifetime, and there would be little point in transmitting them to his children even if he had a chance to do so.
>
> (1977, pp. 123–124)

At the same time, in the USA, there was a post-war crusade by mental health, mental hygiene, counsellors, marriage guidance, psychiatrists, health visitors, and social workers; all emphasising humanistic values of self-acceptance, personal authenticity, self-realisation, and spontaneity in opposition to the dehumanising and atomising effects of industrial society. The ideology of these movements

> promoted a "democratic" conception of domestic life, advocated permissive child rearing, defended the rights of women, attacked sexual repression and censorship, and sought to make the members of the family more responsive to each other's emotional needs, more skilled at communicating their own, and more adept, in short, in the art of interpersonal relations.
>
> (Lasch, 1977, p. 102)

Lasch suggested that local autonomous traditions, often involving resilience against the vagaries of the market, were thus undercut from "both sides" – by the ubiquitous commodification that accompanied consumer capitalism, and from the intrusions of the helping professions and a therapeutic, or rather a "pseudo-therapeutic", culture, from which the radical pessimism of Freud and the psychoanalytic tradition had been surgically removed. Meanwhile, Lasch argued, therapeutic modes of thought and practice, promulgated by the "progressive state", translated collective grievances into personal problems, leading to the disempowerment and impoverishment of more local traditions of self-help and collective resilience, as human relating skills become professionalised, commodified, and "exported" out from depleted communities. They also allied themselves with those forces rendering obsolete parental, and in particular paternal, authority:

> The propaganda of commodities ... undermined puritanical morality and patriarchal authority, subtly allying itself with women against men, children against parents.
>
> (Lasch, 1977, pp. 19–20)

Lasch made the point that "radical" critics were still bemoaning the consequences of industrial modernity, mass society, and patriarchal structures, when these were already being made obsolescent by changes in the nature of capitalism. As we have already seen, for example, the Frankfurt School had tried to link patriarchal family structure, based on repression, to the "authoritarian personality" and to the rise of Fascism when, according to Lasch:

> The dependence of fascism on the family is purely rhetorical and sentimental. Itself the product, in part, of the decay of patriarchal authority, fascism rules not through conscience and guilt but through terror, psychological manipulation, and primitive loyalty to the blood brotherhood.
>
> (1977, p. 91)

Thus left-wing critics, acolytes of a new "therapeutic culture", bemoaned the authoritarian nature of the patriarchal family, itself in part a pre-capitalist institution, as a bastion of reaction, at a time of the dissolution of such a family structure. As Lasch reminds: "Minerva's owl flew out at dusk" (1977, p. 91).

The result of these socio-cultural transformations, he argued, was "that many normal people now displayed many of the same personality traits that appeared, in more extreme form, in pathological narcissism" (Lasch, 1979, p. 239). If in the older personality type the dominant defence was repression (leading to a more neurotic personality structure) then in the contemporary narcissistic personality different, radically split, versions of self and others co-existed without meaningful integration, and usually without in-depth relations with others. Rather, despite loud emoting, everything was on the surface. The default emotional position was not depression, or internal conflict, but emptiness. There was, typically, a strong affiliation with peers, and a difficulty in tolerating solitude. Despite an emphasis on personal authenticity, there was a lack of introspection, and of respect for the separate experience of others. There was, typically, an almost total alienation from the past.

> The prevailing social conditions thus brought out narcissistic personality traits that were present, in varying degrees, in everyone – a certain protective shallowness, a fear of binding commitments, a willingness to pull up roots whenever the need arose, a desire to keep one's options open, a dislike of depending on anyone, an incapacity for loyalty or gratitude.
>
> (Lasch, 1979, p. 239)

Such characteristics were adaptive to the requirements of the market, and also defensive responses to a world felt as no longer the "work of men", but as terrifying, autonomous, and out-of-control. Thus narcissistic modes of thought and relating, Lasch suggested, characterised both the advocates of free-market capitalism and nominally "anti-capitalist" counter-culture movements. On the one hand, this might be expressed as omniscient ideas of conquering external reality through technology, through the Promethean endeavours of science. A disembodied and autonomous man conquering dependency, the physical body, and even death now seemed possible. On the other hand, the inherent limitations, losses, and disappointments of external reality could be circumvented by resource to bountiful nature, to fantasies of fusion with an all-providing symbiotic mother. Lasch saw these fantasies as characteristic of counter-culture "new age" spiritual movements, with their celebration of id over ego, of "oneness" with the world; and their undiscriminating denigration of the "authoritarian" paternal order, and of scientific knowledge:

> Strategies of narcissistic survival now present themselves as emancipation from the repressive conditions of the past, thus giving rise to a "cultural revolution" that reproduces the worst features of the collapsing civilization it aims to criticize. Cultural radicalism has become so fashionable, and so pernicious in the support it unwittingly provides for the status quo, that any criticism of contemporary society that hopes to get beneath the surface has to criticize, at the same time, much of what currently goes under the name of radicalism.
> (Lasch, 1979, pp. xv-xvi)

Such a picture echoes the thoughts of Norman Cohn (1957) on the historical recurrences of millennial thinking. Cohn, in a new edition of his study of millenialism, suggested that mainstream groups on the post-war political left have been predominately practical and governed by politically achievable goals. The appeal of millennial and apocalyptic ideas has primarily been to those societies which are both poor and overcrowded, and which are in the dislocating and alienating throes of an uneasy transition to modernity. Such ideas also appealed, however, to a minority in the developed world, to politically marginal sections of the population, the unemployed and déclassé, and a small number of intellectuals and students. Cohn also made a link with aspects of the radical counter-culture of the time, with those individuals and groups who seek "total emancipation of the individual from society, even from external reality itself". He concludes that "stripped of their original supernatural sanction, revolutionary millennialism and mystical anarchism are with us still" (1957, p. 286).

Lasch's analysis, for its part, was rooted in a specific historical time and place, the America of the 1970s and 1980s, and though influential has been criticised for its "idealisation" of the family and of small-town tradition, in other words for Lasch's alleged "left conservatism". There may be some justice to this and there are aspects of Lasch's analysis that have inevitably dated. Nevertheless,

I believe that his observations remain central to any understanding of powerful psychological, emotional, and intellectual trends in contemporary life. Indeed in a more recent work Susan Long (2008) has gone further than Lasch and argued that some aspects of late capitalism, certainly in its corporate form, are fundamentally perverse. She asserts that there is a splitting of perception, and a willful blind eye turned towards aspects of the truth, and systemic corruption amongst organisations. Long's analysis certainly appears to have been apposite at the time of the credit crunch, where the perversity of areas of "creative" financial activity, siphoned off from the real economy, was exposed like the Emperor's new clothes. However, it is Lasch's contention that narcissistic traits permeate much that is considered radical and "oppositional" in late capitalist society that I believe may be his most important insight.

In the next chapter I draw on my professional experience of mental health care and psychotherapy in the light of what I suggest, following Lasch, are narcissistic trends existing across the political spectrum. The reconceptualising of the "patient" as a "consumer" of "mental health services", promising liberation from the old "paternalistic" doctor/patient model, represented the coming together of the free-market commodity capitalism, and ostensibly progressive ideologies of personal empowerment. I outline the way in which the therapeutic role of the nurse was downplayed to that of a "care provider", and the way in which a consumer model of human relating failed to account for the way in which patients' difficulties are manifest not simply as symptoms but as a relational pattern. I discuss the way in which effective care embodies both maternal and paternal aspects, the provision of empathy, but also the assertion of limits and structure. However, in generic care, and in some of the newer psychotherapeutic approaches, there was a moving away from this oedipal structuring of care, and a tendency to move towards the dyadic world of thin-skinned narcissism, that is, toward the notion of a perfectly attuned therapist.

Chapter 14

Marketisation and subjectivism in mental health care

The importance of the paternal function

In recent years, in line with the trends outlined in the previous chapters, there has been a gradual permeation of market-consumer models of human relations into mental health care. This has been partially determined by government policy and economics, but also reflects an ideological shift away from those more traditional forms of care seen as "institutional", "paternalistic", and "oppressive". There has been any number of books and articles delineating the shift from institutional care, associated with the old asylums and held to be oppressive and dehumanising, to something called "community care", or "care in the community". I trained as a psychiatric nurse in one of these old institutions in its last days. The Victorian hospital had been built in what had then been the green outskirts of the city, though it was now increasingly surrounded by suburban housing (housing that would soon penetrate the perimeter walls). Aspiring young professionals going out on a nightly jog might find themselves, if they were not careful, restrained by burly nurses searching in the dark for an absconded patient. There were acres of walled garden, a full-time gardening team, and a large industrial workshop. Industrial therapy was in its last days, and the setting was indeed paternal and institutional. The nurse in charge, himself an odd and eccentric-seeming individual, would call out "Juice!" every 10.30am, as the insipid watery jugs of orange arrived on a trolley. Soon, industrial therapy was, alongside the asylums themselves, cast into oblivion and history, as an anachronistic and inappropriate exploitation of the labours of the patient.

As is well known, a policy of helping all but the most extremely disabled live in a sometimes idealised "community" replaced the old institutions. In part this was determined by humane aspiration, in part by the need to cut costs. Clinically, it was made possible by the revolution, started in the 1950s, in psychotropic drug treatment of the severely mentally ill, a revolution that allowed people to live relatively symptom free for longer periods of time. The "patient" was redefined as a "client", "service user", "consumer", or even as a "survivor" of mental health services. These changes were also influenced by upward pressure from patient groups and advocates, representing a welcome push for a patient voice in the delivery, structure, and range of services on offer.

There were many positive aspects to the changes in mental health policy and provision; the wish to work in a more holistic and joined-up way, integrating psychiatric and social care, the need for consistent and coherent treatment models linked to research and best evidence, the desire for the patient to be at the centre of treatment and to have a voice in this, and the provision of treatment that would involve the least restrictive option. The need for increased psychological intervention in mental health (a regular consumer demand) was emphasised by the Layard Report (LSE, 2006), leading to an increase in primary care and other community settings of therapists trained in cognitive techniques. This was an important step forward in the provision of a range of psycho-social as well as medical interventions for people with mental health problems.

However, there were some problems, too. There was originally a positive aspect to the idea of "asylum". It was not just that these institutions existed to remove those rightly (and also often wrongly) designated as "mentally ill" from "normal" society, casualties and exiles from the atomised and alienating new mass-industrial society; but the idea that a "retreat" (the name of a famous Quaker asylum in York) from the stresses and strains of the world could offer time for recuperation, and eventual recovery. There had been, in the nineteenth century, the progressive idea of humane, moral treatment of the emotionally unwell. Indeed, it was clear that the old hospitals were themselves communities, with a containing function for both patients and staff. As the psychiatrist and psychoanalyst Henry Rey (1994) said of the Maudsley Hospital in South London, it was "a brick mother". Moreover, for some debilitated patients the opportunity for structured and relatively undemanding work – the excoriated industrial therapy – with the limited social contact this afforded, was indeed therapeutic, and there was little opportunity for this in "the community".

Increasingly, in a process that has continued ever since, only the most disturbed patients were offered intensive intervention in the NHS. This led, along with the socio-cultural changes that are one of the main subjects of this book, to a change in the kind of patients being seen in the psychiatric settings. When I started my psychiatric nursing training, in acute psychiatric in-patient wards in the mid-1980s, there were patients with neurotic difficulties straight from psychoanalytic textbooks, with conversion disorders, hysterical amnesia, and psychogenic paralysis of the limbs. There were patients with acute melancholia. In short, one saw some of the same neurotic problems described by Freud in Vienna at the turn of the century, in the west end of Newcastle, nearly a hundred years later. There were also people experiencing "reactive" or "biological" depression or bi-polar mood disorder. There were people suffering from psychogenic psychosis, or the defect states of schizophrenia. All of these presentations, though often difficult, were to be expected, and were in accordance with our training. The majority of patients were informal and, in my experience at least, the episodes of violence and gross behavioural disturbance were relatively rare.

Increasingly, however, in NHS mental health services, as wider health service and socio-cultural changes took hold, there was a prevalence of people presenting with, "complex, severe, and enduring" mental disorders. Many patients were diagnosed with what was called "co-morbidity": a formal psychiatric "axis 1"

disorder complicated by an underlying personality disorder, frequently of a narcissistic, borderline, or anti-social type. Whilst there are conceptual difficulties
with these phenomological classificatory systems, it is probably fair to say that
an increasing number of patients seen in formal mental health settings presented,
whether formally diagnosed or not, with the narcissistic, borderline, schizoid,
paranoid, and dis-social manifestations of an underlying "borderline personality
organisation". Often coming from extremely disturbed and deprived family and
socio-economic backgrounds, their disturbed and sometimes threatening presentation was frequently complicated by substance and alcohol abuse. There was a
change in atmosphere on the wards, they seemed to become more frightening and
violent places, with higher levels of disinhibition. There were more instances of
what Michael Balint (1968) had called "malignant regression", where breakdown
appeared to be infused with a sadistic wish towards treatment, as opposed to those
situations from where emotional regression, as a concomitant of serious mental
illness, may be in the service of recovery.

The best psychiatric staff have the knack of being able to stay with people in
distress, and to accept, and contain, the violent projection of feelings without too
much distancing, or too much retaliation. To do this requires personal attributes
of resilience, balance, tolerance, and the capacity to exercise appropriate authority, when required. The relationships these staff have with patients, even if they
have had no formal therapeutic training, are deeply therapeutic, and were deeply
undervalued in the new consumer model of "care providers".

In line with the incursion of market forces and consumer models of human
relating, patients were offered "packages of care", rather than "treatment", as they
had been in the bad old paternalist days. In fact, the consumer approach, whilst
bright and shiny and new, seemed imbued with a therapeutic pessimism, as if
treatment was not really an issue. Those psychiatric nurses who were skilled clinicians and able to form therapeutic relationships with disturbed patients increasingly, as their careers advanced, found themselves as "case managers" or "care
co-ordinators", with the relational aspect of the nursing role downplayed. Their
role became increasingly one of brokering this "package of care" for the client.

Thus the modern consumerist models of the individual tended to posit the
self as a rational autonomous agent who, as, for example, in the case of mental
health, is the victim of mental illness (that is, of genetic destiny) on the one
hand, and/or societal stigma and oppressive institutional practices on the other.
These are necessary but not sufficient explanatory factors, as they neglect an
understanding of the way in which the patient's disturbance may be relived as
an unconscious and frequently self-defeating pattern of relating to help. As Jane
Milton remarks:

> This view of human nature sees the application of reason and the right exter-
> nal conditions as sufficient for healing. The assumption is that the patient is
> simply a good and reasonable victim of misunderstanding and neglect. Most
> psychoanalysts, in contrast, see man as subject to complex internal conflicts,

and strong tendencies towards unreasonableness – all needing to be understood and addressed in detail.

(2001, pp. 438–439)

As I have discussed, disturbance is manifest not simply as a set of symptoms but as a relational pattern. One example of this is of those patients who externalise an intra-psychic and interpersonal claustro-agoraphobic (Glasser, 1979, 1998; Rey, 1994) dilemma in their relationship with the psychiatric system. Feelings of distance from others leads to profound feelings of loneliness, isolation, and/or abandonment, and the desire to get closer. Intense neediness is projected into the needed other who is then experienced as engulfing and annihilatory of the self and of identity. The person then moves away from any wished for but threatening closeness, begins to feel lonely, looks to get closer, and the cycle starts all over again.

The psychiatric services are likely to get recruited into such an interactional scenario. Indeed, the patient is likely to seek help when their status quo or psychic equilibrium has been disrupted by other people in their lives getting too close, or too distant. Their hope in seeking help is not necessarily to understand, but to restore the equilibrium. This might be achieved by a quick admission and be threatened again by the prospect of intensive psychological treatment, leading to a claustrophobic reaction, or by discharge, leading to an agoraphobic one.

The traditional psychiatric day hospital, in which I had been working in east London, changed its function to become a new acute day service for people with acute mental illness. Several long-established patients of the old day service had breakdowns when they were discharged, despite the fact that some of them were not really actively involved with treatment. In perhaps a similar way, some patients do well on a psychotherapy waiting list but deteriorate when either being discharged from or taken into treatment. There are patients who cannot tolerate the intensity of regular treatment but benefit from the opportunity for periodic contact, the chance to meaningfully talk with someone, not simply as a review of medication and so on, but a chance to explore emotional difficulties and life problems. For years this was the valuable task of good psychiatrists and community psychiatric nurses – to offer good supportive intervention for people with longer-term vulnerabilities without necessarily expecting significant change.

These essential roles have become devalued, however, and hospital managers, pressurised by cost and the need to demonstrate results, were unable to grasp the essential containing function of such long-term interventions, a function that was also, incidentally, highly cost-effective. This was an example of the way in which good mental health care (which, after all, is dealing with emotional and frequently unconscious processes) is often counter-intuitive. Common sense is certainly necessary, but it is not sufficient.

In psychiatric systems it can frequently be the case, for example, that the more the service gets involved, the more help they offer, the more they try to be reasonable and to "understand", the worse the patient gets. People's attempts to delineate a problem, and to respond helpfully, do not work. Indeed, the patient may get significantly worse, and the worker more anxious – not least because the repara-tive drive to do good, and to help, has been frustrated. This might lead to anxiety, because what is instead unleashed is irritability, gradually shot through with aggres-sion and hate. A sado-masochistic relationship gets enacted, and in the context of modern consumerist notions of "care co-ordination" and "packages of care", it can be difficult for mental health workers to find a language to address these processes.

In some situations a consumer-client model of mental health care can collude with a sense of pathological entitlement, and buttress omnipotent states of minds in which regressed needs can be met by a system that promised to "meet people's needs", thus avoiding the loss and disappointment that are central to development. A patient managed to secure, through her care package, two simultaneous psycho-logical therapies, in so doing repeating an oedipal dynamic in which she felt able to simultaneously maintain an exclusive dyadic relationship with both parents, without facing exclusion and loss, a situation that lead to a state of manic triumphalism but also to a therapeutic impasse. There can be a confusion between what the patient wants and desires, and what she may actually need, which may be a quite different matter. This brings in the issues of conflict between provider and customer, and the reality that the customer, in this instance, may not always be right.

A particular relational dynamic amongst patients with narcissistic-type diffi-culties – a pattern that can be chronic and seriously impact, for example, on the effectiveness of generic psychiatric or medical treatment – is that the help on offer is denigrated and treated with implicit or explicit contempt. This may be partially as a way of defending against the fact that the patient might be dependent upon another human being who has things that they need and want, a situation that may induce intense anxiety and intense envy of the other, also accompanied by fear of feelings of shame and vulnerability.

The question as to where responsibility is located is important, as responsibil-ity for life and development may be projected into the therapist and the treatment situation, leaving the patient identified with a more destructive part of the self. In this way, an internal conflict has been externalised, and this may lead to the patient sabotaging and/or attacking attempts to help. This can have an exciting addictive quality and can push the system into omnipotently seeking to take all control. The desire for improvement, development, and for life then becomes a priority of the system, or a defensive response, as seen by the patient, rather than what the patient is seeking himself. In other words, the impulse towards life and develop-ment is projectively identified with the system, leaving the patient identified with something more destructive and deadly. An internal object relationship has been externalised and enacted with the system, or the therapist.

On the other hand, a recognition of aggressive and destructive impulses can reassure the patient that something is being faced. The patient is helped, too, by the presence of a therapist or a mental health worker who is robust and resilient in the face of these processes, and who he feels can tolerate knowing about these impulses and parts of the self without becoming overwhelmed, who can resist the pressure to take over control and responsibility. This brings me to the importance

of applied psychoanalysis – psychoanalytic psychotherapy and modern derivatives – in the public sector. In this setting, the patient's core personality difficulties
may emerge, not as a set of problems "out there", but embedded in the relationship between therapist and the patient. The therapist has been termed a "partici-
pant observer" in this unfolding process, in which they will inevitably be subject
to the projections, anxieties, longings, and hatreds of the patient. The predictability and continuity of this setting then serve to create a live culture in which there
is the possibility of emotional learning; very different from the conscious striving
for change, or the adoption of cognitive strategies, or even the achievement of
conscious intellectual insight. This process can, of course, take time.

   Psychoanalytic psychotherapy, or practical derivations from it – such as
mentalization-based therapy (MBT) (Allen & Fonagy, 2006) and transference-
focused psychotherapy (TFP) (Yeomans et al., 2015), both aimed at increasing
reflective functioning, the latter also aiming at structural personality change and
integration – are important as discrete treatment options. However, not every
patient is going to need or be able to use formal psychoanalytic psychotherapy, or
other forms of therapeutic intervention. Therefore, as essential to the provision of
effective treatment is the integration of psychoanalytic understandings into psychiatry and generic mental health care; to have an awareness of the importance of
a triangular oedipal structure around the parameters of care, and of the importance
of providing a reflective space for both patients and staff.

   As we have seen, the patient brings his disturbance as a set of internal object
relations to be re-enacted with others, with professionals, and with the psychiatric
system. Staff, and the system as a whole, are inevitably, and necessarily, part of
this complex dynamic. As Glen Gabbard (1994) writes:

> Projective identification operates unconsciously, automatically and with com-
> pelling force. Clinicians feel "bullied" or coerced into complying with the
> role that has been projectively attributed to them. A basic axiom of psycho-
> dynamically informed treatment acknowledges that staff members are more
> similar to patients than different from them. The feelings, fantasies, identi-
> fications and introjections within patients have their counterparts in treat-
> ers. Because those counterparts may be more strongly repressed in staff ...
> they often are experienced as alien forces sweeping over the treater.
>
> (2005, p. 160)

   In Gabbard's terms, staff, in the face of this, can seek to try and understand
what is going on in terms of the core emotional conflicts of the patient, or can
find themselves simply joining in the dance. The main "work" then, is in the team
members' acknowledgement of their own feelings in relation to the patient, and
their different propensities – depending their own backgrounds, personalities, and
experiences – to identify with different projections from the patient. The team
might then be able to provide a containing space in which the projected, fragmented, dissociated, and split-off aspects of the patient's experience can come

together in a more integrated and comprehensible way. And while the patient may not be able, or willing, to hold these aspects of the self together in a more integrated way, it can be the case that if the team, or the therapist, can perform this containing function (without necessarily offering interpretations to the patient – interpretations that the patient in any case is not in a position to hear), there might be the beginnings of a shift. At the very least, with an effective reflective space (where the team might meet, for example, with an external consultant), there is more chance that team members can, for example, address the patient's destructiveness from a position of enquiry and concern, rather than from a position of unacknowledged retaliatory anger; or, more likely, from a position of complete avoidance of taking up the issue for fear of this anger emerging in themselves.

Implicit in this consultative approach is an attempt to maintain an oedipal structure, rather than collapse into a dyadic situation. The clinical rationale for this relates to treatment embodying both maternal and paternal functioning, the symbolic role of the father providing a model for identification and an alternative source of help in the face of the regressive pull towards the maternal object, as sometimes expressed by a hostile and dependent relationship in which there has been a treatment impasse or deterioration. In this way, psychoanalytic understanding and practice can also be embedded in generic psychiatric care, and might, through the understanding of personality development and the dynamics of relations with health-care systems, help inform treatment of different modalities, and underpin organisational structure and systems. I am emphasising here the need to maintain boundaries and limits to treatment, in short to maintain an oedipal structure. It is this attention to structure and setting that helps maintain a reflective space. Given that it is not always possible to create such a space in direct work with the patients themselves, it is all the more important to develop and maintain this reflective space within the treatment team.

Such a concentration on the oedipal structure; the linking of maternal and paternal qualities; the capacity to, as far as possible empathise and stay with the patient's experience without undue distance and/or retaliation; to set realistic limits and parameters of treatment; and to exercise benign authority, was though, increasingly out of kilter with the spirit of the times. Rather, in a highly subjectivist "therapeutic" culture, there was an idealisation of empathy and a denigration of paternal functioning, a difficulty in distinguishing between benign and malign authority. It is to these subjects and their relationship with those wider sociocultural shifts associated with postmodernism and hyper-subjectivism that I turn in the next chapter.

Chapter 15

From dyadic to triadic

The postmodern turn in psychotherapy

I have commented in earlier chapters on the notable contemporary cultural antipathy towards Freud and psychoanalysis. The paradox that the attacks on Freud and the psychoanalytic tradition have been occurring in what Philip Rieff (1966) has termed a "therapeutic" culture in the West is only an apparent one. For whereas classical psychoanalysis stressed that the self is inherently fragmented, that some degree of suffering and conflict is intrinsic to human nature, and that some degree of guilt is both psychologically justified and necessary, newer approaches stressed holism, emotional openness, freedom from inhibition, in a way that appeared to chime with the increased individualism of the times, a trend that was further evident in the proliferation of books on self-help, and positive thinking.

By contrast, psychoanalysis stresses the developmental importance of facing the reality of limitation and loss, and the impossibility of "self-actualisation". In *Beyond the Pleasure Principle* (1920g) Freud famously described a little boy playing with a ball and string as a way of representing and mastering his feelings about his mother's absence, and as "related to the child's greatest cultural achievement – the instinctual renunciation which he has made in allowing his mother to go away without protesting". Writing of the "Moses of Michelangelo" (1914b) he sees Moses as an artistic representation "of the highest mental achievement that is possible in a man, that of struggling successfully against an inward passion for the sake of a cause for which he has devoted himself" (1914b, p. 233). Thus, the relationship between the individual and the social world contains inherent tension and conflict, of which there can never be a full resolution, between reality as it is, and as it is wished to be. Freud saw the instinctual renunciations inherent in the dissolution of the Oedipus complex, in particular the setting up of the superego, with the powerful effect of guilt, as a central to human civilisation – at the cost of a certain degree of inherent conflict and suffering.

In late capitalist culture, however, there is an emphasis on the realisation of desire that goes far beyond Freud's more modest aim of "the transformation of neurotic miseries into common unhappiness" (Freud 1895d, p. 305). As Rob Weatherill (1995) writes: "One wants a better life materially and one's emotional life must become much more exciting and gratifying too" (1995, p. 153), and "the new psychotherapeutic ethic, unlike religion, is flexible, adaptable, essentially populist and client centred" (1995, p. 153). Such a programme was also "totally compatible with capitalism" (1995, p. 153), at least when removed from those awkward Freudian emphases on inherent conflict within the psyche, and between the individual and society, and the need to accept the limitations of biology and reality. As Wetherill notes, "If everything is potentially commmodifiable, why not make a commodity of the self – an ideal self – *psychologically and spiritually?*" (1995, p. 153). It is, of course, in the face of the contemporary injunction to "Enjoy!", one of the salutary truths of the "traditional" psychoanalytic perspective on human nature that we are inevitably divided within ourselves, that we cannot always be "who we want to be", and that though we have multiple unconscious identifications, these are often conflicting. We cannot be everything, and each choice also necessitates a loss. Nor, though we can try, can we simply get rid of parts of the self we do not like.

In the practice of counselling and psychotherapy there has been, as a concomitant of these pseudo-therapies, considerable social, political, and personal pressure to be an idealising and idealised "good object", attentive, empathic, non-discriminatory, and sensitive. In the literature, for example, from mainstream non-analytic counselling and psychotherapy journals, there is exhaustive attention to the importance of not, implicitly or explicitly, "imposing" a view of the world on the other. In these journals there are – and I could quote numerous examples of this – frequent expressions of personal and collective guilt, at times amounting to masochistic self-recrimination and breast-beating, at failures of empathy and non-discriminatory practice, to the unconscious imposition of a "Eurocentric" or "paternalistic" world-view on the potentially re-traumatised client. There appears, too, in the wider progressive milieu, an anxious concern with not giving offence, or being seen as being judgmental in any way, reflecting an anxiety about exercising any authority. This sometimes creates a kind of stultifying emotional correctness in public discourse and a rather forced and inauthentic "empathic" attitude.

Stefan Bolognini (1997) has pointed out that empathy cannot be forced as an attitude, or employed as a method. It cannot arise *cito, tuto, et incunde* (quickly, safely, and agreeably). If so employed in psychotherapy, for example, empathy becomes restricted to fitting the patient's conscious expectations and needs. This may lead to the avoidance of painful truths about himself that the patient may be narcissistically resisting, and to the creation of an idealised dyadic situation, which then becomes held as a beacon of light in the darkness of a malignantly misunderstanding world. In such a situation the psychotherapeutic treatment itself may form an addictive component of a psychic retreat against life.

The more "traditional" psychoanalytic stance runs against the above cultural trend and therein lies its value. It is a stance that is hard to maintain because it is difficult not to moderate, or relieve, or seek to distance oneself from the more uncomfortable projections and communications of the patient. Jane Milton (2001) notes the way that it is possible to be nudged into being more supportive, more educative, and that this may get the therapist away from the uncomfortable feeling of being a bad object for the patient, unable to provide the guidance that he might want, or the relationship he never had. If this analytic stance is collapsed into something more educative or supportive, then immediate anxiety might be ame-liorated, but the opportunity for a new experience may be lost. If, for example, the therapist or worker strives to be therapeutic and empathically attuned to an abnor-mal degree, then he might be temporarily spared the imprecations that fall upon being a failing therapist, but he will have by-passed the opportunity for the patient having to face disappointment – spared the simple but necessary disillusionment that may occur when the therapist, as he must, gets it wrong.

These cultural schisms also influence the way in which mental illness and per-sonality are conceptualised, and, in particular, permeate debate about the underly-ing causes. From most current psychiatric and psychoanalytic perspectives, the prevalence of serious emotional and personality difficulties in any individual is multi-determined, and includes both constitutional and environmental factors. As we have seen, biology and inherent temperament are in a dynamic reciprocal interaction with the lived environment, and for some people the pathogenic factor may be predominately in the environment, whilst for others it may be predomi-nately temperamental, but given the interaction of these factors from the onset of life it can never be exclusively one or the other.

The individual is not a *tabula rasa*, and every individual has a unique genetic, biological, and temperamental endowment. This means that individuals will respond to similar environmental stressors and opportunities differently, and that, for example, the pathogenic impact of trauma cannot be assumed. However, at the same time, the individual's biologically primed potentialities need activation by requisite experience, of a reasonable environment and human care, not "perfect" (which would preclude psychologically necessary disillusionment and would itself would be pathogenic of real development) but good enough. As Mark Solms and Oliver Turnbull point out:

> Environmental and genetic influences are *absolutely inextricable*. The geno-type (the design according to which you are built) is open to a wide variety of manipulations, as it expresses itself in a particular environmental context, which in turn shapes the phenotype ("you" yourself).

> (2002, p. 238)

Despite the unexceptionable common sense of this position, there has neverthe-less continued to be a fundamental tension between predominately environmental and predominately biological accounts of mental distress and disorder, and per-sonality pathology. The aetiological accounts of narcissism, for example, as, on the one hand, the result of innate antipathy to otherness, and, on the other, as a defensive response to environmental trauma or loss, continue to this day, and are implicit in the origins of the term. As Britton (1998, p. 170) points out, Ovid's account of the beautiful youth Narcissus, who rejects all suitors and falls in love with his own reflection, is a solipsistic account of narcissism in which the self-love is primary, accompanied by an innate antipathy and fundamental hostility to the existence of others, with a cautionary tragic and self-destructive outcome. Narcissus ignores Echo, and turning to his ideal self, reflected in the water, can only pine away and die. In the alternative version of the myth, recalled by Pausanias, a Greek traveller and writer, Narcissus was reminded of his beloved dead sister when he looked at his reflection. This second version is, in Britton's terms, a traumatic account, in that the narcissistic development is in response to the traumatic loss of his sister.

Some psychoanalytic accounts side with Ovid; there is a view that in severe narcissistic states there is at root an *innate* hostility to otherness, and to engaging with difference, and with other people, and that this hostility is *primary*. For Britton (1998), there may be at work an innate temperamental disposition against the experience of otherness, of separateness, and desire for the perfectly attuned maternal object. For Kernberg (1984), too, the powerful affective storms that underpin borderline and narcissistic psychopathology are related to constitutional temperamental endowment and may be primary, that is, ontologically prior to any environmental deficits or traumas. Recent research on borderline personality disorder has tended to support this view, suggesting a partially hardwired neurobiological predisposition linked to hypersensitivity of the amygdale to even neutral stimuli. For Peter Fonagy and colleagues (Fonagy et al., 2002), though, as we have seen, there may be a temperamental substrate to emotional difficulties, development is inescapably intersubjective, and there is a need for another available and attuned mind with whom to identify. Emotional deprivation and lack of an attuned reciprocal response can exacerbate underlying temperamental vulnerabilities.

In contrast to the complex dialectic between body/mind and early experience and relationships inherent in the approach of Britton, Fonagy, and Kernberg, for example, many contemporary approaches in mental health, social policy, and in some schools of psychotherapy and counselling appear to persist in seeing people with serious personality disturbance as the simple victims of social trauma; or, in a more subtle though still reductive analysis, the emotional impingements and failings of parents. They side with Pausanias. We can hear in this, perhaps, an echo of Lasch's (1977, 1979) account of developments in America dating from the post-war era and the 1950s, or David Reiff's (1991) description of victim culture, another version of a pathological split in existence since the era of romanticism. What is bad is identified at the macro level with the dehumanising industrial society, with traditional structures of authority – including sometimes the family itself. The good is identified with the innocent child or individual, subject as he is to the inevitabilities of trauma and impingement, or less dramatically, maternal misattunement, of being with parents who "invalidate" his experience. Of the newer approaches to psychotherapeutic treatment most appear – from the literature at least – to see the patient's anger as somehow justified by parental or societal failure. They inhabit, that is, a deficit rather than conflict model of the human mind. This appears true of intersubjective approaches, and of Kohutian (Kohut, 1984) self-psychology.

At the level of clinical theory and practice the tension between deficit and conflict models is perhaps best illustrated by looking at the different approaches of Heinz Kohut and Otto Kernberg. The American psychoanalyst Kohut (1984) famously advocated taking an empathic approach to narcissistic patients, and this has been further developed by self-psychology and relational therapeutic approaches. The patient is traumatised, the therapist has to remain sensitive, attuned and empathic to the patient's experience of the world. Kernberg (1984, pp. 182–189) argues, however, that the self-psychology and relational approaches, at least as they are reported in the literature, do not distinguish normal from pathological grandiosity, and accept rather than analyse the grandiose self. These approaches tend to neglect the interpretation of the negative transference, even artificially fostering idealisation, and adopt a supportive re-educative approach, rather than an analytic stance. As such they can lead to patients rationalising their aggressive reactions as the natural result of failures of other people in the past, or of the failure of the therapist or of society; rather than facing their own destructive feelings (as an activation of unconscious aggression towards an earlier internal object). Such an approach ignores aggression in the transference – except as a product of other people's failures.

Kernberg argued (1984) that the self-psychology approach neglects the analysis of the unconscious aspects of the transference, the defensive nature of the patient's conscious experience of the therapist, and the distortions of the psychoanalytic situation that mediate between the conscious present and the unconscious past. This feeds into the patient's tendency to elaborate the past on the basis of an overly conscious reorganisation of that past, a narrative or personal story, rather than the radical reworking of the unconscious past as evolving in the transference relationship.

There is absolutely no doubt that empathy is the core of any therapeutic work, and a prerequisite to any change. Most clinicians would probably concur that Kohut's stance is necessary (though perhaps not sufficient) in the early stages of treatment with some narcissistic patients, particularly those with demonstrable early environmental and/or interpersonal deficits. Kernberg's writing serves as a useful rejoinder, however, to approaches that see the patient too simply as a victim of social trauma. A balance between the two positions is provided by Bolognini who defines psychoanalytic empathy as:

> properly a condition of conscious and pre-conscious contact characterized as separateness, complexity and a linked structure, a wide perceptual spectrum including every colour of the emotional palette, from the highest to the darkest; above all it constitutes a progressive, shared and deep contact with the complementarity of the object, with the other's defensive ego and split off parts no less than with his ego syntonic subjectivity.
>
> (2007, p. 120)

The reality, however, of the clinical impasse that can occur with severely narcissistic patients has been, perhaps, best described by Britton as one where the therapist feels that if he asserts his own view he is annihilating the subjective reality of the patient, but if he accepts the patient's view he is annihilating his own. The essential factor is that there is no third position available. Britton (1998, p. 43) makes the point that sometimes the best thing the analyst can do is to buy time, to make an interpretation to himself rather than to the patient, or to make what Steiner (1993) has termed an "analyst-centred interpretation" (1993, p. 133). It is not so much the words that are being said that are important, but the emotional position from which they are being spoken, in that if the therapist can tolerate and contain the patient's projections without getting into a battle, then the patient may in time become interested in thinking about his own contribution to the situation, and about more open to exploration. That is, that he might become interested in understanding as well as in being understood. This cannot, however, be forced; it requires time and working through, and in some situations it may never occur.

It is essential, in the face of these pressures (coming both from the patient and the wider social world) to maintain what has been called an "analytic stance". Empathy, then, is necessary, but not sufficient to affect psychic or social change. This is difficult under pressure, and the danger, as Jane Milton (2001) has argued, is in the avoidance of a third position, and the collapse of the oedipal dimension. This is true both at a social and an individual level; there is pressure to collapse an analytic oedipal stance, to move from the triadic to the dyadic.

The conflicts in the world of psychotherapy increasingly echoed, though, larger socio-cultural conflicts. As we have seen, psychoanalytic understandings of projective processes, particularly those occurring in paranoid and/or narcissistically regressed groups, can help the understanding of racism, of the scapegoating of minorities and those seen as in some way "different". This is a hugely important insight, properly applied. However, there are other constellations at work in contemporary life, which also require analysis. Freud's case study (1910c) of Leonardo Da Vinci – however accurate or otherwise it may have been about Leonardo's actual personality and life – exemplifies a certain sort of narcissistic object relationship. Leonardo deals, according to Freud, with the loss of his first love object, mother, by a process of an unconscious identification with her, and loves his apprentices, projectively identified with his own young self, as he himself would have wished to have been loved by mother. Thus, this form of narcissistic relating involves relating to others as vicarious extensions of the self.

In the situations I have been discussing, it may be that the vulnerable, child-like self, exquisitely sensitive, easily hurt, thin-skinned, and subject to traumatic impingement and malignant misunderstanding, is being projected into the vulnerable client, in therapy, or into the excluded or discriminated against "other" in the socio-political world. Clients then become less than robust potential victims, whose needs must be omnisciently met, and who must on no account be re-traumatised by a malignantly misunderstanding or chance remark by a more powerful other. In this context, authority, difference, power differentials, and the imposing of one world view on another, is to be avoided. Although this position presents itself as progressive, this is not the case; the projection of needy parts of the self into others whose needs are then to be omnisciently met is essentially a narcissistic form of relating, in which the other is dehumanised and unconsciously related to as an extension of the self. The danger is of the situation becoming self-perpetuating, a dyadic relationship where paternal authority and limits are denigrated or absent.

I want now, once more, to take a historical perspective and look more closely at the emergence of this culture of subjectivism, a culture that is inseparable from postmodern moral and epistemological relativism – the hostility to all metanarratives and claims to knowledge. To object to the extreme relativism that can be a feature of these movements is not to return to naive nineteenth-century positivism, or to suggest that claims to expertise and truth should not be held to scrutiny. Many critical enquiries, from different philosophical positions and political viewpoints, have sought to expose the partisan, ideological, and self-interested nature of some forms of knowledge: knowledge that can present itself as universal objective truth. All of these critical approaches to social reality and established knowledge maintained their radical stance without jettisoning the idea of truth, or the possibility of more objective knowledge of self and the world. As such, they belonged to the traditions of the Enlightenment, of radical, skeptical, and rational enquiry (Bell, 2009). This applied to the fractured forms of the modernist novel and the cubist portrait, to the explorations of the irrational in Freudian analysis, no less than to critical bourgeois realism and positivistic scientific enquiry. And as David Bell notes, "an underlying credo of the modernist movement is that it is through knowledge that human beings can emancipate themselves". Postmodernism as epistemology, on the other hand, "instead stands in opposition to all claims to knowledge, truth and reality" (Bell, 2009, p. 335).

There have been a number of trenchant attacks on postmodernism and social constructivism in recent years. Most famously, or most notoriously, depending upon one's point of view, Alan Sokal, professor of physics at New York University in 1996, had his parody "Transgressing the boundaries; Towards a transformative hermeneutics of quantum gravity" published as a bona fide article by the cultural studies journal *Social Text*. The subsequent book, *Intellectual Impostures*, which Sokal wrote with his scientific colleague Jean Bricmont (Sokal & Bricmont, 1998), contained devastating analysis of the tendentious, mistaken, and sometimes absolutely meaningless use of scientific concepts – from chaos theory to quantum physics – by a number of leading French postmodernists. Although Sokal and Bricmont were themselves attacked for their alleged "left conservatism", the articles that they exposed have to my knowledge never been defended in any serious intellectual quarter.

And yet, as extreme epistemological relativists do not, in any case, accept the idea of objective truth, it may be that their intellectual discrediting means little, particularly when the motivation for such relativism may be essentially emotional. In short, the influence of these ideas may be out of all proportion to their intellectual credibility – or lack of such – because they chime with the times, with both the needs of consumer capitalism, and with a highly subjectivist contemporary culture of narcissism. Postmodernism as epistemological, moral, and aesthetic relativism is part of the zeitgeist of modern time and is intrinsic to late capitalism, as Jameson (1991) argues. It is, in part, a form of extreme political correctness in which we might be spared the discomfort, and social awkwardness, of conflict, of having to hear a different perspective on things.

In the psychoanalytic world postmodernism has been most influential in inter-subjectivist schools of psychotherapy, mainly based in the United States, in which what is emphasised is the "co-construction" of psychoanalytic "truths". This is put most clearly by Owen Renik:

> Insights are always specific to the analytic couple that produces them. Insight is something co-created by the analyst and patient as much as it is discovered by analyst and patient. To differentiate co-creation from discovery in clinical psychoanalysis is to establish a specious distinction.
>
> (2004, p. 1054)

The point has been well made; however, the problem with postmodern approaches to psychoanalysis is a slippage from the inherent intersubjectivity of the therapeutic encounter (how could it be otherwise?) to a relativistic epistemol-ogy where there is "co-construction" of truths. As Marcia Cavell (2004) argues, the fact that truths can be discovered through an irreducibly creative and non-mechanical interpersonal dynamic does not mean that they were created by this dynamic, or that objective knowledge cannot be reached.

The necessary imbalance of psychoanalysis (and of other forms of psycho-therapy) is embodied not in some absolute difference and inequality between the patient and an omniscient therapeutic "expert" but, more relatively, in the respective roles of the participants. It is embodied, from a practical perspective, in the boundaries of the setting, in an analytic stance that is relatively abstinent, unobtrusive, and which, as Jane Milton (2001) puts it, is counter-intuitive and far from the normal form of social interchange. Indeed, the analytic "expert" who impersonally understands the patient's psychic life surely does not belong to any recognisable strand of clinical psychoanalysis or psychoanalytic psychotherapy. Instead, this figure seems more like a straw man, an omniscient God-like figure to be repudiated and renounced – a God that failed. Rather than this omnisci-ence, the therapist's partial and tentative knowledge comes from his experience with the patient and also comes from his relationship to his own thoughts, to technique, to colleagues, to supervisory structures, internal and external. It is this third position that appears to be by-passed in some more postmodern intersubjec-tive accounts. Indeed, this third position if it is apprehended at all, is identified instead with an omniscient expert imposing his expertise, his dogma, upon the hapless patient. In this sense, postmodern psychotherapy, and postmodernism itself, may be seen as occupying the dyadic world of epistemological narcissism, in which the risk is seen as "false compliance with a powerful object" (Britton,

1998, p. 166); the traumatising impingements of the external world upon the authentic vulnerable self.

To summarise, I have suggested that what is projected into the patient in some postmodern subjectivist forms of therapy may be the narcissistically wounded and thin-skinned self, and what is identified with the conventional therapist, in the guise of a straw man of omniscient scientific expertise (the last dinosaur of the white male canon of authoritative knowledge), is the malignantly misunderstanding paternal object, imposing absolute truths and annihilating the personal reality of the patient. Claims to truth are identified with dogma, omniscience, the imposition of beliefs, and the inappropriate use of authority; in short "truth" (with a small "t") is conflated with absolute "Truth". Absolutist modes of thought are projected and attributed to "positivist science", or to traditional psychoanalysts imposing their dogma on the defenceless patient. As Terry Eagleton (2003) says, "those who do not believe in truth are quite often inverted dogmatists. They reject an idea of truth that no reasonable person would defend in the first place" (2003, p. 104).

In the next chapter I turn to a notable socio-political manifestation of these tendencies.

Chapter 16

Not in our name!

There either were, or there weren't, weapons of mass destruction.

The good-natured crowd, suggesting that we "make tea not war" that wandered down the Embankment were "warmly inclusive and endlessly upbeat" (Harris, 2008), proceeding with typically English reasonableness and self-restraint, in orderly fashion up the Mall, to Hyde Park. In an impressive display of the unity of the disparate, the masses were united. "Not in our name!" The people on the rally were against the Iraq war, and, of course, and, it might be argued, they had good reason to be. However, if it was clear what they were against, it was much less clear quite what they were for, and indeed, in a practical sense, what they proposed to do.

The millions who were so impressively mobilised (under the exegesis of the Stop the War Coalition) were coming together against war on an oppressive, authoritarian, and quasi-fascist regime that was also responsible for well-documented and evidenced acts of genocide against sectors of its own population. Thus, we had the strange phenomena of a right-wing American administration, supported by the populist governments of Aznar in Spain, Berlusconi in Italy, and the inveterate free-marketers and anti-Communists of Poland, proposing the violent overthrow of a "fascist" government – even if for the "wrong reasons"; and being opposed by large sections of the "progressive" left, in the name of non-interventionism and in some cases an avid anti-Americanism that clearly extended to the view, in some more extreme quarters that "my enemy's enemy is my friend". On the wider shores of relativism, Bush, and by extension, Blair and his government, were no better than Saddam.

No matter, for Prime Minister Tony Blair had long since thrown his hat in the ring with the Bush administration. The vilification that he then received only served to strengthen his cause, and his will to power. For Tony Blair had always seemed more comfortable taking on his own side, ministering unpalatable realistic "truths" to the "deluded" legions of the old left, telling it like it is, on Clause IV and numerous other issues, or admonishing the old public sectors and professional groups, than he did taking on any of the real inequalities of class and power. Sometimes, in taking on this role, Blair was right; difficult realities, changing conditions had to be faced, ideas and principles needed to be flexible and to move with the times, rather than fall back into the unthinking regurgitation and retreat into the old comfort zones.

Tony Blair's premiership had many achievements, as the Herculean feat of winning three consecutive election campaigns for the Labour party attested. The Prime Minister's apparent character also chimed with the times, and partially helped to explain his popularity. He argued from passion, from personal conviction, particularly when he had an "established interest" to fight against, usually one of the old left or the professional middle classes. He was talented at emoting and arguing from personal charisma and authority, the dominant mode being of sincerity and feeling rather than analysis. He echoed the changes in society highlighted by the response to the death of the Princess of Wales: the prevalence of an emotive feeling- based and pseudo-therapeutic democratic and popular culture, ranged against the stiff-upper-lip paternalism of the old authoritarian culture and identified with the older members of the royal family, and the old established professional groups, such as the medical profession.

The demand for rights and equalities against the old bastions of power and privilege, and the assertion of feeling authenticity against "cold reason", were expressed, despite the government's queasiness on this issue, not in terms of citizenship or social solidarity, but through the prism of consumer empowerment and economic individualism. Traditional expertise and knowledge associated with the old professions tended to be denigrated at worst, or discounted at best. In the NHS, as we have seen, bewildered frontline staff had to negotiate the permanent revolution of organisational change, the packaging and commodification of health-care service in the name of patient as consumer, and of market reform. The government, having further opened the Pandora's box of entitled consumer individualism, hastened to slam the lid back on by the insistence on "responsibilities" as well as "rights", but by now the narcissistic baby was out with the bath-water.

Tony Blair conveyed a sense of inner conviction in relation to Iraq. He gave the impression that on this matter his mind was made up early, and the question of evidence appeared secondary to the decision to follow a certain course of action, a course determined, it would appear, by moral conviction, by feeling. The search for the, as it turned out, mythical "smoking gun" had the feel of an add-on, a legalistic justification for something already decided. Giles Tremlett in his book *The Ghosts of Spain* (2006) quotes from Don Quixote in explaining Prime Minister Aznar's fatal preoccupation with the Basque terrorist group ETTA as being responsible for the Madrid train bomb, when it was clearly the outcome of a fundamentalist reprisal for Spain's involvement in Iraq: "What I say is true and you will see it presently" (2006, p. 250).

This seemed to be, also, Tony Blair's position on the Iraq war. However, what was much more worrying, in relation to Iraq, was that from what we could see, Tony Blair's ultimate judge and arbiter would not be the cabinet, or the Labour Party, or the country, although he undoubtedly was wounded by the opposition that existed, or the United Nations, but instead would be God, and "History", with a capital "H". That is, his relationship was not with something ordinary, another human perspective, the verdict of reality, but with something special and extraordinary. This was what was so dangerous about this new twentieth-century form of liberal interventionism. The hotline was with a personal God, not with everyday reality, the government or the electorate.

In the face of the rush to war, the emergence of the spontaneous anti-war demonstrations that descended on Hyde Park might be seen as an impressive display of social solidarity, rather than of atomised apolitical liberal, tolerant, and vaguely hedonistic individualism held to be typical of the times. Yet it was hard not to escape the impression that here we had an expression of identity and moral outrage, rather than of practical engagement with the issues; with the developing of any coherent alternative strategies that might engage with the realities; of what policy to follow in the middle east; of how to think about and respond to a new brand of nihilistic terrorism. Rather, there was the repeated mantra, "Not in our name!"

The journalist and author Nick Cohen (2007) described this as the most narcissistic political slogan in recent political history. He has a point: the phrase hints at moral self-regard, suggests the primary importance of maintaining a pure view of the self – a self potentially sullied by association with unpopular government policy, but maybe a self, too, that wants to avoid the difficult, morally compromising decisions that do need to be made at times of crisis. Perhaps above all, what the crowds at Hyde Park could not quite engage with was what to do in the presence of evil, or, if we do not like to think in such fundamentalist terms, primary human destructiveness that cannot be contained by reason. And in this context, as the fictional neurosurgeon Henry Perowne from Ian McEwan's novel "Saturday" (2005) – in which an artistic, sensitive, guitar-playing middle-class family is menaced by a caricatured working-class lout whom the surgeon then saves from death – comments:

> All this happiness on display is suspect. Everyone is thrilled to be together out on the streets – people are hugging themselves, it seems, as well as each other. If they think – and they could be right – that continued torture and summary executions, ethnic cleansing and occasional genocide are preferable to an invasion, they should be somber in their view.
>
> (2005, pp. 69–70)

In fact the Stop the War movement soon lost the early momentum that had been acquired by the huge anti-war rally at Hyde Park in London, by making demands for the resignation of Tony Blair. They allowed themselves to be painted into a corner, as if they were defending a fascist dictator against a progressive popular front. They appeared to conflate the crime of Saddam Hussain with that of George Bush, another example of postmodern moral relativism. In some quarters in the anti-war movement, there was a regressive anti-Americanism, and, also, a flavour of the old anti-Semitic anti-capitalist associations that one, perhaps naively, thought had been consigned to history.

From the vantage point of history and the Chilcot report, it could be argued that the war was "wrong", though not simply for the reasons that many of its

opponents claimed. The pursuit of war was misguided because there was a serious lack of planning about the aftermath, the hard part after the predictably
straightforward military victory. There were some serious mistakes, such as the
disbanding of the army and Baathist police force. As many of the old pan-Arabists of the foreign office had suggested all along, the war was likely to make a
bad but relatively stable situation much worse, and much more unstable. And,
as many people who were not languid Old Etonian pan-Arabists at the foreign
office instinctively knew, remove a strong and charismatic, if tyrannical, leader
from a country, together with the state apparatus for maintaining order that surrounded him, and who knows what atavistic tensions you might release and call,
once more, into being. Most of all, the war was wrong, from these perspectives,
because the Bush administration appeared to be conflating two forces that, in fact,
were in opposition to each other – fundamentalist Islamist terrorism, including
Al-Qaeda, and the secularist tyranny of Saddam's Baathist regime. Tony Blair,
whatever he thought privately, echoed this position, a line that ended up creating
the very conditions which had not existed prior to the war, a coming together of
these very hitherto warring factions, as Iraq became a crucible of nihilistic terrorism, of horrific, sadistic, sociopathic violence.

Iraq is important in itself clearly, but also because in the run-up to the Iraq
war, all the arguments, self-contradictions, and ideological battlegrounds of the
modern world were laid bare. In the one corner was the humanitarian, rationalist
scepticism of Hans Blix, the United Nations chief weapons inspector, a scientist,
an exemplar of scientific positivism, and disinterested logical enquiry. In the other
corner was Tony Blair with his rhetorical emotive assertion of truth and personal
conviction. The anti-war lobby of the progressive left, as we have seen, had early
momentum and potentially strong arguments, but was prey to alarming moral
relativism, and to wishful thinking. Their position became quickly marginalised.
It was Hans Blix, however, who was in the prime pole position to bring in the
verdict of reality, of how things were as opposed to how people wanted them to
be. Either there were or there were not weapons of mass destruction. It is hard to
be certain, but we had to establish the best available evidence of the truth of the
claim – that there were indeed weapons of mass destruction. "Wait!" Hans Blix
was saying. The investigation of truth takes time and requires diligence; there will
be threats, resistances, and obstacles in our way, but this investigation might produce the information that we need, although we cannot absolutely rule out error
or successful deception. "Let me have some more time."

Hans Blix's air of melancholic matter-of-factness suggested that he knew that
the decision had already been made, that he was being asked to provide a smoking gun to justify a course of military action that had already been decided upon,
and that, in the absence of his producing such a gun, he would be shunted into
retirement and irrelevance, as he in fact was. And Blix's carefully worded suc-
cinct masterpieces of reportage increasingly indicated that there was likely to be
no smoking gun; his dry reportage of the facts, as we might best understand them,
was increasingly drowned out with more rhetorical and dramatic voices.

In the time of the postmodernist assertion of the truth of feelings over rationality and objectivity, so well-represented in many ways by the figure of Tony Blair himself, some assertions of truth are more powerful than others. In the face of Tony Blair's and George Bush's particular wish-fulfilment in this incident of historical time, joined at the hip as they were, then the ministrations and depredations of reality, as delivered by the four-square Hans Blix was just so much chaff in the wind – unless it delivered the wished-for result.

Perhaps the sanest view of all, however, came from the old pan-Arabists of the Foreign Office, now out of office, and out of favour in the Tory party. Yes, Saddam was a terrible man. Maybe, though, we might have to face the fact that there is little we can do about evil in the world. Sometimes our actions make things worse, even if our intentions are good. And, perhaps what was most dangerous of all was the naive, teleological, liberal providentialism, seeking by fair means or foul to secure a world of democracy and free markets, all at a time when the sky was full of economic chickens coming home to roost.

Chapter 17

Everything is permitted, restrictions still apply

By the early 1990s, in a process given huge impetus by the fall of Communism, the doctrines of light-touch regulation, competitive tax environments, and market flexibility had become the ideology without a name of Western governments, of right and left alike. As late as summer 2007 lavish praise was being heaped upon the city and its institutions. Alongside this, as we have seen, was the curious neglect, in the UK and the USA (though not in countries such as Germany) of the manufacturing base, and the need to invest in and develop productive capacity. This was the economic concomitant of the socio-cultural denigration of the industrial working class and its institutions, a process that, as we have seen, was not confined to the political right.

However, whilst the public, and the public sector, were repeatedly told to "tighten their belts", it was becoming increasingly clear that the culture of the financial markets – in the context of government policies fetishising the free market and encouraging tax breaks and light regulation, became one of excess, greed, and rampant individualism, rather than responsible investment. From the outside at least, the actions of the unregulated financial market resembled nothing so much as Freud's large group, operating by the herd instinct, capricious, contradictory, easily suggestible, governed by primary human motivations of greed, anxiety, fear, and panic, and unmediated by a sense of trust or restraint. Thus, it seemed, markets had been built upon leverage deals, an inverted pyramid in which all but the base of the pyramid was borrowed money, such schemes tending to collapse in a domino effect when loans were called in. Periods of catastrophic collapse and dire apocalyptic predictions alternated with periods of high and heady euphoria.

All of this bore an unclear relationship with something called the real economy, and the world where most people live, except that it was becoming increasingly clear that the market collapse in the USA had its roots in the overvaluation of the housing market and the giving of irresponsible loans. The system had given out credit and the banks had grown their loans much faster than the rate of economic growth. This had created a credit and property-price bubble.

Paul Mason (2010) has described how the American International Group (AIG), for example, admitted in 2005 that it had faked $500m of transactions, and "misclassified" another $3bn in order to fool its auditors and inflate its profits.

The Valukas report revealed that Lehman Brothers had been insolvent and hid its liabilities during 2008. Goldman Sachs was charged with civil fraud over the allegation "that it had defrauded its own clients by selling them a package of sub-prime debts effectively designed by a hedge fund manager who wanted to bet that they would lose money" (Mason, 2010, p. xi). Lies and manufactured rumours were spread about companies in order to drive down their shares and pocket a profit – as happened with the bank HBOS, the UK's largest mortgage lender in March 2008, when shares fell seventeen per cent in thirty minutes. Will Hutton (2009) suggests that there are likely to have been very many other examples of such practices, most of which will never see the light of day.

The echoes of Rosenfeld's "narcissistic organisation" (1971) and of the psycho-analytic theories of perverse indifference to, and twisting of, reality, are inescap-able. Further, all of this could only have taken place in a context where there was an abnegation of proper systems of authority – a failure of paternal authority at a societal level, in this case a responsible regulatory system, thus allowing any activity to be indulged in, and for the growth of a situation in which manic activity is further and further removed from reality. Mania always comes crashing down.

The consequences of this was a loss of over four trillion dollars in the world financial system. Globalisation and interconnectedness meant that "contagion" wiped millions of dollars off the value of shares. World trade declined by nine per cent in a year. The inherent savagery of this process, the savagery of the market, saw the populace view the state not as oppressor but as security. The net result of these crises was that it was the state that bailed the financial system out, in what was to become a pattern of privatisation of profit and socialisation of loss.

The reaction to the credit crunch and the bail-out betrayed the contradictions that had always underpinned free-market ideology, and the wider emotional investments of economic individualism. Technically, the credit crunch had roots in the repeal of the 1933 Glass-Steagall Act in the USA, which prevented invest-ment bankers betting deposits on the buying and selling of tradable financial secu-rities. After moves by the Thatcher government in 1986 to loosen this restriction, and "liberate" the city from financial shackles, in 1987, after intense banking lob-bying, the American Federal Reserve relaxed the ruling, so that five per cent of a bank's deposits could be so used. This was extended to twenty-five per cent in 1997. The act was finally abolished in 1999. Regulators also accepted the bank-ers' arguments in creating "collateralised debt obligations", the bundling up of income-generating assets into one security, and insuring them against the risk of default. This led to a situation where some banks had balance sheets thirty times bigger than their capital base, and in which it was no longer possible for them to insure against their own systemic failure (Hutton, 1999). One trillion dollars of subprime debt had been bundled into various categories of structured tradable debt. This system came crashing down when American house prices began to decline in 2007.

Mason (2010) outlines how in the USA, the 158-year-old Lehman Broth-ers investment bank, having lost seven billion pounds in a year, as the value of property-related investments fell, filed for bankruptcy. The American government took the decision that it could afford to let Lehman's fall – it was less structurally involved with the wider market. A right-wing, free-market, Republican administration then, in effect, nationalised the giant mortgage firms, Fanny Mae and Freddy Mac, as it did the world's biggest insurance firm, AIG, after a fall in its share value of seventy-four per cent. Further shockwaves then forced the government takeover of Merrill Lynch, the largest nationalisation outside of the Communist world.

After the febrile meltdown of markets, a right-wing free-market, Republican administration had made the biggest public intervention in the private sector since the Great Depression by a $700bn (£382bn) bailout of Wall Street; it was characterised as socialism or even as Bolshevism by dyed-in-the-wool Republican free-market right wingers. Let the market sort it out, and flush out the dead wood, they clamoured. However, from another perspective the bailout, known as the Troubled Assets Relief Program (TARP) was, presented as an article of inequality, bailing out the rich, rewarding the failed bankers and investors, and doing nothing for hard-pressed householders and the small shopkeepers of "Main Street". The population saw the bill, as it first appeared, as an unaccountable bailout for the rich, without any real reforms to the system; and contrasted this with the habitual lack of bailouts for the poor, and for "uneconomic" heavy industry.

Thus the opposition to TARP, occurring during election year, exerted a powerful influence on those Congressmen and women, Democrat and Republican, up for election. The issue was one of fairness, and perceived fairness. Why should the taxpayer foot the bill for the failures of high finance and casino capitalism? The mantra that the weak or the uneconomic – the miners, the shipbuilders, and the struggling small business – should be allowed to fail and should not be bailed out by the state, had been one of the cornerstones of free-market orthodoxy since the Reagan and Thatcher years. Yet here, policy appeared, when push came to shove, to be going in quite the opposite direction, with certain institutions offered an exemption from the normal rules and conditions.

For many people, on both nominal left and right, and all places in-between, such a special arrangement stuck in the craw. However, these inequities and contradictions were not accidents due to the malfunctioning of the system; it might be argued that, at a structural level, they were intrinsic to it. And yet, given that we had long been told that there was no alternative to this system, then people had to swallow their feelings, and with a heavy heart put their vote in the yes box, pray that the scheme might work, and leave the reckoning until later.

Mason (2010) makes clear that in the UK there was a parallel process. As it turned out, major British banks and building societies, such as HBOS and Royal Bank of Scotland (RBS), had also been subordinating normal lending and balance-sheet banking to money-market trading and risky investments. The UK had an exposure to loans, investments, cash injections, and guarantees to the banking system of £1.3 trillion, the IMF calculated. The leader and letter pages of the *Daily Express*, and the *Daily Mail*, and middle England harangued the "spivs and speculators" of the City. They called for the regulation of the City, the curtailing of bonuses based on speculation, and a restriction of hedge fund selling and buying – in short of asocial predatory activity – such as short selling, borrowing shares and then selling them, with the hope of buying them back again at a reduced price, leading to price instability. Gordon Brown, and his cabinet, belatedly rediscovered their roots and raison d'être and cottoned on, gingerly at first, to the public mood.

The public mood was not rabidly anti-market but recognised, unlike many politicians and intellectuals, that there was a hegemonic crisis, a sea-change in the air. For most ordinary people, the market was essential for funding projects and enterprises, but they had little sympathy for those bankers and investors who, like Ben Jonson's (1606) Mosca and Volpone, overreached themselves, borrowing over thirty times their capital to finance their deals, and, in the interests of greed, putting not just themselves at risk, but the whole economy. It was as if we had stumbled, as if in a waking dream, on to the essential inequalities and contradictions of capitalism, at least of its free-market variant.

Had things changed with the evident objective failures of this system, or was it more, as Paul Mason has suggested, a case of "cognitive dissonance" (2010, p. 250)? That is, amongst the political classes, if not the population as a whole, was there a psychological inability to accept the reality of the limitations, and indeed failures, of a particular political paradigm; and at a deeper level, a reluctance to relinquish the "culture of narcissism" underpinning, I would suggest, both late capitalism and its anti-capitalist critics?

The light-touch deregulated model appeared to have been blown out of the water, given that the system was only saved by massive public and state intervention, including nationalisation of major financial institutions. Whilst this was recognised, or appeared to be, in the immediate aftermath of the credit crunch, there was also a wish to resume things "as they were", as if the crunch were a temporary blip in the smooth running of the free market. In a remarkable example of politically convenient displacement, the massive state intervention resulted not in changes to the banking system, but in bankers carrying on as normal, with massive bonuses, once the situation had been tenuously stabilised; there was a new rally on the stock markets, and an excoriation of the "waste" of the public sector, leading to conservative appeals for the further shrinking and privatisation of the state – an appeal that resonated with some voters' instinctual doubts about "living beyond your means".

However, the problem was that a crisis of the banking system and of private debt had become a crisis of the nation state, and that it had become too much for some states. There had been a failure, over the boom years, of easy credit and generous loans, to invest in and diversify industry and technology, and to train the workforce. There were inefficiencies and cronyism in some state bureaucracies and, in some countries, a basic failure to collect taxes. However, continued policies of austerity could not reduce the debt if they did not address the issue of growth and investment. If all countries were simultaneously pursuing austerity then there was a loss of export markets, in a vicious spiral, redolent of the failed financial orthodoxies of the 1930s.

Meanwhile, the real structural problems of the UK economy were not limited to the idealisation of the free market, and the light touch deregulated financial sector. The boom years now appeared (as had been clearly evident for many years to anyone who cared to have looked) to disproportionately rely on the housing bubble, massive personal debt, and to have lost sight of the old art of actually producing things. The actions of some investors and bankers were shown to involve trickery, a sleight of hand, in which, as we have seen, massive pyramid schemes were built on bad debt, on a foundation of sand, or precisely nothing. They made massive bonuses and profits for themselves, but they contributed nothing to the banks' essential function: allowing individuals and organisations to invest in creative enterprise. It took not an ostensibly left-wing politician but the "establishment" figure of Lord Turner of the Financial Services Authority to say that such actions were at best "socially useless" and at worst positively destructive.

Wolfgang Streek (2014) has identified a number of the "disorders" of contemporary late capitalism. I will mention four of them here. The first is stagnation, an excess of capital, and the relative failure of low or even negative interest rates to stimulate real recovery and investment. Of course, low or no growth does not preclude high profits. The second is oligarchic redistribution; inequality depresses growth, easy money blows up the financial sector and invites speculative rather than productive investment, with redistribution to the top. This is an international process – from this perspective there is no need to worry about national growth rates. The third is the plundering of the public domain through underfunding and privatisation. The tax state has become the debt state and now the austerity state. Attempts to reduce public deficits relied mainly on cuts to government spending – social security, infrastructure, and human capital. However, evidence has suggested that the consolidation of public finances by austerity is likely to depress growth. We therefore see a pattern of declining economic growth, rising inequality, and the transfer of public to private ownership.

Streek's fourth point is that of corruption; he points out that Max Weber had identified the values of restraint, self-discipline, postponement of gratification, sobriety, the rational ordering of life, methodological effectiveness and stewardship as necessary to ensure that capitalism is not simply greed. This requires a certain structure of personality and superego, as Lasch suggested, but also bureaucratic restraints. This changed, however, with the rise to dominance of the financial rather than productive sector. There is a fine line, in this regard, between innovation and creativity on the one hand, and rule bending and semi-legal activities on the other. The deep interconnection between the biggest firms, regulatory bodies, and governments have led to blurred lines. The revelations of 2008 were of the reality of toxic loans, of off-shore banking and tax evasion – in other words of the moral decline of capitalism.

There is no doubt that, seen in historical terms, globalised capitalism brings many changes for the better. However, the aspects of consumer capitalism highlighted by the credit crunch appeared highly perverse. This perversity might be seen as being at the core of a system that asserts exchange value over any question of intrinsic worth, and in which increasing areas of public, private, and socio-cultural life, including many venerable traditions, were hollowed out and rendered obsolete, or repackaged as self-conscious commodities. To question these forms of late consumer capitalism is not to advocate a Luddite return to primitive conditions in which life really was, for most people, "nasty, brutish and short". It is not to turn one's back on scientific and technological innovation, or indeed on globalisation. As Eric Hobsbawm (2000, pp. 61–93) pointed out, globalisation is related to electronic technological revolutions, and these represent creative human endeavours that go beyond a particular form of late capitalism, and it seems both likely and desirable that they will continue.

Looking at it now, the position of extreme economic individualism and free-market fundamentalism, as advocated by Rand, Hayek, and Friedman, carried on by Margaret Thatcher and her supporters in the UK, and enshrined in much neo-liberal policy, seems permeated with the kind of "thin-skinned" narcissism described by Ron Britton (1998). As we have seen, in this psychological configuration the supreme value is in the "authentic individual", and the danger is one of "compliance with a "false object". The "bad object" was the state, imposing its heavy, iniquitous, bureaucratic hand into every corner of dynamic activity. The prototype of the state as the "false object" was, of course, the Soviet Union, and the collapse of Communism brought to a head the crisis of mainstream social democracy. Such beliefs had a religious intensity and seemed impervious – or frankly hostile to – rational argument or empirical evidence.

At the same time, pathological splitting amongst some opponents of capitalism led to, for example, an idealisation of the natural world and all things "natural", and a denigration of all the "artificial" forces of modernity and technological innovation that undoubtedly made life better for people. Many of the criticisms of consumerism contained unlikeable elements of Puritanism, of intellectual and class snobbery. "Ethical" or abstentious consumers proclaimed their moral superiority over the masses, whilst others jetted across to France to binge on wine and crêpes as a protest against the election of Margaret Thatcher. However, it was not so much consumerism that was the problem but the increasing commodification of everyday life and human relationships. This could be seen as involving a severe impoverishment of personal and civil relationships, and as a contributory factor to a decline in civility and an increase in narcissism in everyday life. These trends could not, however, be split off and located in the inequities of the capitalist system imposing its ways on the innocent masses. Rather, they arose from the complex and often contradictory dialectical relationship between the individual and society; a pull towards states of pathological entitlement, or the automatic right to happiness and material satisfaction, are also in the psyche of the individual. These individuals were exercising a choice, albeit with limited alternatives.

Reality will out, however, and the fundamentalist and utopian notion, shared across sections of right and left alike, that markets left to their own devices are self-regulating, that the activities of individuals following their own rational self-interest leads to a trickle-down, a world where all must have prizes, was exposed by the 2007/8 credit crunch, and the long recession that followed, as being as much a form of wishful thinking as the old faith in the command economy. The response though, was not the emergence of a new paradigm but a falling back towards older explanatory systems, and to familiar narratives, which also, of course, served particular interests. Thus, for the right a crisis that started in international banking and the deregulated credit markets became redefined as a crisis of national government and public expenditure, part of a process that has aptly been termed the privatisation of profit and the socialisation of loss. The response was the politics of austerity, which had no prospect of addressing the crucial underlying problem of low or stagnant growth, the balance of payments deficit, and the rebalancing of the economy towards production. At the same time, on the left, nostalgic harkening back to the "triangulated" thinking of the Blair years on the one hand, or resort to increasingly intemperate cultural wars with soft-target socially conservative groups on the other, did little to present compelling counter-narratives.

The presence of protest tents outside St Paul's Cathedral prompted masochistic self-recrimination from sections of the Church of England but hardly seemed to amount to new thinking. In fact the protesters seemed to deliberately eschew the dirty work of evolving new policies, and it was not clear if, in their righteous "occupation" and disavowal of "oppressive" hierarchies, they offered the inchoate beginnings of something new or the last gasps of a defunct system. The election of Jeremy Corbyn as leader of the Labour Party in the UK, taken together with the rise of Syriza in Greece and Podemos in Spain, gave succour to the notion of a rejuvenated left. However, the fate of Syriza, reduced to privatisation and penury as the price for remaining in the Euro, only appeared to confirm the impression that it had been the ideologues of free markets and privatisation that had been able to reframe the dominant narrative.

Streek, in his recent work (2017) has argued that although neo-liberal capitalism is in decline, this process could take many years to play out, and this is occurring without there being as yet any available systematic alternative. He adds that in the interregnum between the disappearance of one system and the emergence of an as yet unknown other, various morbid symptoms are appearing – the election of Donald Trump being one of these. Marine Le Pen and the Front National in France might be another; the rise of populist authoritarianism in Turkey and some parts of Eastern Europe still another. In this context "progressive" movements of the centre, right, and left find themselves assailed by what they describe as a new "post-truth" populism, and against which they are driven to reassert their pluralist, liberal, and rationalist values. However, Streek (2017) cautions that the term populism can be used to denigrate or pathologise, and makes the point that there have, in historical terms, been many forms of progressive populism. Here we return to themes we visited in the discussion of millennialism – distinctions have to be made, the crowd is not always a regressed mob, and on some issues may be in the right.

It is to these subjects that I turn next.

Chapter 18

Post-crash, post-truth

"Post-truth" – the new word of the year in 2016 – has been defined in the Oxford English Dictionary as an adjective "relating to or denoting circumstances in which objective facts are less influential in shaping public opinion than appeals to emotion and personal belief". "Fake news" is taken to denote a more specific and conscious spreading of hoaxes and misinformation, most usually via the electronic media. That these terms are descriptive of the circumstances leading to Brexit, and to the election of Donald Trump as President of the USA, is itself rapidly becoming a truism. Indeed, in this narrative both events are conflated as manifestations of the same underlying trends; the promulgation of fanciful claims, of mutually contradictory analyses and policies to meet the expectations of different audiences, at worst the pedalling of lies, at best the assertion of emotional "truth" at the expense of expertise and knowledge, and an outright contempt towards rationality and evidence. These are the features, it is argued, that underpin the new populist nationalism, a force that has swept America, the United Kingdom, and threatens to sweep across Europe too, and which has its core support amongst the "left behinds", the poor and the déclassé, the ill-educated and the elderly. At best, in such a characterisation, these "low information" groups are "dupes" for demagogues and the right-wing media and web, for the promulgators of conspiracy theories and "fake news". At worst, they are outright xenophobes, the embittered "déplorables" of contemporary life.

Post-truth and "fake news" tendencies are, of course, ubiquitous in human beings, organisations, cultures, and social institutions. Over recent years there have been numerous examples of such tendencies, across the political spectrum, of a wilful disregard for the claims of evidence, and manifest most egregiously as conscious lying and corruption. A recent notorious example in the UK is the falsifying of evidence and covering up amongst sections of the South Yorkshire police force, revealed after the Hillsborough enquiry into the deaths of Liverpool football supporters during the 1989 FA Cup semi-final. Such tendencies are also evident in the ubiquitous tendency, conscious and unconscious, to cherry-pick data to fit a preconceived argument. The exposure of such phenomena – as in the case, as we have seen, of the decontextualised "facts" that were used to make the case for the Iraq War – might well lend credence to the view that it is most rational and wise to have a healthy scepticism towards "establishment" expertise and claims to truth.

Perhaps most crucial of all though, has been the crisis of the fundamentalist neo-liberal free-market ideology that emerged from the fall of Communism and the decline of the post-war social democratic settlement. This was no less an ideology for proclaiming itself ideology-free, common sense, or simply "the way things are"; it is in the nature of ideologies, particularly the ideologies of the powerful, to present themselves in just such a way. Here, long before the election of Donald Trump, we were in a world where everything was permitted, and restrictions did not apply. Here reality could be willed to power by those with the resources to do so. As David Harvey (2010) caustically notes – there has long been a problem in the relationship between representation and reality in late capitalism.

The failure of large swathes of the political and economic establishments across the developed world to predict the financial crisis, and the wish of many to resume the way things were, in the process of which a failure of neoliberal economics with its origins in banking and deregulated markets was reconceptualised as one of public expenditure, might be said to constitute the primary post truth of the current age, from which subsequent post-truth responses follow.

Such a situation has contributed to a pervasive distrust of official expertise, a distrust that from this point of view has a realistic basis, and more recently contributed to the scepticism towards the "project fear" warnings, or rather threats, of economic Armageddon that would immediately follow a "No" vote in the European Referendum, delivered by the vast swathes of the economic and political establishment. That those supporting "Remain" could also reasonably point to similar exaggerations and fanciful claims on the "No" campaign side only further confirmed that post-truth tendencies cross the political divide.

Nor were such tendencies confined to the United Kingdom. Notwithstanding the progressive aspirations and achievements of the European Union, it could be argued that one of the most striking contemporary political examples of wish fulfilment being asserted over recalcitrant reality in the face of repeated evidence to the contrary, is that of continued adherence to the notion of a single currency across widely divergent economies, at a time when there is no political will or democratic mandate for greater political convergence. The costs of such a policy in southern Europe, and in Greece in particular, are only too evident, and may have been insufficiently cited as a background factor contributing to the outcome of the European Referendum in the UK and the rise of the "populist" parties and politics elsewhere.

In historic terms there have been both progressive and regressive forms of populism, and many of the achievements of liberal pluralist society were only achieved against the odds by populist pressure. That "populism", however, was mainly employed as a term of derogation in these accounts, pointed to the inescapably partial and politicised nature of these invocations of truth, rationality, and expertise; to which the obvious response was that it depends where you are sitting. For some sections of the population, a version of globalised liberal capitalism with free movement of goods and labour, allied to a pluralist and tolerant culture, offered the self-evident best of all possible worlds; whilst for others the same system was experienced as the evisceration, hollowing out, and impoverishment of tradition, community, and opportunity. It was not that one version was "true" and the other "false" but that both simultaneously applied, and were different manifestations of the same underlying forces.

Moreover, as we have seen, there had long been, amongst sections of progressive and radical opinion, a retreat from the universalist rationalist traditions of the Enlightenment, a retreat that had gone beyond the critical realism of modernism, into the relativisation of all truth claims. These trends, I suggest, form the emotional and intellectual backdrop to today's "post-truth" society. Such tendencies have contributed to a highly subjectivist culture, and a radically relativistic world of rhetorical assertion, freed from constraints, in which the power of a compelling emotional narrative trumps the authority of professional expertise and established knowledge. It might be argued that Donald Trump is merely the latest example of these trends.

Such are the contradictions I would suggest, of the "post-truth" world, a term used by self-described "progressives" to characterise their "reactionary" or even "fascist" opponents but which is also highly pertinent to their own practice and which has its roots, socio-culturally, in the politics of identity; in the extreme relativism and post-modernity that has in the words of Frederic Jameson (1991) long been the "cultural logic of Late Capitalism" – and its critics.

Such trends are deeply embedded in late capitalism and neo-liberalism. I have suggested in this chapter that perhaps the fundamental post truth of the current age, from which all else follows, was that of the neo-liberal house of cards that was erected on the basis of mortgage leverage, pyramid schemes, and other financial sleights of hand following the collapse of Communism. Although the bankers and financiers were seen as the prime villains, as it were, there was the sense that for most people during that time there had been a turning of a blind eye, the replacement of reality with a degree of wish fulfilment, a sense of knowing and not knowing. This was the world where everything was permitted, in which, it seemed, restrictions did not apply. The corollary of this was the neglect and denigration of manufacturing, engineering, and the associational communities that serviced these industries. Once the subject of idealisation, they became the subject of opprobrium, and cultural denigration. As I have argued, such attitudes were not confined to the free-market right, and, indeed, particularly permeated sections of progressive liberal-left opinion.

These attitudes have not gone away, and indeed may have strengthened since. They have been all too evident in the response to the European Referendum in the UK and the election of Donald Trump in the USA, which too often has replaced the need for sober analysis with shrill moral condemnation and sneering sarcasm. I want to make clear that here I am talking about dominant but not exclusive trends – there have been and continue to be many thoughtful attempts to understand these phenomena. Even some of these accounts, however, have seemingly worked from the assumption that it is the irrationality of these movements that requires sympathetic understanding, and that, implicitly, the views that go alongside them are ipso facto misguided whilst the author's own remain enlightened and rational. I believe that this, irrespective of the "objective" merits of the argument, is part of the problem and in part an explanation for why the situation is self-perpetuating – in psychoanalytic terms a failure of social attunement, a process of invalidation that serves, as it does in the clinical situation, to perpetuate a split and to produce further fragmentation.

It could be argued that it is not necessary to advance complex political and psychoanalytic understandings of why people may feel and vote as they do. The answer, as it usually does, resides in the state of the economy, the underlying material fundamentals. Christopher Caldwell (2017), in his discussion of the work of the French geographer Christopher Guilluy, identifies a number of related urban trends: globalisation brings benefits in efficiency but also increases inequality, demographic upheaval, and cultural disruption; some urban areas benefit highly from "metropoliticisation" and become hotbeds of financial, commercial, entrepreneurial, scientific, cultural, and educational activity, helped by the provision of cheap, often immigrant, labour, low tariffs, and new overseas markets; other urban areas become deserted, with empty shopfronts and blighted inner cities. The successful cities, such as Paris, London, and New York, are overwhelmingly populated by particular social groupings – millionaires, immigrants, tourists, and the young, often students. Other groups, the less educated and affluent, including some strata of the middle class, are excluded, and the urban property-market prices mean that there is no realistic possibility of this process being reversed: they remain confined to the periphery. Nor is there a realistic prospect of the emergence of a new middle class. Thus the laws of unintended consequences, and of uneven development. Thus, on the one hand, cities full of art, of street food from all around the globe; on the other, deserted, windswept high streets, full of charity and pound shops.

Caldwell (2017) suggests, following Guilluy, that in France it has been immigrants who, by and large, have occupied the public housing stock vacated by the "traditional" working and lower middle classes, and it has been immigrants who now do most of the jobs associated with servicing the new rich; as nannies, gardeners, nurses, care assistants, cleaners, security guards; all of this, for the most part, on low wages and insecure temporary contracts. These are the jobs many French workers are reluctant to do. In this context the relationship between inequality and diversity, economics and identity are uneasy and intertwined. The unrestricted movement of goods and labour benefits some groups, but most certainly damages others.

Amongst the periphery there is an alienation from the larger political project, in part because decisions have been made about the make-up and nature of society that have never been put to the electorate, in part because parties of the liberal left have distanced themselves from the "reactionary" cultural attitudes of their old natural constituencies, turning instead to seeking to obtain support from a coalition of minorities and those that have been the beneficiaries of globalisation.

The policies they pursue offer little more than minor variations on a neo-liberal continuum, and are only nominally of the left.

For significant sections of the population, therefore, the system is not working, and has not been working for some time. The assumptions of the post-war settlement, those of increased standards of living, the probability of a better quality of life for the next generation, the provision of an effective welfare state for the protection of individuals and communities from the exigencies of life and of the market, of capitalism red in tooth and claw, have been reversed. The basis of the post-war "democratic consent", as Streek (2014) has put it, of liberal capitalism, has been breached. We are seeing a situation where for some sections of the community – in particular those left stranded by the withdrawal of productive work to other parts of the world – life expectancy is now decreasing. Such is the case amongst sections of the community in the old dust-bowl states of the USA. There is an echo of this to be heard in mental health work in the north-east of England. There is much that is lively and vital about the area. There is a natural resilience amongst people and in the cultural life. There is also a creative coming together– for example, in the old working-class district of Byker – of indigenous locals and recent immigrants. However as Jonathan Lear (2007) suggests, if cultural belief and practices are no longer rooted in a lived life then they no longer have meaning or intelligibility. There are also localities in the North-East, as there are everywhere, where there are indications of cultural collapse and social implosion, of which there are, most definitely, morbid symptoms – social withdrawal, apathy and inertia, de-politicised states of diffuse despair.

The late Peter Mair (2014) has analysed a sense of a democratic crisis and disconnect with origins in the 1960s. He outlined the decline of political parties and institutions formed on the basis of mass membership, shared social experience, and collective hopes, functioning as effective intermediaries between the individual, community and state. Mair suggested that, increasingly, differences between parties became blurred, although an appearance of opposition was maintained. At the same time, in part linked to changes incurred by the growth of individualism, the decline of social associations, and a fragmentation of collective identities there was a growing level of citizen disengagement.

Mair (2014) shows how changes in human subjectivity interact with globalisation; a decline in long-term commitments increased short-termism and volatility, an explosion of choice, and the assertion of personal taste and style, the establishing of voluntarist connections across social media, rather than identifications of class or locality. Such new connections can, of course, be easily severed. Social bonds have been reconstructed as a matter of taste and choice rather than obligation. It is in this context that, for good or bad, or, most likely, both, communities and political movements can quickly form over specific issues. Such a situation lends itself, however, to highly subjectivist assertions of reality and truth, the seeking of like-minded individuals, and a world in which a different perspective can be quickly deleted.

Here we have a world where everyone can have his own reality, where there is no higher authority – or, as I have suggested earlier, no paternal presence – and everyone is seen as having the right to his own truth. Any challenge to this is experienced as a violation, or invalidation. Here we are once more in the word of thin-skinned narcissism. This is another example of the way in which post truth, which has always been with us, is intrinsic to late capitalism – and its critics.

At the same time, the changes incurred through globalisation, in particular the declining ability of national governments to shape autonomous policies, strengthened a mindset in which politicians and political parties were viewed as irrelevant to the essential issues, impotent in the face of global forces, and, fundamentally, "all the same". There was, and is, a degree of reality to these views, and to the generalised scepticism towards "establishment" assertions of expertise and truth. Rather than offer clear and distinct policy choices, there has been a tendency to accentuate apparent cultural differences, whilst at the same time retreating into state institutions, and to non-democratic forms of technocratic depoliticised "management", to central banks, and so on. The emergence of new populist parties is therefore linked to these changes and to the abandonment of the parties of the centre-left of their old constituencies, in favour of consensual coalition policies. In the long term, however, as Slavoj Žižek (2006, p. 41) writes, "participation by the far Right (in government) ... is the price the Left pays for ... accepting that market capitalism as 'the only game in town'".

In this context, how will future historians see the current polarisation in the UK between the more ardent "Remainers" and "Brexiteers", and the level of vituperative abuse that has accompanied this? Will it be seen as an issue of seismic proportion, or a diversion from the key problems of the age? The former is certainly how some people on both sides currently see it. Some "progressive" Remainers have made it very clear, for example, that they would scupper the chances of a socially egalitarian Labour government being elected, if this was the price they had to pay for the chance of a second referendum, or an end to Brexit. Or will it be seen as the modern equivalent of those violent religious schisms of the Middle Ages based on arcane and obscure doctrinal differences? Will it be seen, in the context of the decline of neo-liberalism and its consequences (a process that will continue whether or not the UK remains in the European Union), as the equivalent of fiddling whilst Rome burns?

My own view is that there are, clearly, substantive issues but that there are underlying emotional motivations and projective processes that are also at work, emotional motivations that have gone well beyond the surface issues. To take the central substantive issue first: in an age of globalisation, is it better to be connected to a larger body, as a refuge and bulwark against the extremes of market forces and their consequence, the growth of authoritarian nationalism? Is this the best protection against the atomising of individuals and hollowing out of communities, against the possibility of a narcissistic or paranoid large-group regression? Here, the strong argument is that the European Union has helped maintain the post-war peace – not least in formalising an alliance between France and Germany – and that the Union and, less, national sovereignty, represents a bulwark against volatile financial markets and the power of the USA and China.

On the other hand it might be argued, as Lilla (2014) suggests, that the European Union's neo-liberal approach to economic integration threatens the principles of democratic self-government that were restored after the Second World War. As Lilla argues, since the 1980s the European Union has been dominated by neo-liberalism, a particular form of libertarianism in which the rational choices of the economic individual are idealised, and those of the state denigrated, born in part out of some of the real limitations of the social democratic settlement. There has been a blindness to the impact of the neo-liberal model, particularly on economic integration, as it has moved from ideology to dogmatic certainty, as simply "the way things are". As the EU has demanded more austerity and privatisation, citizens have felt that they are losing control of their fate. What we have seen is, in some cases, democracies replaced by technocratic experts, and a situation where a democratic vote – such as that made by the people of Greece in their referendum rejection of austerity – was not allowed to have an impact on policy.

From this perspective it is important to recognise, though we might wish it were not so, that the historical reality is that modern constitutional democracies have only developed within the context of the nation state. This is perhaps not perfect, but nonetheless represents a compromise in that, as Lilla (2014) puts it, "it is large enough to encourage people to think beyond their local interests, but not so large that they have no control over their lives". It provides a focus for collective action, for accountability and also for identification. As such, it combats the pull towards narcissistic regression. This is no mean feat and maybe the best that can be done. For without a sense of shared identity there may be little opportunity for altruism, for a sense of the common good. As Paul Collier, writing in the *Times Literary Supplement* puts it (2017), "a world composed of global citizens would not be the universalist utilitarian paradise that liberals lazily imagine but the brutally atomistic world of unchecked individualism". And, as we have seen, a sense of national identity is not the same as a sense of shared ethnic identity – a nation state can be pluralistic, cosmopolitan, and progressive. From this point of view, global citizenship without empowered national citizenship is unviable. It is in this context that the Western liberal contempt for nationalism may be particularly misplaced; "faced with extremist religious and ideological identities it should be evident that the pertinent social menace is fragmentation into oppositional identities sustained by the echo chamber of the social media" (Collier, 2017).

The issues raised here are substantive and my own view on them remains a conflicted one. However, I think that it is surely significant that these issues have rarely been voiced, rarely heard, in my experience at least, in public and political debate. The divide has become, as is the way of things in the late capitalist world, one of identity and culture, of moralism, to the exclusion of political analysis, or psychological understanding. Thus, in the progressive liberal picture, in which the European Union as an institution and Europe as a historical entity have become increasingly conflated, we see, on one side, rational cosmopolitan internationalists, on the other, defensive "post-truth" isolationists and xenophobes – the hooligans and wreckers come to the world party again. This picture reveals a class and culturally based contempt that leads to the working class being reconstituted as an "embittered", "left behind" interest group, an attribution that is actualised by massive projective processes, in the main through cultural denigration and provocation. Such a mind-set amongst sections of "progressive" opinion defends against internal conflict, against the cognitive dissonance that might occur if the contradictions and limitations of the liberal position were more honestly faced. For example, the free movement of labour and capital can have beneficial aspects, but can also have deleterious effects, not least on the country being left.

The conclusion I draw is not that a progressive political force must pander to prejudice or xenophobia, but that the real anxieties underpinning social dislocation need to be treated seriously, and the feelings of "ordinary people" should not be patronised as inherently misguided or ripe for populist exploitation, or as the product of foreign interference and fake news. Many people have thought through the issues. There of course remain strong economic and political arguments to support staying in the European Union – arguments that should command respect, as should, in a democratic society, the contrary position. This, though, is not the central issue. The central issue is the continued vituperative denigration of the "deplorables" upon whom one has to keep an ever-vigilant eye in case something nasty emerges from under the carpet. As Streek has noted, "elites" have, in promoting the globalisation of which they are the beneficiaries – the winners – also assumed a position of moral superiority. The corollary is that the losers are reconceptualised as, at best, fodder for post-truth populism and, at worst, as outright xenophobes and fascists. That there are worrying manifestations of such tendencies – the "alt-right" in the USA and, in the UK, amongst a small minority, a continued visceral hostility towards immigration – does not diminish the reality of the level of denigration and contempt visited on the great unwashed. Meanwhile what has been much less talked about is a phenomena arguably much more worrying than Brexit, or even Donald Trump – the growth of neo-fascism and authoritarian populism in parts of Europe and in Turkey. Sections of the European Union as a response appear increasingly set on greater supranational integration. In an era of globalised dislocation of "traditional" communities and social identifications and the rise of authoritarianism, the question remains, however, as to whether this is part of the solution or part of the essential problem.

Chapter 19

Conclusion

A plea for a measure of universalism

I have written this book from a psychoanalytic perspective, and emphasised that mourning involves the relinquishment of what has been lost as an external object, as a precondition for being internalised within the self, and as a source of memory and personal identification. The ongoing work of mourning also involves toleration of normal ambivalence, the presence of loving and hating feelings, without too much self-reproach, and the capacity to relate to others as separate individuals rather than as extensions of the self. If, however, what has been lost has been denigrated and/or rendered invisible and thus not available for representation, then the scene is set for pathologies of mourning. These might be manifest as an immersion in the past, or as a manic denial that any loss has taken place. I have particularly focused in recent chapters on the way in which the changes associated with deindustrialisation of the "traditional" centres of manufacturing and the decline of their associational communities have been accompanied by cultural denigration. I have discussed the rise of an intensively subjectivist culture, and of the concomitant politics of identity and competitive victimhood, in place of the universalist socio-economic, civic, and class perspectives of the "traditional" left.

The attacks, noted earlier, on football and its supporters, in the absence of any real evidence for the prosecution, appear to be merely part of a righteous disapproval displayed towards the "masses", and in particular to a denigrated indigenous "white working class". To take another topical example: "Islamophobia" has been held to be rampant in the UK. There have been disgraceful incidents but these have been, even allowing for the spike in reported incidents following the European referendum, relatively small in number – though no less worthy of condemnation. It could be argued that what has been most noticeable in historical terms has been the measured and, in a positive sense of the word, discriminating approach of the population as a whole to the rise of fundamentalist terrorism and what was, and is, the reality of an ongoing threat. The fueling of the spectre of Fascism and mass racism on the basis of relatively isolated incidents is, in sections of progressive opinion, though, a parallel process to that of sections of the right holding all Muslims somehow as being responsible or linked to the pathological destructiveness of a few individuals.

How do we understand such phenomena in psychological terms? I believe that in such a situation we are in the presence of a particular form of projective identification, all the more powerful for masquerading as being in the service of progressive emancipation and traducing those who question it as bigots and reactionaries – or at worst, fascists. The recipient can be made to feel, and indeed often does feel, that he is being prejudiced or unreasonable, as one who finds himself doubting the veracity of a story of abuse can feel, or be made to feel, that such doubts are collusive with the abuse, and indeed, if voiced, become a perpetuation, a further violation. Indeed, we are now in a culture in which the rightful investigation of abuse, the proper bringing of perpetrators to legal account, and the recognition of the need for justice for victims, has been accompanied by an abandonment of due process, of the assumption of innocence until proven guilty, and by trial and sentence through electronic media. Such a process is dangerous in the extreme and does nothing to achieve real justice and redress.

I am not seeking to pathologise what are real issues, nor to deny the reality of actually existing racism, or abuse, but to point out that there is also an emotional component at work that is distorting perception and, indeed, exacerbating the process. I have already made the point that self-designated political labels cannot be taken at face value and that, in my view, some of those claiming to be on the progressive or the liberal left could be seen, in practice, as neither liberal nor on the left. Equally, there may be some forms of populism that are progressive, of nationalism that are inclusive.

Here I repeat the crucial distinction between a genuine liberal pluralism and cosmopolitanism, and the contemporary hyper-subjectivism that remains preoccupied with narratives of righteous victimhood and identity. In the former there is tolerance of difference, at the same time as acknowledgement of areas of disagreement and conflict, and the reality that in ordinary life people may get it wrong, or rub up against each other the wrong way, or that there might be mutual misunderstanding. There is an acceptance that people might say things in the heat of the moment that they may later regret, but also that there are painful things that sometimes have to be spoken. Here we have to accept the contingency of our convictions in the here and now, and the reality of conflicting views. Uncertainties and conflicts may be impossible to resolve – we have instead to find a way of living with them, and allowing a degree of plurality. Most of all we have to accept that in a private capacity people have the right to different opinions, and the right to be "wrong".

Increasingly, however, in contemporary culture, there is an expectation of total agreement, a thin-skinned hypersensitivity, and a tendency to be traumatised by a different perspective. The fact that these positions are buttressed by a righteous position, in which moral outrage is the dominant emotional currency – manifest as the ubiquitous Twitter storm that takes place when some unwitting celebrity says, or is taken to have said, the wrong thing, or where a triumphant scientist wears the wrong sort of "sexist" jumper, this being almost inevitably followed by a tearful and shamed retraction – makes them more difficult to challenge.

Increasingly such movements are characterised by a hypersensitive subjectivism and solipsism. Such trends simultaneously display a tendency towards extreme relativism – all universalising metanarratives should be treated with suspicion – and states of affective certainty. The proponents become convinced not only of their own righteousness, but that they represent the truth, and to question this is to add to the trauma of the disbelieved. These trends are divisive and self-perpetuating in that they relentlessly concentrate on injustice and grievance, and, through projective processes, unconsciously provoke that which divides people rather than what might unite them.

Joanna Williams (2016) critiques the hypersensitivity and subjectivist concepts of micro-aggressions, micro-invalidations, and micro-assault that serve to constantly foreground issues of identity and inequality. She points out that the more these things become reified in this way, the more entrenched they become. The actual impact is not progressive but a regressive re-socialising, away from the universalism of campaigners such as Martin Luther King in which, perversely, to not judge someone because of their skin colour, in other words to see and treat them first and foremost as a human being, becomes a form of micro-invalidation. This is a culture where people become emotionally tied to narratives of victimhood, and in which acknowledging the real progress in fighting racism (never complete but, in historical terms, substantial) serves only to threaten their identity. The growing influence of this type of identity politics in education means that, potentially, students are denied access to emancipatory knowledge. Here we have the pseudo-progressive notion that students need to see their own identity reflected in the curriculum, a process that itself demonstrates the racism and reductionism it purports to combat; "the world of knowledge is judged on the skin colour of its originator rather than the intellectual and artistic insights it offers into the human condition" (Williams, 2016, p. 27). Similar processes are evident in relation to other forms of reified and exclusionist identity politics.

The present preoccupations with cultural appropriation and micro-invalidations represent emergent, but not exclusive, psychological trends in contemporary life. From a psychoanalytic perspective, they share, together with some other forms of extreme political correctness, features in common with religious fundamentalism. There is a pathological splitting of self and others, dividing the world between the righteous and the profane, the terror of the psychic catastrophe that might be the consequence of bringing together subjective and objective, maternal and paternal, in other words of allowing the oedipal couple to come together. Under states of high emotional arousal there is the same fidelity to concretised textual truths, and the same difficulty with flexible symbolic reflective thinking, and with entertaining, or even allowing, a different perspective.

This is the world of the thin-skinned narcissist as described by Ronald Britton (1998), most accurately identified by the nature of the counter-transference of the therapist, or mental health worker, in feelings of being taken over; of being in a world where his own internal reality and that of the patient remain incompatible, and where the assertion of one reality is felt to entail the annihilation of the other.

There is no short-term "fix" to such a dilemma. The best the therapist can do, as Britton outlines, is to make his key interpretations of what might be going on to himself, and to try to find a way of accommodating in his mind both his own experience and that of his patient – until such time as the latter may become more interested in understanding, rather than solely in being understood.

Optimally, if the coming together of the parental couple and of subjective and objective experience can be tolerated by the patient, such a situation provides conditions for growth, and the evolution of what Britton calls "the third position" – the capacity to see yourself as well as being yourself, to be able to put yourself in someone else's shoes whilst still being yourself:

> If the link between the parents perceived in love and hate can be tolerated in the child's mind it provides the child with a prototype for an object relationship of a third kind in which he or she is a witness and not a participant. A *third position* then comes into existence from which object relationships can be observed. Given this, we can also envisage being observed. This provides us with a capacity for seeing ourselves in interaction with others and for entertaining another point of view while retaining our own – for observing ourselves while being ourselves. I call the mental freedom provided by this process *triangular space*.
>
> (1998, pp. 41–42, emphasis added)

It is this triangular space, this third position, that is increasingly difficult to maintain in the self-perpetuating and self-reinforcing culture and identity wars that characterise much of contemporary life.

I have considered in this book some of the historical psycho-social forces that might be driving these essentially narcissistic trends – the decline of the post-war settlement, the rise of neo-liberal capitalism and its mirror image on sections of the liberal and radical left, postmodern relativism and hyper-subjectivism. I have stressed that, looking forward, pessimism is not always warranted. At an individual level change is possible, regressive outcomes are not inevitable. Many patients with narcissistic and other personality difficulties can be helped, and evidence is increasingly showing that change and development is possible. Indeed, this can occur with maturity, and with the right kind of circumstances, a creative form of work, a supportive personal relation, or a good network of friends – even without long-term treatment. For those with more intractable difficulties the process is inevitably fraught – though not necessarily without hope.

Overall, the interplay of internal and external factors in the multi-determined aetiology of serious personality disturbance, in narcissistic and borderline states, for example, is well described by John Steiner: "Traumatic experience with violence or neglect in the environment leads to the internalization of violent disturbed objects which at the same time serve as suitable receptacles for the projection of the patients own destructiveness" (Steiner, 1993, p. 4). The relative preponderance of innate and environmental factors will lead to a different kind of presentation.

It may be that there is an innately destructive process at work in the more malignant states that is not the case for those people whose difficulties predominately lie in a deprived and/or abusive early environment.

There may be socio-political correlates to these distinctions. In the classic BBC TV series *The Ascent of Man* (1973*)*, Jacob Bronowski is seen standing in the ash pools of Birkenau, noting that this is what happens when you treat people as things, turn everything to undifferentiated matter, and are convinced of your own rightness. Reaching for the right words, he turns to the reported last words of Oliver Cromwell: "I beseech you, by the bowels of Christ, consider that you might be mistaken." A key feature of Fascism was – and is – its explicit repudiation of the very humane, liberal, and reality-orientated values that might have underpinned any negotiation, dialogue, and understanding of it, echoing the idealising of instinct and "the will", and the denigration of logical thought and rationality also evident in the millennial and apocalyptic movements of the Middle Ages as identified by Cohn (1957). Michael Rustin (1991), in a discussion of "Racism and Anti-Racism", quotes Jean-Paul Sartre's essay *Anti-Semite and Jew* to capture the omnipotent triumph inherent in this position, its thick-skinned and grandiose narcissistic invulnerability, and its contemptuous denigration of normal human concern:

The anti-Semite has chosen to live on the plane of passion. The anti-Semite has chosen hate because hate is a faith; from the outset he has chosen to devalue words and reason. How entirely at ease he feels as a result. How futile and frivolous discussions about the rights of the Jews appear to him. He has placed himself on other ground from the beginning. If out of courtesy he consents for a minute to defend his point of view, he lends himself, but he does not give himself. He tries simply to project his intuitive certainty on to the plane of discourse.

(Sartre, 1948)

The above passage has been much quoted and for good reason, for though the fascist mentality may wear different clothes in different eras – including the clothes of progressive righteousness – its essential elements remain constant throughout the ages. A major implication of this analysis, if it is correct, is that it is of limited value to spend time and energy trying to understand these ideologies on their own terms, intellectually incoherent, shallow, empty, and self-contradictory as they frequently are, as the real emotional motivations reside elsewhere. We might want, rather, to better understand the nature of these emotional motivations and the sort of psychological, socio-cultural, and political conditions in which they emerge and thrive.

I want here to turn to the neglected subject of fairness. As Eric Rayner (1999) pointed out, fairness is a social concept, based in our need to function relatively harmoniously in social groups, increasing our chances of survival, utilising mutuality, attunement, and trust. Fairness involves people feeling that they are treated equitably, without bias, as separate, different, but also equivalent. Developmentally and philosophically, fairness precedes the more complex concept of justice. When fairness is ruptured, then strong feelings are induced; indignation, outrage, bitterness, vengeance, grievance, sometimes full of violence.

Grievance, Steiner says, can be seen as a form of pathological mourning. There is a "very intense tie to the object". Thus, in states of grievance there is a holding on to the object of attack. This failure of mourning has both individual and socio-cultural manifestations. Freud wrote, in "Some character-types met with in psychoanalytic work" (1916d), of people who regard themselves as "exceptions" to normal life, as having special status, linked to a perception of having suffered unique injury, that makes them exempt from the necessity of having to undergo normal suffering. This sense of grievance might be linked developmentally to the process of weaning, to being expelled, as the patient may have experienced it, from the symbiotic Eden of the maternal relationship. Often this is associated with the arrival of a younger sibling. A modern variant of this is the parental separation, promising the child exclusive oedipal access to the remaining parent, only to find defeat emerge from the jaws of victory as the parent finds a new partner, not the patient, or has another child. The upshot is that something unforgiveable is felt to have happened. The emotional tie with the parental object remains (and indeed is not mourned and relinquished) but is now suffused with hatred and the desire to make this "object" suffer:

> A wound results which may become so invested with narcissism that it is denied the opportunity for proper healing. In these cases the patient comes to believe that the objects that have wronged him are so totally bad that they never can be forgiven, and his own hatred, and his wish for revenge, are so total that they are equally unforgiveable. Subsequently even if the loss seems bearable, the injury is nursed in order to keep the sense of injustice alive and to defend against any sense of responsibility. The pathological organisation supports the patient and helps him to evade guilt which is felt to be appropriate for the object rather than the patient to feel. At the same time the conviction that the guilt is unbearable leads to an extremely stuck situation where change is resisted and progress in the analysis is blocked.
>
> (Steiner, 1993, p. 76)

There are a number of things that can be said about Steiner's formulation. A pervasive sense of grievance, resentment, and entitlement, with its origins in early life, may be projected into the social world. This is accompanied by pathological spitting and denial, so that the badness that resides in the self, or in idealised objects, is projected into all bad oppressive socio-political structures. There may be some objective truth to these attributions, as these socio-political structures may well have objectively oppressive characteristics that make these projections appear persuasive and reasonable. There is a fit, a valency, between internal processes and external socio-political realities. However, all discrimination and flexibility of thinking becomes lost in this polarised all-or-nothing characterisation of innocent victim and oppressive structure.

Writing about working with survivors of the Omagh bombing in Northern Ireland, Raman Kapur (2002) comments on the way in which experience of the trauma lent itself to the rigid defence-identification of self with the trauma, and with self-righteous victimhood: "Traumatic events attack the core of self-identity and at the same time can accentuate psychotic aspects of the personality which can become addicted to destructive processes" (Kapur, 2002, p. 324). The traumatic event becomes the source of perverse forms of self-esteem, and this is very difficult to challenge without feeling the patient is being re-victimised in some way. "To take away any source of attention that the injury gave to the individual patient was like robbing them of all they had left" (2002, p. 325). The therapist's attempts to understand this situation, on anything other than concrete terms, were experienced by these patients with fury and as proof of the therapist's incapacity to understand and to see justice. Yet it was just this position of self-righteous competitive victimhood that sustained the bloody momentum of the conflict.

People, family systems, larger groups, and nations may move in and out of this aggrieved position in a more flexible way, or may become fixed as part of a pathological structural organisation. As Richard III allegedly uses his spinal deformity as a justification for cruelty, so historical wrongs can be used as justification for nihilistic terror. Such terror has no coherent or realisable political objective. It is an end in itself.

An appreciation of these sorts of dynamics, at once intra-psychic and intrapersonal, may help with the understanding of, and response to, pathological politics of identity and victimhood. The most extreme manifestations of this mindset, it might be argued, can be seen in some contemporary forms of terrorism. Whereas in the past there may be coherent if conflicting political demands in political terrorism, in more modern manifestations there seems to have been a more nihilistic component. The aim is to keep alive and to terrorise, to disable, to inflict pain. In this sense, there is no coherent or achievable political objective, in this world at least. Rather, the acts of terror are ends in themselves. The recipients of these attacks may be unconsciously seen as a maternal and/or paternal body, perceived to have unforgivably wronged the attackers, and so deserving of eternal punishment. Real and/or imagined historical traumas and injustices, many going back generations, are recruited in service of these grievances, and political demands, such as they are, are apocalyptic and not deliverable, thus ensuring that the grievance continues. The attacked group is nudged via behavioural provocation and mass projective processes into overreaction and violent responses so that more grievances are collected, and "the guilt which it is felt more appropriate for the object rather than the patient to feel" (Steiner, 1993) is then felt not by the original aggressors but by the victims.

As well as overreaction from the attacked group to the provocation, there is also a danger of under-reaction and underestimation of the real threat. If the attacked group are themselves feeling a historical "bad conscience" related to guilt at their own relative privilege, or from other factors, they may show a tendency to maso-chistically submit to their attackers, and to berate themselves for what they might have done that was wrong such as to merit such an attack. This response – the "Stockholm syndrome" – also defends them from an open expression of their own aggression and rage. This response, and less extreme versions of it, mean that, at best, the aggression of the attackers is not taken up and confronted, and, at worst, that a sadomasochistic *folie à deux* takes place. On the other hand, if they do counter-react aggressively they may "play in" to the projective identification, actually becoming an abusive violent oppressive force, thus actualising the fantasy. It is here that an integrated and applied psychoanalytic perspective (Volkan, 1988) can be helpful, in providing a space for reflection. As John Alderdice (2002) has written, however, there are no quick fixes; change, if it occurs, takes a long time, and may be subject to regression:

> It is not the content of a solution that is critical but the process of achieving it. We know in our clinical work that merely telling the patient where the problem lies, or giving them an analytic text to read, is rarely a healing intervention. It is taking the patient through the analytic process that is transformational.
>
> (2002, p. 13)

Correspondingly, at a socio-political level, in the field of conflict resolution, there is a need to establish an inclusive social setting, with all the parties involved in attendance, and where everything is "open to be talked about, without commitment" (Alderdice, 2002, p. 13). There is some evidence, as with the case of Northern Ireland, that, with time, change is possible. However, Alderdice cautions that it is also necessary to maintain differentiation between, for example, the uses of terror that have a political aim, and terror that is used to perpetuate a split, to maintain a deadly psychological and political status quo.

Responses and attempts at understanding appear beset, however, by the characteristic problem of contemporary socio-political analysis – a relative ignorance of psychodynamic factors, of unconscious emotions, and their psychosocial precipitants, and a tendency to overvalue the explanatory powers of the professed ideology of the perpetrator. These beliefs may have motivational force but are, as we have seen from the earlier discussion of millennialism and Fascism, shallow, contradictory, and intellectually risible. The implication of this is that a response to acts of terror based on the notion that the perpetrator is acting out of rational motives will likely be inadequate; for this involves the attribution of meaning and normal propositional thought to acts that are emotionally motivated, and for which ideology serves as a rationalisation. In the case of Andreas Breivik, Carine Minne and Matthias von de Tann (2011) suggested that he may have been suffering from an extreme personality disorder, during which he appeared, to outside observers, as sane, if a little eccentric. Within this personality structure may have been an encapsulated psychotic core. The psychosocial determinants are likely to be multiple – an absent father, a possibly narcissistic mother, an insecurely established masculine identification, the presence of powerful defences against the experience of shame and vulnerability, the latter of which is projected into victims. For understandable emotional reasons the tragedy arising out of human pathology and destructiveness was turned, however, into something politically resonant and comprehensible. Breivik's ideological beliefs do require analysis. Such a stance, though, risks colluding with the grandiosity, the "delusion of sanity" (Minne & Von de Tann, 2011) of the perpetrator. Further, in emphasising, and sometimes engaging with, the overt "political" ideology and demands of these individuals, such responses tend unwittingly to give these beliefs an unmerited credibility.

There is a need for ongoing research into links between certain sorts of psychopathology, social structures and ideology formation. Angelique Chrisafis (2015)., for example, makes the point that the disaffected perpetrators of the "Charlie Hebdo Paris atrocity attackers were born, raised and radicalised in Paris", some in the nineteenth arrondissement, in a locale that is a mixture of gentrification, working-class streets, and gang-blighted high-rises. They had poor school records and chaotic family lives. As adults they were often unemployed, involved in petty crime, theft, drugs, and trafficking. They lived in a world that was so near yet so far from the gilded riches and desirable lifestyles of late capitalist life. Immature, marginalised, and enthralled by a young guru figure, their Islamic belief and knowledge does not appear to have run very deep. Death fantasies and notions of martyrdom were stimulated by the second Iraq war. Ideology was minimal; inchoate rage against the USA combined with limited introspection and a search for a sense of identity. Chrisafis suggests that the appeal of fundamentalism is more likely to take root where there is a sense of malaise and personal unimportance. In this sense the defining social context is not poverty as such, but the decay of social order, the absence of the state, the seeming irrelevance and unattainability of liberty, equality, and fraternity – instead the omnipresence of a youth culture of fast money, robbery, drugs, and guns. In such a fast track culture paternal authority is absent, ineffectual, or marginalised. Fathers arriving typically from the Maghreb, North Africa, and working in poorly paid jobs were no longer seen as sources of positive identification.

Such a picture has support from recent studies in which we see a pattern of alienation and estrangement from the world of the father, immersion in the virtual worlds of the electronic media, a mindset that is postmodern rather than medieval, an indifference to questions of actual political injustice, and in which there is a wish to go out with all guns blazing (Roy, 2017). Such a picture accords all too well with many variants of home-grown terrorism, and with the unpredictable actions of the "lone wolf".

Perhaps the most disquieting thought, though, is that although ostensibly in opposition to "Western values", contemporary forms of fundamentalist terrorism appear as a nihilistic variant of Western "identity politics", infused by resentment, grievance, and a sense of personal trauma and shame, identified with national and religious humiliation, redeemed by an act of purifying violence and self-immolation.

I have argued in this book that the identity politics of nominal left and right are narcissistic mirror images of each other, that they are, through projective processes, self-perpetuating, and are based on emotional needs, including the need for group affiliation, and the denial and externalisation of inadmissible internal conflict. Here I briefly return to my earlier discussion of human subjectivity. We have noted earlier the essential difference between inclusive cosmopolitan versions of the nation state and those based on fictive notions of ethnic identity. From a psychoanalytical perspective, too, at a deeper level, all claims to identity rest on shaky ground. We are never entirely secure in our positions, never entirely settled. We have multiple conflicting identifications – passive, active, loving, aggressive, feminine, and masculine; and these combine together in dynamic interaction with a changing environment. The psychoanalyst Joyce McDougall in her book *Plea for a Measure of Abnormality* (1990) notes the ambivalence people inevitably feel towards the claims of reality and normality. There may be a wish to earn the approval and love of parents, but also a wish to circumvent and transgress. There may be in every human being "ordinary", neurotic, psychotic, perverse, and psycho-somatic solutions to the problems attendant upon facing reality, and in particular the reality of the oedipal situation.

Whilst the presence of different and often competing parts of the self may give rise to conflict it is also the case that our multiple identifications allow us to be able, potentially, to identify with the experience of others who are ostensibly very different, because there may be a part of us that identifies with the feeling and/or experience. Furthermore, although everyone is unique and individual difference is irreducible, people generally have more in common than they have in difference. All human beings, though they may have to do so in very different circumstances and socio-historic conditions, have to face the existential facts of life that exist outside of human culture and wishes – the nature of human vulnerability, the terror that may accompany dependence on others, and the reality of ageing and loss. As the Italian philosopher Sebastiano Timpanaro wrote:

> love, the brevity and frailty of human existence, the contrast between the smallness and weakness of man and the infinity of the cosmos, are expressed in literary works in very different ways, but still not in such different ways that all reference to such constant experience of the human condition as the sexual instinct, the debility produced by age (with its psychological repercussions), the fear of one's own death and sorrow at the death of others, is lost.
> (Timpanaro, 1975, p. 50, cited in Eagleton, 2000, p. 110)

It is a key finding of psychoanalysis – though, of course, not only of psychoanalysis – that a central factor in human development is the quality of early relationships and attachments. At a social level, it is a secure attachment to a sense of continued tradition, as a source of meaning, value, and emotional identification that provides the optimum conditions for the development of empathic identification with others from different backgrounds – that is, for the possibility of moral universalism. Whilst change is inevitable and has to be come to terms with, this is made much more difficult if it comes too quickly, or if the pressures associated with adjustment are concentrated on already disadvantaged social groups. It is made much more difficult, too, if the world that has been lost is rendered invisible or made subject to cultural denigration. In these circumstances we can see the conditions for the growth of regressive narcissistic and paranoid group processes as outlined earlier. Such an outcome, however, as we have also seen earlier, is by no means inevitable, and is conditional on such factors as class, economics, culture, ideology, the presence or absence of effective leadership, and the realistic possibility or otherwise of achieving political reform and securable objectives.

In the light of these factors it has been a calamity of the first order that sections of "progressive opinion", essentially the liberal left, have retreated from the universalist concerns of class, inequality, economics, and social justice, and from the rationalist Enlightenment values that underpin these concerns, to the toxic politics of identity and sectional interests. The limitations of this, merely as electoral policy, were only too evident in the failure of Hilary Clinton to defeat Donald Trump. The democratic campaign seemed to exemplify the trends that I have highlighted in this book; the liberal-left abandonment of the universalist socio-economic preoccupations of the traditional left for an acquiescence with global capital, marketisation, and privatisation, and its replacement of politics with self-perpetuating narratives of cultural difference. It is, of course, an unanswered question as to whether if the Democrats had opted instead for Bernie Sanders – a man from a very different intellectual and social tradition, someone who did make across-board socio-economic appeals, for example, to the farmers of the mid-west – they might have won. In the United Kingdom the 2017 Labour Party election manifesto hit a similar note by stressing universalist social democratic economic priorities rather than appealing to the politics of cultural difference and identity, and in so doing helped to significantly raise the party's vote – in stark contrast to the fate of nominally social democratic parties elsewhere in Europe.

This book has not, however, been written as a party political tract, or as an outline of a political programme. Rather I have sought to focus on common emotional trends and motivations that have been operating across the political spectrum – and indeed within the wider culture. These trends, coming to a head at the time of the fall of the Soviet Union, posited an end of history and a world where everything was permitted, and restrictions did not apply. Fundamentalist ideologies of individual autonomy and liberation characterised some forms of radical counter-cultural thinking no less than they did extreme free-market individualism. They have increasingly involved in their decline, I have suggested, an essentially narcissistic retreat into narratives of identity and victimhood, buttressed by states of pathological certainty. In such a "post-truth" mindset the power of a compelling emotional narrative is given primacy over the claims of tradition, expertise, and disinterested knowledge. However, as we have seen, wishes conflict, between people, and social groups, and within individuals. In the more narcissistic trends, which have been the subject of this book, though, conflict is denied and/or projected into others, and real mourning and internalisation do not take place, as reality, not least the reality of irreducible conflict, has not been faced. In the slow protracted demise of neo-liberalism we are seeing the emergence of new class configurations, and new conflicts of interest. In the post-war years, for example, there was a highly creative alliance between the working class and sections of the progressive liberal middle class, securing many economic and civil reforms that we now tend to take for granted. It may be, though, that the interests of these two groups no longer so readily coincide: one group are the beneficiaries of a system in which the other are the losers, and the internal conflicts and cognitive dissonances that might arise from a recognition of this situation, have been denied and mystified, in part through the reconcepualisation of economic privilege as moral and cultural superiority.

Although I have suggested that a progressive political project requires the reassertion of universalism, located in a secure sense of shared and inclusive history and tradition, there is no pain-free, or conflict-free, solution. Hard choices sometimes have to be made, at both a personal and political level, and each choice also involves a loss, a recognition of roads not taken. I started this book with a reference to modernity and modernism. It is a feature of our contemporary world that many different realities co-exist, even within small geographical areas. The question is whether we can emerge from the narcissistic bubble in which we mistake our small slice of reality for the whole picture.

References

Adorno, T. W., Frenkel-Brunswik, E., Levinson, D. J., & Sanford, R. N. (1950). *The Authoritarian Personality.* New York, NY: Harper.

Alderdice, J. (2002). Introduction. In: C. Covington, P. Williams, J. Arundale & J. Knox (Eds.), *Terrorism and War: Unconscious Dynamics of Political Violence* (pp. 1–16). London: Karnac.

Allen, J. G., & Fonagy, P. (Eds.) (2006). *Handbook of Mentalization-Based Treatment.* Sussex: John Wiley.

American Psychiatric Association (2013). *Diagnostic and Statistical Manual of Mental Disorders (DSM-5)* (Fifth edition). Arlington, VA: American Psychiatric Association.

Anderson, B. (1983). *Imagined Communities: Reflections on the Origin and Spread of Nationalism.* London: Verso.

Arendt, H. (1951). *The Origins of Totalitarianism.* London: Penguin, 2017.

Arendt, H. (1963). *Eichmann in Jerusalem: A Report on the Banality of Evil.* New York: Penguin, 2006.

Balint, M. (1968). *The Basic Fault: Therapeutic Aspects of Regression.* London: Tavistock.

Barnett, B. (2007). *"You Ought To!": A Psychoanalytic Study of Superego and Conscience.* London: Karnac.

Bauman, Z. (1989). *Modernity and the Holocaust.* Cambridge: Polity.

Beckett, S. (1958). *Krapp's Last Tape.* In: *Samuel Beckett: The Complete Dramatic Works.* London: Faber & Faber, 2006.

Bell, D. (1999). *Psychoanalysis and Culture: A Kleinian Perspective.* London: Duckworth.

Bell, D. (2009). Is truth an illusion? – Psychoanalysis and postmodernism. *International Journal of Psychoanalysis, 90*: 331–345.

Berman, M. (1982). *All that is Solid Melts into Air: The Experience of Modernity.* London: Penguin.

Bion, W. R. (1961). *Experience in Groups.* New York, NY: Basic.

W. R. Bion. (1962). A theory of thinking. In: *Second Thoughts.* London: Karnac, 2007.

Blake, W. (1804). *Milton: A Poem.* London: The Tate Gallery and the William Blake Trust, 1993.

Bolognini, S. (2007). *Psychoanalytic Empathy.* London: Free Association.

Breuilly, J. (1993). *Nationalism and the State* (2nd Edition). Manchester: Manchester University Press.

Britton, R. (1998). *Belief and Imagination: Explorations in Psychoanalysis.* London: Routledge.

Britton, R. (2003). *Sex, Death, and the Superego: Experiences in Psychoanalysis.* London: Karnac.

Bronowski, J. (Writer) (1973). *The Ascent of Man* (TV series). London: BBC.

Caldwell, C. A. (2017). French fracture: a social thinker illuminates his country's populist divides. *New Statesman*, 11 May.

Campbell, B. (1994). The shipbuilders' swansong. *The Independent*, 13 November.

Campbell, D. (1999). The role of the father in a pre-suicide state. In: R. J. Perelberg (Ed.), *Psychoanalytic Understanding of Violence and Suicide* (pp. 73–86). London: Routledge.

Campbell, D., & Hale, R. (1991). Suicidal acts. In: J. Holmes (Ed.), *Textbook of Psychotherapy in Psychiatric Practice* (pp. 287–306). London: Churchill Livingstone.

Caper, R. (2008). Envy, narcissism and the destructive instinct. In: P. Roth & A. Lemma (Eds.) *Envy and Gratitude Revisited* (p. 44). London: Karnac.

Cavell, M. (2004). Truth, mind and objectivity. In: J. Mills (Ed.) *Psychoanalysis at the Limit: Epistemology, Mind and the Question of Science.* Albany, NY: State University of New York.

Chase, D. (Writer and Executive Producer) (1999–2007). *The Sopranos* (TV series). New York, NY: HBO.

Chasseguet-Smirgel, J. (1985). *The Ego Ideal.* London: Free Association.

Chasseguet-Smirgel, J. (1986). *Sexuality and Mind: The Role of the Father and the Mother in the Psyche.* London: Karnac.

Chasseguet-Smirgel, J. (1990). Reflections of a psychoanalyst upon the Nazi biocracy and genocide. *International Review of Psychoanalysis*, 17: 167–176.

Chrisafis, A. (2015). Charlie Hebdo attackers: Born, raised and radicalized in Paris. *The Guardian*, 15 January.

Clekley, H. C. (1941). *The Mask of Sanity.* St. Louis, MS: Mosby.

Clement, D., & La Frenais, I. (Writers) (1973–74). *Whatever Happened to the Likely Lads?* (TV series). London: BBC.

Cobb, R. (1998). *Paris and Elsewhere: Selected Writings* (edited and introduced by David Gilmour). London: John Murray.

Cohen, N. (2007). *What's Left? How the Left Lost Their Way.* London: Harper Perennial.

Cohn, N. (1957). *The Pursuit of the Millennium: Revolutionary Millenarians and Mystical Anarchists of the Middle Ages.* Oxford: OUP, 1970.

Cohn, N. (1967). *Warrant for Genocide: The Myth of Jewish World Conspiracy and the Protocols of the Elders of Zion.* New York, NY: Harper & Row.

Collier, P. (2017). How to save capitalism from itself. *Times Literary Supplement*, 25 January.

Colls, R., & Lancaster, B. (Eds.) (1992). *Geordies: Roots of Regionalism* (2nd edition). Newcastle: Northumbria University Press.

Conrad, J. (1907). *The Secret Agent.* Oxford: OUP, 2004.

Cronin, A. (1996). *Samuel Beckett: The Last Modernist.* London: Flamingo.

Damasio, A. (1999). *The Feeling of What Happens: Body and Emotion in the Making of Consciousness.* New York: Harcourt Brace.

Defoe, D. (1719). *Robinson Crusoe.* Canada: Broadview, 2010.

Dibdin, M. (2007). *Endgames.* London: Faber & Faber.

Dicks, H. V. (1972). *Licensed Mass Murder: A Socio-Psychological Study of Some SS Killers.* Sussex: Heinemann.

Dostoevsky, F. (1880). *The Brothers Karamazov.* New York, NY: Random House, 1996.

Drake, E. (Writer) (1961). "It was a very good year" (Song). Reedlands Music Corp.

Eagleton, T. (2000). *The Idea of Culture*. Oxford: Blackwell.

Eagleton, T. (2003). *After Theory*. London: Penguin.

Eichinger, B. (Writer and Producer) (2004). *Downfall (Der Untergang)* (Motion Picture). Munich: Constantin Films.

Eliot, T. S. (1922). The Wasteland. In: *Collected Poems 1909–1962*. Faber & Faber: London, 1974.

Elliot, L., & Atkinson, D. (2016). *Europe Isn't Working*. New Haven, CT: Yale University Press.

Ellmers, C., & Werner, A. (1988). *London's Lost Riverscape*. London: Viking.

Engels, F (1845). *The Condition of the Working Classes in England*. London: Penguin, 1987.

Evans, R. J. (2005). *The Third Reich in Power: How the Nazis Won Over the Hearts and Minds of a Nation*. London: Penguin.

Evans, R. J. (2008). *The Third Reich at War*. London: Allen Lane.

Fagen, D. (2013). *Eminent Hipsters*. London: Jonathan Cape.

Fonagy, P., Gergely, G., Jurist, E., & Target, M. (2002). *Affect Regulation, Mentalization and the development of the self*. New York: Other Press.

Frank, T. (2002). *One Market Under God: Extreme Capitalism, Market Populism and the End of Economic Democracy*. London: Vintage.

Freud, A. (1936). *The Ego and the Mechanisms of Defence*. London: Karnac, 1993.

Freud, S. (1895d). *Studies on Hysteria. S. E., 2*: 1–335. London: Hogarth.

Freud, S. (1910c). *Leonardo da Vinci and a Memory of his Childhood. S. E., 11*: 57–137. London: Hogarth.

Freud, S. (1914b). The Moses of Michelangelo. *S. E., 13*: 209–236. London: Hogarth.

Freud, S. (1914c). On narcissism: An introduction. *S. E., 14*: 67–102. London: Hogarth.

Freud, S. (1915c). Instincts and their vicissitudes. *S. E., 14*: 109–140. London: Hogarth.

Freud, S. (1916d). Some character-types met with in psychoanalytic work. *S. E., 14*: 318–24. London: Hogarth.

Freud, S. (1917e). Mourning and melancholia. *S. E., 14*: 237–258. London: Hogarth.

Freud, S. (1920g). *Beyond the Pleasure Principle. S. E., 18*: 1–64. London: Hogarth.

Freud, S. (1921c). *Group Psychology and the Analysis of the Ego. S. E., 18*: 65–143. London: Hogarth.

Freud, S. (1923b). *The Ego and the Id. S. E., 19*: 3–68. London: Hogarth.

Freud, S. (1926d). *Inhibitions, Symptoms and Anxiety. S. E., 20*: 75–174. London: Hogarth.

Freud, S. (1930a). *Civilization and its Discontents. S. E., 21*: 57–145. London: Hogarth.

Friedlander, S. (2013). *Franz Kafka: the Poet of Shame and Guilt*. New Haven, CT: Yale University Press.

Frosch, S. (1987). *The Politics of Psychoanalysis: An Introduction to Freudian and Post-Freudian Theory*. London: Macmillan.

Gabbard, G. O. (1994). *Psychodynamic Psychiatry in Clinical Practice — The DSM-IV Edition*. Arlington, VA: American Psychiatric Publishing.

Gabbard, G. (2000). The integration of psychoanalytic and neurosientific thought in the realm of personality. In: J. Sandler, R. Michels & P. Fonagy (Eds.), *Changing Ideas in a Changing World: The Revolution in Psycho-Analysis. Essays in Honour of Arnold Cooper* (pp. 155–162). London: Karnac.

Gellner, E. (1983). *Nations and Nationalism* (2nd Edition). Oxford: Blackwell.

Gilman, S. L. (2005). *Franz Kafka*. London: Reaktion.

Gilmour, D. (1998). *Richard Cobb: Paris and Elsewhere*. London: John Murray.

Ginaite, S. (2008). *The Protests of a Veteran Jewish Partisan*. Jewishcurrents.org (September 2008 issue).

Glasser, M. (1979). Some aspects of the role of aggression in the perversions. In: I. Rosen (Ed.), *Sexual Deviation*. Oxford: OUP, 1998.

Glasser, M. (1998). On violence: a preliminary communication. *International Journal of Psychoanalysis, 79:* 887–902.

Glenny, M. (1992). *The Fall of Yugoslavia* (3rd edition). London: Penguin, 1996.

Glinert, E. (2000). *Guide to Literary London*. London: Penguin.

Grunberger, B. (1989). *New Essays on Narcissism*. London. Free Association.

Hanly, C. (2009). On truth and clinical psychoanalysis. *International Journal of Psychoanalysis, 90:* 363–373

Harris, J. (2008). The day politics stopped working. *The Guardian*, 15 February.

Harvey, D. (2010). *The Enigma of Capital and the Crisis of Capitalism*. London: Profile Books.

Hirschbiegel, O. (Director) (2004). *Downfall (Der Untergang)* (Motion Picture). Munich: Constantin Films.

Hobsbawm, E. (1994). *The Age of Extremes: The Short Twentieth Century 1914–1991*. London: Abacus, 1995.

Hobsbawm, E. (1997). *On History*. London: Abacus, 2002.

Hobsbawm, E. (2000). *The New Century*. Abacus.

Horkheimer, M., & Adorno, T. W. (2002). *Dialectic of Enlightenment: Philosophical Fragments*. Stanford, CA: Stanford University Press.

Houellebecq, M. (2005). *The Possibility of an Island*. London: Weidenfeld & Nicolson.

Hughes, R. (1993). *Culture of Complaint: The Fraying of America*. Oxford: OUP.

Hutton, W. (1999). New Keynesianism and New Labour In: A. Gamble & T. Wright (Eds.), *The New Social Democracy*. Oxford: Blackwell.

Hutton, W. (2009). High stakes, low finance. *The Guardian Review*, 2 May, p. 8.

Jackson, M., & Williams, P. (1994). *Unimaginable Storms: A Search for Meaning in Psychosis*. London: Karnac.

Jack, I. (2011). So much in Glasgow has changed, but violence against women persists. *The Guardian*, 12 March.

Jacques, E. (1955). Social systems as a defence against persecutory and depressive anxiety. In: M. Klein, P. Heimann & R. Money-Kyrle (Eds.), *New Directions in Psychoanalysis* (pp. 478–498). London, Karnac, 1985.

Jameson, F. (1991). *Postmodernism: Or, the Cultural Logic of Late Capitalism*. London: Verso.

Jones, S. (1993). *The Language of the Genes*. London: Harper Collins, 2000.

Jonson, B. (1606). *Volpone*. Manchester: Manchester University Press, 1983.

Joseph, B. (1982). Addiction to near death. In: M. Feldman & E. Bott Spillius (Eds), *Psychic Equilibrium and Psychic Change: Selected Papers of Betty Joseph* (pp.127–138). London: Routledge, 1989.

Judt, T. (2007). *Postwar: A History of Europe since 1945*. London: Pimlico.

Judt, T. (2009) *Reappraisals: Reflections on the Forgotten Twentieth Century*. London: Vintage.

Judt, T. (2010). *The Memory Chalet*. London: Heinemann.

Junge, T. (2004). *Until the Final Hour: Hitler's Last Secretary*. New York: Arcade.

Kafka, F. (1925). *The Trial.* London: Hesperus, 2005.

Kapur, R. (2002). Omagh: The beginning of the reparative impulse? In: C. Colvington, P. Williams, J. Arundale & J. Knox (Eds.), *Terrorism and War: Unconscious Dynamics of Political Violence* (pp. 315–328). London: Karnac.

Kernberg, O. (1984). *Severe Personality Disorders: Psychotherapeutic Strategies.* New Haven, CT: Yale University Press.

Kernberg, O. (2003). Sanctioned social violence (part 1). *International Journal of Psychoanalysis, 84*: 683–698.

Kernberg, O. (2004). *Aggressivity, Narcissism, and Self-destructiveness in the Psychotherapeutic Relationship.* London: Yale University Press.

Kershaw, I. (1985). *The Nazi Dictatorship: Problems and Perspectives of Interpretation* (3rd Edition). London: Hodder Education.

Kershaw, I. (1987). *The "Hitler Myth": Image and Reality in the Third Reich.* Oxford: OUP, 2001.

Klein, M. (1975). *Envy and Gratitude and Other Works.* London: Hogarth.

Kohut, H. (1984). *How Does Psychoanalysis Cure?* Chicago, IL: University of Chicago Press.

Ladd, B. (1997). *The Ghosts of Berlin: Confronting German History in the Urban Landscape.* Chicago, IL: The University of Chicago.

Lasch, C. (1977). *Haven in a Heartless World: The Family Besieged.* New York, NY: Norton.

Lasch, C. (1979). *The Culture of Narcissism: American Life in an Age of Diminishing Expectations.* New York, NY: Norton.

Lasch, C. (1984). *The Minimal Self: Psychic Survival in Troubled Times.* London: Picador.

Layard, R., Clark, D., Bell, S., Knapp, M., Meacher, B., Priebe, S., Turnberg, L., Thornicroft, G., & Wright, B. (2006). The Depression Report: A new deal for depression and anxiety disorders. London: The Centre for Economic Performance's Mental Health Policy Group, London School of Economics and Political Science.

Lear, J. (2005). *Freud.* New York, NY: Routledge.

Lear, J. (2007). *Radical Hope: Ethics in the Face of Cultural Devastation.* Cambridge, MA: Harvard University Press.

Levi, P. (1963). *Is This a Man/The Truce.* London: Abacus, 1987.

Lilla, M. (2014). The truth about our libertarian age: why the dogma of democracy doesn't always make the world a better place. *New Republic,* 18 June.

Lilla, M. (2016). The end of identity liberalism. *New York Times,* 18 October.

Long, S. (2008). *The Perverse Organisation and its Deadly Sins.* London: Karnac.

Lousada, J. (2006). Glancing over the shoulder; racism, fear of the stranger and the fascist state of mind. *Psychoanalytic Psychotherapy, 20*: 97–104.

Main, T. (1967). Knowledge, learning and freedom from thought. In: J. Johns (Ed.), *The Ailment and other Psychoanalytic Essays.* London: Free Association, 1989.

Mair, P. (2014). *Ruling the Void: The Hollowing of Western Democracy.* London: Verso.

Malik, K. (1996). *The Meaning of Race: Race History and Culture in Western Society.* New York, NY: New York University Press.

Malik, K. (2001.12.18). The trouble with multi-culturalism. www.spiked-online.com

Manne, A. (2015). *The life of I: The New Culture of Narcissism.* Melbourne: Melbourne University Press.

Marx, K., & Engels, F. (1848). *Manifesto of the Communist Party.* London: Penguin, 2002.

Mason, P. (2010). *Meltdown: The End of the Age of Greed*. London: Verso.

Mazower, M. (2004). *Salonica, City of Ghosts: Christians, Muslims and Jews 1430–1950*. New York, NY: Harper Collins.

McDougall, J. (1990). *Plea for a Measure of Abnormality*. London: Free Association Books.

McEwan, I. (2005) *Saturday*. London: Vintage.

McGrath, M. (2003). *Silvertown: An East End Family Memoir*. London: Harper Collins.

Menzies-Lyth, I. (1959). The functioning of social systems as a defence against anxiety. In: *Containing Anxiety in Institutions: Selected Essays*. London: Free Association, 1988.

Metcalf, S. (2017). The big idea that defines our era. *The Guardian*, 19 August, pp. 29–31.

Milton, J. (2001). Psychoanalysis and cognitive behaviour therapy: rival paradigms or common ground. *International Journal of Psychoanalysis, 82:* 431–447.

Milton, J. (1667, 1898). *Paradise Lost*. New York, NY: Harper.

Minne, C., & Von de Tann, M. (2011). Opinion. *The Guardian*, 22 August.

Money-Kyrle, R. (1968). Cognitive development. *International Journal of Psychoanalysis, 49:* 691–698.

Nairn, I. (1966). *Nairn's London*. London: Penguin.

Panksepp, J. (1998). *Affective Neuroscience: The Foundations of Human and Animal Emotions*. Oxford: OUP.

Pasolini, P. (1955). *Ragazzi di Vita* (translated as *The Street Kids* by A. Goldstein). New York, NY: Europa.

Pasolini, P. (Writer and Director). (1962). *Mamma Rosa*. (Motion Film). Arco Film.

Pinker, S. (2002). *The Blank Slate: The Modern Denial of Human Nature*. London: Penguin.

Pinker, S. (2011). *The Better Angels of our Nature: Why Violence has Declined*. New York, NY: Viking.

Potter, D. (Writer) (1978). *Pennies from Heaven* (TV drama). London: BBC.

Potter, D. (Writer) (1986). *The Singing Detective* (TV drama). London: BBC.

Prusin, A. V. (2010). *The Lands Between: Conflict in the East European Borderlands 1870–1992*. Oxford: OUP.

Quinidoz, J. (2004). *Reading Freud: A Chronological Exploration of Freud's Writing*. London: Routledge, 2008.

Rayner, E. (1999). Some functions of being fair and just – or not in clinical psychoanalysis *International Journal of Psychoanalysis, 80:* 477–492.

Reid Meloy, J. (1998). *The Psychopathic Mind*. Lanham, MD: Jason Aronson.

Renik, O. (2004). Intersubjectivity in psychoanalysis. *International Journal of Psychoanalysis, 85:* 1053–1064.

Rey, J. H. (1994). *Universals of Psychoanalysis in the Treatment of Psychotic and Borderline States*. London: Free Association.

Rice, A. K., (1969). Individual, group and inter-group processes. *Human Relations, 22:* 565–584.

Richie, A. (1998). *Faust's Metropolis: A History of Berlin*. London: Harper Collins.

Rieff, D. (1991). Victims all? Recovery, co-dependency and the art of blaming someone else. In: S. Sontag & R. Atwan (Eds.), *The Best American Essays* (pp. 253–267). New York, NY: Ticknor and Fields, 1992.

Rieff, P. (1966). *The Triumph of the Therapeutic: Uses of Faith after Freud*. London: Chatto & Windus.

Rose, J (2002). *The Intellectual Life of the British Working Classes.* New Haven, CT: Yale University Press.

Rosenfeld, H. (1964). On the psychopathology of narcissism: a clinical approach. *International Journal of Psychoanalysis, 45:* 332–337.

Rosenfeld, H. (1971). A clinical approach to the psychoanalytic theory of the life and death instincts: An investigation into the aggressive aspects of narcissism. *International Journal of Psychoanalysis, 52:* 169–178.

Rosenfeld, H. (1987). *Impasse and Interpretation.* London: Routledge.

Roth, J. (1929). Strawberries. In: *Collected Shorter Fiction of Joseph Roth* (pp.134–165). London: Granta, 2002.

Roth, J. (1935). The bust of the Emperor. In: *Collected Shorter Fiction of Joseph Roth* (pp. 235–258). London: Granta, 2002.

Roy, O. (2017). *Jihad and Death: The Global Appeal of Islamic State.* London: Hurst.

Rude, G. E. (1964). *The Crowd in History: A Study of Popular Disturbance in France and England 1730–1848.* London: Serif.

Rustin, M. (1991). *The Good Society and the Inner World: Psychoanalysis, Politics and Culture.* Verso: London.

Samuel, R. (1998). *Island Stories: Unravelling Britain, Theatres of Memory Vol II.* London: Verso.

Sartre, J.-P. (1948). *Anti-Semite and Jew.* New York: Schocken.

Sebald, W. G. (1990). *Vertigo.* London: Harvill.

Sebald, W. G. (1992). *The Emigrants.* London: Harvill, 1996.

Sebald, W. G. (1995). *The Rings of Saturn.* London: Harvill, 1998.

Sebald, W. G. (2001). *Austerlitz.* London: Penguin, 2002.

Sebald, W. G. (2003). *On the Natural History of Destruction.* London: Hamish Hamilton.

Segal, H. (1997). *Psychoanalysis, Literature and War.* London: Routledge.

Segal, H. (2002). Disillusionment: the story of Adam and Eve and that of Lucifer. In: N. Abel-Hirsch (Ed.), *Yesterday, Today and Tomorrow.* Abingdon, Oxon: Routledge, 2007.

Sennett, R. (2003). *Respect: The Formation of Character in an Age of Inequality.* London: Penguin, 2004.

Shakespeare, W. (1603). *Othello.* London: Penguin, 2005.

Siegel, D. (Director) (1956). Invasion of the Body Snatchers (Motion picture). New York: Monogram Pictures.

Shengold, L. (1988). *Halo in the Sky: Anality and Defense.* New York, NY: Guilford Press.

Sinatra, F. (Performer) (1965). "It was a very good year" (Song). Reprise Records.

Sodré, I. (2005). The wound, the bow and the shadow of the object: notes on Freud's "Mourning and Melancholia". In: R. J. Perelberg (Ed.), *Freud: a Modern Reader.* London: Whurr.

Sohns, L. (1985). Narcissistic organization, projective identification, and the formation of the identificate. *International Journal of Psychoanalysis, 66:* 201–213.

Sokal, A., & Bricmont, J. (1998). *Intellectual Impostures.* London: Profile.

Solms, M., & Turnbull, O. (2002). *The Brain and the Inner World: An Introduction to the Neuroscience of Subjective Experience.* London: Karnac.

Nicholas Stargardt (2008). The losses at Kursk. *Times Literary Supplement,* 10 October, pp. 8–9.

Steiner, J. (1993). *Psychic Retreats: Pathological Organizations in Psychotic, Neurotic and Borderline Patients.* New York, NY: Routledge.

Streek, W. (2014). How will capitalism end? *New Left Review, 87,* May-June.

Streek, W. (2017). The return of the repressed. *New Left Review, 104,* March-April.

Storr, A. (1979). *Solitude.* London: Flamingo.

Thomson, I. (2008). Zozzo Mondo. *Times Literary Supplement,* 21 November, p. 7.

Thompson, E. P. (1993). *Witness Against the Beast.* Cambridge: Cambridge University Press.

Timpanaro, S. (1975). *On Materialism.* London: Verso, 1980.

Tremlett, G. (2006). *The Ghosts of Spain: Travels through Spain and its Silent Past.* London: Faber & Faber.

Trilling, L. (1947). In: L. Shengold. *Halo in the Sky: Anality and Defence.* New York, NY: Guilford, 1988.

Turquet, P. (1975). Threats to identity in the large group. In: L. Keeger (Ed.), *The Large Group: Dynamics and Therapy* (pp. 87–144). London: Constable.

Volkan, V. D. (1988). *The Need to Have Enemies and Allies: From Clinical Practice to International Relationships.* Northvale, NJ: Jason Aaronson.

Watt, I. (1957). *The Rise of the Novel: Studies in Defoe, Richardson and Fielding.* Middlesex: Penguin, 1970.

Weatherill, R. (1995). Violence and privacy: What if the container fails? *Free Associations, 34*: 150–170.

Williams, J. (2016). Racial awareness – why higher education should not become a vehicle for identity politics. *Times Literary Supplement,* 14 October, p. 27.

Williams, R. (1968). *Culture and Society: 1710–1950.* New York, NY: Columbia University Press, 1983.

Wright, P. (2009). *A Journey Through Ruins: The Last Days of London.* Oxford: OUP.

Yeomans, F. E., Clarkin, J. F., & Kernberg, O. (2015). *Transference-Focused Psychotherapy for Borderline Personality Disorder: A Clinical Guide.* Arlington, VA: American Psychiatric Association.

Yorke, C., Freeman, T., & Wiseberg, S. (1989). *Development and Psychotherapy: Studies in Psychoanalytic Psychotherapy.* New Haven, CT: Yale University Press.

Zimmer, O. (2003). *Nationalism in Europe, 1890–1940.* Hampshire: Palgrave MacMillan.

Žižek, S. (2006). *The Universal Exception.* New York, NY: Continuum.

Žižzek, S. (2016). *Migrants, Racists and the Left.* Interview with Ella Whelan. www.spike-donline.com (May 2016).

Index

For Product Safety Concerns and Information please contact our EU
representative GPSR@taylorandfrancis.com
Taylor & Francis Verlag GmbH, Kaufingerstraße 24, 80331 München, Germany